JAPANESE
POLITICAL STYLE

AN INTRODUCTION TO THE GOVERNMENT AND POLITICS OF MODERN JAPAN

WARREN M. TSUNEISHI

YALE UNIVERSITY

HARPER & ROW
Publishers

NEW YORK AND LONDON

IST OF TABLES

CONTENTS

PREFACE

I have entitled this book *Japanese Political Style* to underscore the fact that the government mechanism of Japan bears a characteristic and distinctive stamp quite different in many respects from western counterparts. While the rubrics under which the discussion is carried on are familiar—the executive, legislative, and judicial branches; political parties, elections, and pressure groups —the content of the terms in some cases proves to be unexpectedly different. This is certainly true, for example, with respect to pressure groups.

This book is an attempt at a descriptive political science of Japanese government and politics in terms of concrete local experience. It is not an exposition of what the political system could be if only the Japanese were wise enough to adopt not only the external forms but also the inner spirit of western-style democracy. As far as possible, I have tried to analyze objectively the main institutions and processes in contemporary government and politics and to describe them in their own terms, not according to certain idealized standards presumed to be characteristic of western institutions and behavior. Comparisons are made, of course, especially with British and American practice, but for the purpose of drawing instructive parallels, and not for moralizing. I do not believe that western styles of democracy, however defined, are necessarily superior to the Japanese manner, insofar as the particular needs of the Japanese people are concerned. Each people must define its own democracy on the basis of its own past experience, its present condition, and future expectations, and Japanese democracy is no exception.

I open my discussion with the basic historical, economic, and social conditions that influence contemporary government. I then move on to the individual branches of government, include a study of parties and elections, and conclude with a section on foreign relations.

In the transcription of Japanese names, the normal order is followed: family name and given name (Prime Minister *Sato* Eisaku). But the western order is followed for Americans with Japanese names or Japanese authors cited for their English-language works (Professor Nobutake *Ike*, J. *Masumi*).

I have often cited prices and costs in yen without giving dollar equivalents. A quick approximation (based on the exchange rate of ¥360 = $1.00) may be obtained by utilizing this formula: ¥100 = $.28. Thus ¥1,000,000 is roughly $2,800 (actually $2,777.777).

I am indebted to Mr. Nozumi Fujio, formerly of the administrative staff of the House of Councilors, for arranging numerous fruitful interviews with members of the National Diet staff; to the Secretariat of the Prime Minister's Office for making available the published results of public opinion surveys of the past decade and a half on numerous political issues; to Mr. Nisihira Sigeki of the Tokyo Institute of Statistical Mathematics for providing survey materials on the Japanese national character; to Mr. Toshiyuki Aoki of the Yale University Library staff for information on informal aspects of government operations not readily available in written sources; and to my mentor, Professor Chitoshi Yanaga of Yale University for guidance over many years of learning about the Japanese political process. I am especially grateful to Mrs. Dorothy Reed, who, before she typed the manuscript, offered innumerable editorial suggestions. Despite the help I have received, I alone remain responsible for any lapses in fact or interpretation.

This book is dedicated to Julia, Kenneth, David, and Betty, who have been frightfully neglected during the time I was closeted with my typewriter and notes in my out-of-bounds study.

                                                                    W.M.T.

JAPANESE
POLITICAL
STYLE

CHAPTER ONE

Socioeconomic Determinants of Japanese Politics

FROM THE TIME of Marco Polo Japan has excited the wonder of the West and surprised occidentals with unexpected or unusual developments. In large measure, this has been due to an aura of mystery—deepened by lack of knowledge—that has surrounded the Japanese islands and her people. Columbus, seeking the "very great island" of Cipangu—located vaguely by Polo 1500 miles east of Cathay—where gold was "abundant beyond all measure," [1] discovered, instead, the New World. In more recent times, westerners have been beguiled by her arts, her architecture, and her aesthetic sensibilities; startled by her sudden emergence as a great power following the Russo-Japanese War of 1904–1905; shocked by the perfidy of Pearl Harbor; and astonished by the economic "miracle" which has transformed Japan in the last decade and a half from a nation with no future to the industrial giant of the East.

The transformation of the Japanese state from a military dictatorship at the time of the surrender in 1945 to a nation commonly referred to as a "democracy" in 1966 is no less a miracle. But the most cursory investigation will immediately reveal that Japanese democracy differs considerably from the classical western

[1] Henry Yule (ed.), *Book of Marco Polo*, J. Murray, 1903, vol. 2, p. 253.

models after which it has been patterned. Indeed, it may be said that the Japanese have evolved a distinctive style of government which, from our point of view, appears to abound in paradox and which cannot be subsumed under any of the traditional categories—though some of the paradoxical elements vanish when the system is examined in terms of the Japanese political experience. Japan, for example, may be classified as a limited monarchy, but it is a monarchy in which the sovereign has not exercised effective governmental power for over a millennium; in this respect it far antedates British constitutional development. Again, Japan may be regarded as a parliamentary democracy in structure and form, but it is strikingly bureaucratic in spirit and operation. Thus, we may observe the sovereign people attempting to exercise formal control over the government through party, parliament, pressure group, and public opinion, but we see at the same time that a great deal of this effort is vitiated by countervailing forces springing from or working through the administrative mechanism of the state. One reason for this state of affairs is the inadequate development in both the people and officialdom of those internalized controls which are rooted in a firm commitment to such democratic values as individualism, majoritarianism, and egalitarianism and which constitute the ultimate bulwark against authoritarian regimes. Finally, in terms of economic ideology, Japan is a country where the word *capitalism* is anathema to a preponderant majority of the people; where the incoming conservative Prime Minister emphasizes the welfare aspects of his policy; and where government and private interests are merged in a complex and intimate relationship to an extent perhaps unknown in the West.

Japan, in short, constitutes a unique polity, which should not be surprising given the particular forces that have molded and shaped her over the centuries. These forces have been both physical and cultural; they include her geographical background and location at the very edge of the Sinic node of civilization; her economic foundations and human resources; and certain pervasive features of her historical past which impinge upon her present constitutional structure and political processes.

Geographical Background

Japan's volcanic islands—part of the "rim of fire" ringing the Pacific Ocean basin—lie in strategic waters off the northeast coast of Asia. From prehistoric times, the overwhelming cultural influence has been Chinese, as reflected in such disparate elements of her civilization as her writing system, arts, religion, social conventions, and premodern forms of government. Even today, Japan cannot escape the influence of the giant at her doorstep, and how she is to come to terms with Communist China constitutes one of the top political problems of the day.

The Japanese island arcs are the upper portions of submerged mountains. Connected in prehistoric times with the Asian continent, they are now separated from the mainland by the Japan Sea, a true ocean basin registering depths as low as 10,000 feet. The crests of the ranges rise about 20,000–30,000 feet above the Pacific Ocean floor (the highest, Mount Fuji, peaks at 12,327 feet above sea level); east of the islands lie deep submarine trenches. Crustal movements, seismic disturbances, and volcanic activity, therefore, are common occurrences. Another consequence is that the terrain is generally mountainous and hilly, and there is a relative scarcity of flatlands large enough for cultivation, urban settlement, and industry. Only 16 percent of the small land area is arable (*vs.* 53 percent in Italy).

Defeated in war, Japan was stripped in 1945 of territories and island possessions which she had acquired in 50 years of conquest. She now occupies a total land area approximately 4 percent that of the United States, though it is still larger than West and East Germany combined, and than the United Kingdom. Her population, roughly half that of the United States, is confined to the four major islands that comprised the empire in the middle of the nineteenth century.

The Japanese islands, stretching from Hokkaido in the north to Kyushu and the Ryukyu Islands in the south, lie in the temperate zone from about latitude 25 to 45 degrees North. If situated off the eastern seaboard of North America, the islands would curve southward from about Halifax, Nova Scotia, to the tip of Florida. Winter and summer monsoons govern the weather, which generally resembles that of the Atlantic seaboard. Severely cold Siberian air masses brought by the northwest winter monsoon are moderated somewhat by warm air carried by the Black Current sweeping up from the south. In early summer, moist air from the Pacific brings rain and high humidity. Tokyo, located in mid-Japan, has winter and summer temperatures comparable to those of Winston-Salem, North Carolina. The great industrial-urban complexes surrounding the cities of Tokyo-Yokohama, Nagoya, Osaka-Kyoto-Kobe, and Kita (North) Kyushu are located in the midlatitudes, far from the severe snows of the northern island of Hokkaido and the enervating heat of the subtropics.

Japan is blessed with abundant rainfall, important both to her agriculture with its emphasis on paddy (wet) rice culture, and to industry, which relies heavily for its energy resources on hydro-electric power. Factors favorable to agricultural development—mild climate, length of the growing season, and adequate water supply—are often counterbalanced by negative factors: the topography which hinders large-scale mechanization, geologically young and impoverished soils requiring frequent and heavy applications of organic and inorganic fertilizers, and natural catastrophes. Geological and climatic factors work to produce periodic disasters of major scope: earthquakes, volcanic eruptions, *tsunami* (seismic waves), landslides, and typhoons. Exclusive of man-made damage and typhoons, Japan was struck by an average of one major disaster every four years during the period 1847–1964, the greatest of the recent ones being the earthquake and fire that leveled the Tokyo-Yokohama area on September 1, 1923, with a loss of some 143,000 lives. The most recent earthquake, on June 16, 1964, struck the city of Niigata and left 25 dead and 338 injured. Of the natural catastrophes, however, typhoons coming at the height of the growing season probably do the most damage. From September, 1945 to September, 1961, there were eight major typhoons, with death tolls ranging from 200 to 3600 persons.[2]

2 R. Isida, *Geography of Japan*, Kokusai Bunka Shinkokai, 1961, pp. 110–113.

One consequence of these frequent seismic and agrometeorological disasters is that the Japanese have long become accustomed to speedy relief and reconstruction measures. Such experience vastly speeded up the rebuilding of her cities and industrial plants, large segments of which had been bombed to rubble during World War II.

Resources and Economy

Nature did not cut the resource pattern of Japan on a scale befitting a great power.[3]

The fundamental problem of the Japanese nation can be expressed in the simple terms of too many people, too little land, and too few natural resources.[4]

The conventional view of Japan's natural resources, typified by these two quotations, tends to emphasize her poverty, and it is true that with some exceptions—such as bituminous coal and cement—Japan must import practically all of her industrial raw material needs: petroleum, iron ore, coking coal, bauxite, rubber, cotton, and wool. Substantial foreign supplies of nonferrous minerals, timber, wood pulp, and fibers must also be found to supplement lean domestic production. With regard to foodstuffs, she is self-sufficient only in rice and must rely upon imports for 70 percent of basic grains such as wheat and soya beans. Recently, as her diet has changed, substantial quantities of meat and dairy products have also joined the import list.

The unprecedented prosperity of the last decade has brought about a significant change in attitude toward the question of resources. The writings of the late 1940s and early 1950s are characterized by pessimistic projections about the country's economic future, often with little hope for any recovery beyond the subsistence level. But by 1964, Japanese economic analysts

[3] G. T. Trewartha, *Japan: A Physical, Cultural and Regional Geography*, University of Wisconsin Press, 1945, p. 3.

[4] From a 1952 address by Joseph M. Dodge, financial adviser to General Douglas MacArthur, as cited in J. B. Cohen, *Japan's Postwar Economy*, University of Indiana Press, 1958, p. 11.

were discounting lack of industrial resources as a serious deterrent to further expansion.

This change in attitude was, of course, prompted by Japan's astonishing recovery; it has also brought about a more sophisticated analysis of the resource problem. Increasingly, economists have come to realize that subsurface minerals and land constitute only a part of a nation's total resources. People, for example, are also an economic asset or a debit according to their ability or inability to function effectively in a modern industrial society. In the case of Japan, her educated and industrious population with its advanced training and technical skills is regarded as constituting her most important resource.

This new view is the basis of a recent publication of the governmental Resources Commission embodying the results of a comprehensive survey of Japan's total resources.[5] The Commission points out that such natural and geographic features as favorable rainfall, light, temperature, wind, and tide must be counted among available resources, as well as such cultural and human assets as existing capital investments, state of technological development, strategically located industrial plants, adequate supplies of skilled labor, and viable economic and political organizations.

One example should suffice to illustrate this new outlook. The major industries are strategically located along coastal areas and are easily serviced by mammoth bulk carriers at relatively cheap rates. Thus the lack of indigenous supplies of materials is not too important as long as the international situation permits free access to outside sources. Two cases in point are iron ore and crude oil, both in extremely short supply domestically. In the case of iron ore, the overall supply picture has been changing as highly profitable mines have been developed in Africa, South America, and Australia in recent years and mines in North America and Europe, which had been readily accessible to the steel mills of the West, have become depleted. Price differences, decisive in the past and requiring protection of native industries,

[5] Japan, Kagaku Gijutsucho, Shigen Chosakai [Science and Technology Agency, Resources Commission], *Nihon no Shigen* [Resources of Japan], Daiyamondo Sha, 1962.

have become less of a factor. For example, delivered prices of ore in 1963 averaged: Japan, $13.60 per ton; West Germany, $9.80; Italy, $11.00; and France, $10.30.[6] Because freight costs are kept down by bulk carriers, and because of the adoption of the latest technological advances, Japan's competitive position has been improved as against U.S. and European mills operating in the hinterlands and served by relatively expensive rail and barge transport and, in some cases, with outmoded facilities.

This view of Japan's resources problem has immediate and far-reaching consequences on foreign policy: any sudden break in her commercial relations with the outside world can be fatal. As a result, Japan's foreign policy must be based first, last, and foremost on the preservation of international stability and order. She is therefore a member and strong supporter of such international organizations as the United Nations, the Organization for Economic Cooperation and Development, and the International Monetary Fund. At the same time, she seeks to expand her economic ties with the Communist world, especially with China, a convenient source of such raw materials as iron ore, coking coal, pig iron, and soya beans, and ultimately a market of considerable importance for her finished products. Japan's current espousal of interdependence is in sharp contrast to her prewar international economic philosophy, which was greatly influenced by the supposed need for self-sufficiency. This in turn constituted the economic rationale for her drive for expansion—first to the continent of Asia and then southward to the Philippines and the East Indies, an expansion which brought her directly into war with the Allied powers in 1941. Foreign relations will be treated in greater detail in Chapter Eleven.

The Economy

When Japan surrendered in 1945, her shattered economy, operating at less than 60 percent of the prewar level, showed little promise of revival. Moreover, her already large population was suddenly increased by the repatriation of millions of her overseas

[6] *Japan Economic Journal,* Oct. 20, 1964, p. 12.

soldiers and civilians crammed into a territory reduced by about one-half.

The economic growth that has transformed Japan into a mass-consumption, "leisure-boom" society rapidly approaching western standards has been phenomenal. For the period 1952–1963, the average annual growth rate was about nine percent (1925–1939 average: 4.6 percent), and during fiscal 1963–1964 the real growth rate of her gross national product climbed to an astonishing 12.3 percent, giving rise to fears of an "overheated economy."

The technical economic reasons for her sustained growth are many and varied. According to Professor J. B. Cohen, they include such factors as the $6 billion in U.S. funds poured into Japan during the first postwar decade, the attitude and know-how of the people, the industrial boom stimulated by the Korean War, world-wide prosperity, monetary and fiscal policies correctly applied, high capital investment, an increase in the absorptive capacity of the domestic market, high savings ratio, technological innovations, expansion of exports, and sharp decrease of military expenditures. In addition, the economic historian G. C. Allen has pointed to other fundamental factors such as the cohesion of Japanese society during the period of revolutionary change, her comprehensive educational system which facilitated relatively easy innovation, a competent civil service, and a capacity for assimilating needed political and economic reforms necessary to stimulate the economy.[7] Above all, there is the one factor which economists often overlook but politicians always put first: stable government. This was epitomized by Prime Minister Ikeda, whose campaign slogans in the November, 1963, general elections included the boast, "I am the Premier who made Japan prosperous." Despite the self-serving nature of the slogan, there can be little doubt that government actions skillfully applied over an extended period of time by a succession of conservative cabinets have been generally beneficial to the nation's economy, and the party in power may well take credit for the overall prosperity.

Along with the impressive rise in production have come an

[7] Cohen, *Japan's Postwar Economy, op cit.*, p. 18; G. C. Allen, *A Short Economic History of Modern Japan*, Praeger, 1963, pp. 190–191.

advanced standard of living and a steep increase in consumption levels. Per capita income in 1964 approached the Italian standard ($526 *vs.* $557), an unprecedented high for Japan, although still approximately one-half that of Great Britain, West Germany, and France ($1000–1150) and about one-fourth the U.S. average ($2300). Television sets, washing machines, and electric refrigerators have become commonplace. The giant department stores of Japan's cities are jammed with well-dressed shoppers, and their streets are clogged with traffic. Prosperity even extends to the hinterland farms, which are increasingly mechanized.

In spite of her general prosperity, however, there exist grave imbalances and weaknesses in the economic structure. There is, for example, the problem of a dual economy characterized by giant modern enterprises utilizing the latest technological developments (e.g., steel; chemicals) on the one hand, and relatively inefficient small and medium industries, undercapitalized and utilizing outmoded facilities, on the other. As a result, according to a 1961 survey, while concerns employing from 30 to 299 workers accounted for 93 percent of all enterprises and gave work to 52 percent of the total labor force, they nevertheless accounted for only 37 percent of the total added value production. The disparity in productivity and wage levels has been decreasing in recent years for at least two reasons: (1) the smaller businesses have been forced to modernize because of the increasing shortage of skilled labor; and (2) over a period of years, the government has actively aided the modernization of these enterprises through subsidies, establishment of special credit and financing facilities, the promotion of small business trade associations, and guidance in management and technology. Though these techniques are not unknown in the United States, they are more actively promoted by the government and more readily accepted by business firms in Japan.

Agriculture, Forestry, Fisheries

Agriculture, until recent decades, was regarded as the foundation of the empire, and indeed it was agricultural surpluses drained off in the form of land taxes that supplied the necessary capital for Japan's industrialization in the nineteenth century. Agriculture has steadily declined, however, as reflected in such figures as percentage of total labor force engaged in farming and proportion of gross national product contributed by primary industries. In 1872, at the beginning of Japan's experiment at modernization and industrialization, almost 80 percent of the total labor force were engaged in the primary industries (agriculture, forestry, fisheries), with only 4 percent in manufacturing and about 7 percent in commerce and trade. The 80 percent had dropped to about 25 percent of the labor force by 1963, with about 12 million still engaged in agricultural pursuits.[8] Moreover, about 75 percent of farm workers had auxiliary positions in non-agricultural occupations, and of this number some 41 percent counted their auxiliary jobs as their main source of income.

The total agricultural labor force had long remained stable in the 15 million range, but in the past few years, it has undergone a steep decline, reflecting a large-scale exodus of farm workers to urban areas. The primary cause of this movement is the wide disparity between rural and urban income levels due in turn to increasing industrial productivity as against a lesser (though remarkable in its own terms) rise in productivity on the farm. Agriculture's share of the national income dropped from 18 percent in fiscal 1955 to 10 percent in fiscal 1962, and the decline shows no signs of stopping.

The ruling Liberal-Democratic Party finds its basic support in the rural conservative masses, and accordingly there have been and will be no end to political solutions to agrarian problems. The remarkable rise in farm production during the last decade in the face of a declining farm population has been caused mainly by increasing mechanization and capital investments. Such investments have been supplemented by public loans; during the decade of the 1950s the government accounted for nearly 20 percent of the fixed capital formation on the farms.[9]

[8] *Japan Statistical Yearbook*, 1963, p. 50. About 33 percent of the total population are classified as farm-connected, as against approximately 7 percent of the United States.

[9] T. Ashikaga, *Agriculture in Japan*, Japan FAO Association, 1963, p. 7.

The present Basic Agricultural Law of 1961 stresses autonomous efforts on the part of farmers and their organizations (with generous government aid) to modernize agriculture, raise productivity, rationalize marketing and distribution of products, stabilize prices, and secure welfare benefits. By 1964, as the farm population continued to decline, the Liberal-Democratic Party was calling for the establishment of a Farmland Control Agency to coordinate efforts to consolidate Japan's tiny average landholdings (2.5 acres per family) and hence permit further mechanization of farm production.

The fishing industry has also benefited from government aid, especially in the modernization of port and docking facilities carried out with state funds. Because of the miniscule size of Japan's livestock industry, her fisheries are of prime importance as a food source; two-thirds of the animal-protein component of the national diet is supplied by marine products. In addition, Japan, the world leader in fisheries with Peru, counts heavily on fish products for foreign exchange.

Industry and Commerce

It is in her secondary (mining and manufacturing) and tertiary (commerce, service, government) industries that Japan has made the most noticeable gains since the war, creating a vast and modern industrial plant embodying the latest technological developments (more often than not imported through licensing arrangements or purchases of patent rights). Production has been stepped up sharply in heavy and chemical industries: machinery, shipbuilding, automobiles, iron and steel, chemicals and fertilizers, and petrochemicals. In synthetic and natural textiles, she has maintained her prewar eminence, and in electronics (transistor radios, TV sets, electron microscopes), and optical goods (cameras, binoculars) she has created whole new industries.

Drastic changes have also occurred in her export trade. In prewar days cotton goods and raw silk accounted for about 40 percent of the nation's exports, but these had declined to about 25 percent in 1963, while machinery, steel products, chemicals, and other manufactured goods had taken up the slack. Her markets have also changed with profound consequences for her foreign policy. Although in prewar days Chinese and Korean buyers accounted for roughly 60 percent of her total exports, by 1963 her sales to Asian countries had shrunk to 34 percent while exports to Europe and the United States had risen sharply. Today, her largest customer by far is the United States, accounting for 28 percent of her total exports (vs. 16 percent in 1941).

Economics and Politics

In spite of her unprecedented growth and prosperity, Japan always seems to be on the verge of economic crisis. At the beginning of 1965, for example, while the governmental Economic Planning Agency was issuing the usual rosy picture of continued expansion, the bankruptcy rate in the last quarter of 1964 had reached alarming proportions; and, partly as a consequence, the Bank of Japan liberalized its tight money policies to stimulate the economy. In recent years, Japan's political problems, both foreign and domestic, have been primarily economic ones. Thus her main concern in economic diplomacy has been to maintain and expand trade with her best customers in the West while, at the same time, further developing her trade with the Communist bloc through such means as extension of credits and deferred payments to the Soviet Union and promotion of private economic ties with Communist China.

Domestically, successive conservative governments have sought to ensure a steady growth of the economy [10] without an excessive rise in prices; to increase investments in social capital (transportation network, housing, water supply, sewage systems) without dampening trade expansion; to decrease disparities between urban

[10] Currently projected through a new five-year plan to expand at the real rate of about eight percent as against the 1963 rate of almost 13 percent. Imbalances created by too much success in the original 10-year Income Doubling Plan of 1961 necessitated a new shorter term five-year plan in 1964. It is to be noted that Japanese "plans" are merely governmental guidelines for development and are different in substance from the enforced plans characteristic of Communist states.

and rural productivity, wages, and income; to overcome the persistent unfavorable balance in invisible trade; to encourage modernization and rationalization of the underdeveloped sectors of her economy; to counteract the suffocating effects of over-concentration of population in existing industrial centers by regional dispersal; [11] and to maintain her balance of payments position and avoid an extensive number of bankruptcies as a result of increasing liberalization of trade.

In her day-to-day politics, therefore, it is economic issues that are of paramount importance; it is these which, day after day, consume the attention of the government and the people. This has been especially evident during the cabinets of Ikeda Hayato (1960–1964), the first Prime Minister to focus the center of his governmental policy on economic growth. The conservative program obviously has the support of the populace, since in election after election the Liberal-Democratic Party is returned to power with overwhelming majorities. Only some unforseen catastrophe can elevate the opposition Socialists to supremacy.

The Japanese People

POPULATION

Japan's inhabitants totaled approximately 98.5 million in 1964 as compared to the U.S. total of 192 million. Japan has about twice the number of inhabitants of metropolitan France, about 40 million more than the United Kingdom, and about 20 million more than East and West Germany. In 1966, the population is expected to exceed 100 million and then rise steadily to about 113 million in the year 2000. Thereafter, it is probable that it will subside and stabilize around the 105 million level.[12]

The combination of a small land area and a large population places Japan among the most densely populated countries in the

[11] By 1963, urban-rural income disparities were creating social and cultural disparities as well. In this situation, pressures developed to strictly control the further growth of such metropolitan centers as Tokyo and promote new urban centers in "underdeveloped" regions of Japan. See Kiuchi Shinzo, *Nihon no Toshika* [Urbanization of Japan], Kokin Shoin, 1964, p. 173.

[12] Japan, Kagaku Gijutsucho, Shigen Chosakai, *Nihon no Shigen, op. cit.,* p. 48.

world, averaging 259 persons per square kilometer as against 215 in the United Kingdom and West Germany and 19 in the United States. The contrasts are far more striking with regard to density per cultivated square mile: Japan's 4519 is far greater than the United Kingdom's 1826, and the United States' 221. The population, moreover, is not evenly distributed among the four major islands but is heavily concentrated in the two central islands of Honshu and Kyushu. In 1960, the population densities of these islands were 310 and 308 per square kilometer as against 220 for Shikoku, and a low 64 for sparsely settled Hokkaido, the target for pioneer development for almost a century and still the preserve of a special Development Agency of the national government. In Honshu and Kyushu, the population has become increasingly concentrated in giant metropolitan complexes, and the 1960 census showed that approximately 44 percent of the people live in "densely inhabited districts"—defined as areas having densities of 4000 persons or more per square kilometer.[13] The number of administrative units designated as "cities" (*shi*) rose from 47 in 1890 to 556 in 1960; the percentage of urban dwellers jumped from 7.8 percent to 63.5 percent during the same period and shows no signs of diminishing. There are now seven cities with populations in excess of one million: Tokyo (with 10 million people; the largest city in the world), Osaka, Nagoya, Yokohama, Kyoto, Kobe, and the recently designated city of Kita (North) Kyushu. Together with their satellite towns, they concentrate the population of Japan into the four great "conurbations" of Tokyo-Yokohama, Osaka-Kobe-Kyoto, Nagoya, and North Kyushu, which contain roughly half the population and 1 percent of the land area of Japan.

Japanese population growth fits the low birth and death rate pattern typical of developed western countries. According to government forecasts, during the decade of the 1960s, a disproportionate number of teenagers will enter the labor market as the postwar baby crop matures. After 1970 there will be a sharp drop in the group of productive workers (15–59 years of age); at the

---

[13] Japan, Office of the Prime Minister, Bureau of Statistics, 1960 *Population Census: Densely Inhabited District, its Population, Area and Map*, 1961, vol. 1, p. 9.

same time there will be an increase of those 60 years or older. Since the high rate of economic growth—characterized by massive labor requirements—is expected to continue, it will lead inevitably to a shortage of workers in the productive category and a surfeit in the older brackets.

By 1963 the pinch in the supply of young workers had already begun to develop, some seven years ahead of schedule, and both industry and government began to seek solutions to the problem. One possibility was retraining older men for new jobs; in this effort the government characteristically took the lead, setting up a three-year project with the object of establishing basic standards for individual capacity and adaptability in the face of revolutionary changes brought about by automation and technological innovation. The study is being carried out jointly by the Science and Technology Agency and the Ministries of Labor and of Welfare.[14] The results are being eagerly awaited by modernization-conscious business leaders whose scarce capital resources do not permit large research and development budgets, compared to U.S. standards. We may observe in passing that this is one more example of the tendency of business leaders to look to the government for leadership in a situation in which their American counterparts might very well turn to commercial or academic researchers for solutions.

High population densities, demographic changes, rapid urbanization, and alterations in employment fundamentally affect the people. Because they are universally regarded as amenable to government action, they are inevitably drawn into the vortex of national politics. For example, there is an urgent need for more urban housing, which has been in short supply since the war. Because private mortgage lending and borrowing are virtually nonexistent, builders are heavily dependent upon government subsidies and loans for new housing. The role of the central government is paramount in providing for higher education and job retraining to meet the new needs of the modernizing industrial establishment. Government action at the highest level is also required to provide more generous social security and welfare benefits for an increasingly aging population, and a more com-

[14] *Japan Report,* June 15, 1963, p. 8.

fortable and pleasant physical environment in every way, from
improved highways and mass transportation networks to modern
public sanitation facilities.[15] Urbanization has also created a political problem not unknown in the West. For years the need to
reapportion election districts now grossly weighted in favor of
rural constituencies has been self-evident, but in spite of legal
requirements calling for periodic redistricting, political difficulties have stopped all attempts to correct this imbalance.[16]

NATIONAL CHARACTER

"National character," according to Professor Alex Inkeles, "re-
fers to relatively enduring personality characteristics and patterns
that are modal among adult members of a society." [17] Behavioral
scientists generally accept the proposition that national character
so defined forms the substratum that nurtures, shapes, and supports the political regime of a nation. In other words, it is generally held, though not yet conclusively shown, that the wide-
spread distribution of a given personality type will reveal itself
in the nature of the regime it supports. For example, the presumed prevalence of a relatively open, individualistic, egalitarian,
and autonomous personality type is regarded as supportive of
such stable democracies as Great Britain and the United States.
On the other end of the spectrum, the wide distribution of
closed, rigid, aggressive, and hierarchically oriented personality
types is equated with the existence of such authoritarian regimes
as those of Nazi Germany and presurrender Japan.

When we apply this sociopolitical equation to contemporary
Japanese society, we are immediately confronted with a number
of difficulties, not the least of which is the relative sketchiness
and incompleteness of the empirical data on modal personality
traits. Postwar Japan, furthermore, is in a state of flux marked

15 One critic asserts that while Japan boasts 15 million TV sets, the
highest ownership rate in the world after the United States, only 10 percent
of her roads are paved; and that while Tokyo may have six television stations,
its sewage and water supply facilities are grossly inadequate for the needs
of the largest city in the world. See *Japan Report*, Nov. 30, 1963, p. 4.

16 See Chapter Seven for further discussion.

17 Alex Inkeles, "National Character and Modern Political Systems," in
F. L. K. Hsu (ed.), *Psychological Anthropology*, Dorsey, 1961, p. 172.

by a transition from traditional values to newer and more democratic conceptions of the ideal role of the individual, the group, and the state. Despite these difficulties, the imperfect data supplied by a number of recent sociological studies in depth, as well as opinion-attitude surveys, suggest a general personality configuration fairly indicative of current Japanese behavior. Authoritarian characteristics still are important, although they are being eroded away, especially among the youth of the nation. In the process, it would appear that a new identity is being created in which such traits as individualism and rationalism are more highly prized than previously.

In postwar Japan, the traditional values have been under constant attack and, as a consequence, have been modified considerably. The attack was initiated by U.S. occupation forces who sought to democratize not only autocratic political institutions but also the supportive social mechanism. It continues to be carried on by such groups as the intellectuals, youth, and opposition political parties. In a study of the attitudes of farmers, the sociologist R. P. Dore found a remarkable persistence in rural Japan of such traditional attitudes as submissiveness to authoritarian leadership and acceptance of hierarchical status distinctions, although there is no longer unquestioned acceptance of these modes of behavior. Holistic tendencies, in which the individual willingly sacrifices his own needs to the good of the community and in the presumed higher value of "harmony," continue to hold sway, while extreme nationalism appears to be on the wane.[18] D. E. Mendel, in his study of the relationship between public opinion and foreign policy in post-treaty Japan, found that while the traditional view of a government that exalts the official and degrades the people [19] still exists, it is being modified by a growing expectation on the part of the people that their views should be considered in the formulation of policy. Professor Mendel also found wide public support for free expression of even the most extreme political ideas.[20]

[18] R. P. Dore, *Land Reform in Japan*, Oxford University Press, 1959, pp. 393 ff.

[19] Expressed in the phrase *kanson mimpi* [the official respected, the people despised], which has had currency since the nineteenth century.

[20] D. E. Mendel, *Japanese People and Foreign Policy*, University of California Press, 1961, pp. 29, 37.

The tenacity of traditional values in the face of vigorous forces working for change shows up clearly in a series of nationwide opinion-attitude surveys conducted by a special committee on the national character of the Institute of Statistical Mathematics in Tokyo.[21] Findings on attitudes bearing on political behavior, scattered throughout the data, may be summarized as follows:

1. *Submissiveness to authority.* In 1953, some 43 percent of the respondents agreed with the statement that the work of national reconstruction should be left to the pre-eminent politicians who had emerged in postwar Japan, rather than to the people working through deliberative bodies. Five years later this percentage had dropped to 35 percent, still uncomfortably high—even though the poor wording of the question might have contributed to the result—for a nation ostensibly committed to parliamentary democracy. Attitudes differed according to sex, age, and education, with men, youth, and the highly educated demonstrating less submissiveness than women, the middle-aged, and those with minimal education, as shown in the following tabulation:

"Leave Reconstruction to Politicians"

		Agree	Disagree
National average, 1953		43%	38%
National average, 1958		35	44
By sex	Men	29	52
	Women	39	37
By age	20–30	29	55
	50–60	45	30
By education	Elementary	48	26
	College	17	63

SOURCE: Tokei Suri Kenkyujo [Institute of Statistical Mathematics], *Nihonjin no Kokuminsei* [Japanese National Character], 1961, pp. 444, 502. ("Don't knows" not shown.)

Another dimension of this tendency toward submissiveness became evident from a question in which the respondents were asked to choose between "discipline" and "freedom" in the rearing of young children. Some 63 percent preferred discipline while

[21] Tokei Suri Kenkyujo [Institute of Statistical Mathematics], *Nihonjin no Kokuminsei* [Japanese National Character], 1961.

a scant 16 percent opted for freedom.[22] The sex, age, and educational level variables followed the same pattern as in the replies to the previously discussed question.

2. *Hierarchy.* The respondents were also asked whether they preferred the variety of Japanese pronouns indicating status or the neutral "I" and "you" of English. Some 60 percent of the respondents felt the distinctions were good, and only 28 percent that they were bad. On this question, there were no statistically significant variations according to age, sex and education.[23]

3. *Holism.* Questions regarding the relative importance of the individual as against the nation elicited a substantial willingness to subordinate individual wishes to the needs of the higher group. In 1953, some 68 percent of those interviewed agreed with the proposition that individual happiness is contingent on prior improvement of Japan, or that making individuals happy and improving Japan amount to the same thing. In contrast, only 25 percent felt that attempts to improve Japan should begin by improving the lot of the individual. The spirit of "individualism" was found to be higher among men than women, among the 20–30 age group than those above 50 (28 percent *vs.* 21 percent), and among university graduates than those who had only finished elementary school (35 percent *vs.* 23 percent).[24]

These questions were not repeated in the 1958 survey. Instead, respondents were asked to choose between the prewar type of life centered on the family and nation as against the supposed postwar pattern centering on the individual. Some 50 percent preferred the prewar style as against 37 percent who opted for individualism. Here the variations by sex, age, education, employment, and political party affiliation are worth noting in detail. They are given in the following table.

There has been a notable widening of the gap between generations, with 54 percent of the 20–30 age group (only 28 percent in 1953) giving first preference to individualism. Differences according to education, occupation, and political party are especially marked.

22 *Ibid.*, p. 485.
23 *Ibid.*, p. 500.
24 *Ibid.*, p. 496.

"Family and Nation *vs.* Individual"

		Individual	Family/Nation
National average		37%	50%
By sex	Men	41	50
	Women	34	50
By age	20–30	54	37
	60 and over	22	56
By education	Elementary	27	56
	College	56	33
By occupation	Professional	51	37
	Farmers	27	60
By party	Lib.-Dem.	30	61
	Socialists	50	39

SOURCE: Tokei Suri Kenkyujo, *Nihonjin no Kokuminsei*, 1961, p. 496. ("Don't knows" not shown.)

4. *Ethnocentrism.* One component of prewar national psychology was the belief in the superiority of the Yamato race destined by divine right to rule the world. Racial arrogance still survives, with 52 percent of the respondents agreeing (and only 31 percent

"Differences in Racial Capacity"

		Agree	Disagree
National average		52%	31%
By sex	Men	53	38
	Women	49	26
By age	20–30	44	44
	60 and over	49	18
By education	Elementary	54	17
	College	46	48
By occupation	Professional	44	54
	Small business	60	32
	Farmers	54	26
By party	Lib.-Dem.	60	28
	Socialists	48	42

SOURCE: Tokei Suri Kenkyujo, *Nihonjin no Kokuminsei*, 1961, p. 514. ("Don't knows" not shown.)

disagreeing) with the statement that differences in racial abilities exist and that it is in the natural order of things for the strong to dominate the weak. The breakdown by variables is shown above.

Although there are the usual differences according to age, educational level, etc., preponderant opinion in all categories supports the traditional view, and this would appear to constitute a formidable barrier to the rise of the egalitarian spirit.

5. *Ideology.* It is too early to say whether the Japanese people are yet committed deeply to any ideology. "Democracy" evokes a favorable response, but "capitalism" prompts a distinctly unfavorable reaction. "Liberalism" and "Socialism" are regarded favorably by 34–35 percent of the respondents. The usual differences according to age, sex, etc., show up again, except in the case of the unfavorable response to "capitalism," which is uniformly held in low esteem.[25]

What emerges from this series of opinion-attitude surveys is a fairly coherent picture of the contemporary Japanese national character. It has in it substantial elements of the old order which emphasized the family and nation over the individual; discipline, duty, and obligation over freedom; distinction in status over equality; and racial arrogance over egalitarianism. The younger generation and the better educated, however, are slowly moving toward individualism and commitment to "democracy," but the movement is uneven, with strong survivals of ethnocentric, hierarchical, and holistic attitudes. The youth of Japan, moreover, are a generation away from control of political power.

In balance, present trends if continued would appear to augur well for the future of Japanese democracy, the viability of which has been a particular point of concern to American observers. There is, however, some doubt that the Japanese conception of democracy will ever reach the ideal levels postulated by its western adherents. There is no historical inevitability about any political process, and it is more likely, as has been indicated previously, that the Japanese government will develop along its own characteristic lines and will always contain a heavy component of elements regarded as basically inimical to the development of a healthy, western-style of democracy.

[25] *Ibid.,* pp. 503–504.

CHAPTER TWO

National Foundations

Historical Background

THE PAST impinges upon the present, molding and influencing contemporary events in any country; but it is in the nonwestern nations that historical forces stand most clearly revealed, perhaps because the contrasts between the old and the new seem so extravagant. In Japan, such antique theatrical forms as the *no* drama, created in the fourteenth century, are still regularly performed, and the classic verse form first anthologized in the eighth century continues to have its adherents. But creative artists from novelists to poets to painters work in westernized genres, and the masses spend their leisure hours in motion picture theaters, coffee houses, and pinball parlors. In such museum cities as Nara and Kyoto, once tranquil temple retreats swarm with sight-se'ers so numerous that they all but obliterate the sights, yet Tokyo and Osaka are modernized metropolises scarcely distinguishable from their western counterparts. The language itself is constantly acquiring foreign words when perfectly good native terms exist—"leisure boom," "vacances," "bargain sale"—even "rice." In the political sphere, the historical legacy is evident not so much in the forms of government, which are completely western in outward appearance, but rather in the spirit that moves the machinery of government. Japan, as has been noted previously, is a parliamentary democracy with an authoritarian coloration inherited from her feudal past, and it is not likely that she will lose this tinge in the near future.

The autocratic streak in Japanese national life is of the most ancient pedigree. The archetypal leader is the benevolent despot, and it is no exaggeration to state that such leaders flourish even today as the leaders of party factions. According to the *Kojiki* [Records of Antiquity] and the *Nihon Shoki* [Chronicles of Japan], the oldest written accounts of Japanese history, both compiled around the year 700 A.D., Japan was a theocratic state ruled by a divine emperor descended directly from the Sun Goddess. As the high priest interceding in behalf of the people with the gods, the Emperor stood at the center of national veneration. Indeed, the early word for government was *matsurigoto*, which connotes supervision of religious observances. When, in the latter half of the seventh century, Japan's leaders began to reshape the administration of the country after the model of the T'ang Empire, they scrupulously followed the Chinese pattern in all but one or two vitally important respects. The theory that a virtuous king rules by the mandate of heaven (and conversely that a wicked ruler loses his mandate and may be overthrown by popular revolt) was rejected by the Japanese, who insisted that the Emperor occupied the throne on the basis of descent alone. Again, while the Chinese bureaucracy was generally ordered by merit, in the Japanese scheme appointment to high office was based first on birth, then on character, and only last on ability.[1]

The military government (*bakufu*), installed in 1192 by the victorious general Minamoto no Yoritomo at provincial Kamakura in eastern Japan far from the effete court in Kyoto, introduced a new type of dualism into the governmental structure, which had long been dominated by hereditary civil dictators of the Fujiwara clan. Military supremacy over civilian rule—or at the very least, relative freedom from civil control—has been a feature of the government ever since, emerging in naked form in the 1930s.[2] Militarism brought with it also the typical ethic of the warrior in which loyalty to one's master, self-abnegation, and mindless duty became the supreme virtues.

The code of the warrior was reinforced by the adoption of neo-Confucianism of the Chu Hsi school as the official philosophy of the Tokugawa shogunate in the early seventeenth century. Japan,

[1] George Sansom, A *History of Japan to 1334*, Stanford University Press, 1958, p. 69.

[2] To be discussed in the next section.

torn by a century of civil war, had finally been unified by Tokugawa Ieyasu in 1600. Ieyasu, a military leader, saw in the ethical
system of the Chu Hsi school the necessary rationale for his
dictatorship. The school, named after the eminent Sung neo-Con-
fucianist, emphasized proper relationships—between ruler and
subject, father and son, husband and wife, older and younger
brother, and between friends. This had been a feature of Con-
fucius' teachings from the beginning; but in feudal Japan, Chu
Hsi's teachings, with their further emphasis on loyalty and duty,
took on a decidedly authoritarian cast. A corollary was the har-
monious adjustment of disagreements even to the point of sacri-
ficing one's own individual interests.

This world view, essentially Chinese and Confucian with distinctly Japanese modifications, gave coherence to Tokugawa
society in its splendid isolation. In providing a code of behavior
for lord and loyal vassal, it ensured the stablity of the regime
headquartered in Edo (now Tokyo) for more than two and a half
centuries. It laid down or reinforced patterns of behavior that
have not been effaced to this day.

Constitutional Beginnings

A constitution may be regarded in functional terms as an instrument designed to restrain the capricious exercise of government
power, which, if unchecked, can easily lead to despotism.[3] This
is especially evident in British constitutional development, in
which the landmarks all relate to the checking of royal tyranny
by people and parliament: the Magna Carta, which King John's
barons extorted from their sovereign and which set England on
the constitutional road; the Petition of Right of 1628 granted by
Charles I, which represented the power of Parliament and the
common law as a restraint to the exercise of absolute regal power;
the Habeas Corpus Act of 1679, which guaranteed freedom
against arbitrary arrest and imprisonment; and the Act of Settle-

[3] C. J. Friedrich, *Constitutional Government and Democracy* (rev. ed.),
Ginn & Co., 1950, p. 121.

ment of 1701, which guaranteed judicial independence, to name but a few.

Japanese constitutionalism, on the other hand, is the product of an entirely different history. Traditionally, the state has been viewed as a kind of extended family with the divine and benevolent Emperor as paterfamilias to whom all subjects owe unswerving loyalty. In the nature of the system there can be no confrontation between Emperor and people, who comprise a single corporate entity, the Japanese state. There can be no parliament representing the people pressing for redress of individual wrongs trampled upon by arbitrary exercise of the royal prerogative. There can be no eventual or logical culmination in the concept that the majority will of the people exercised through parliament should rule rather than an aristocratic and authoritarian bureaucracy that has plumbed the mind of the divine ruler. Thus individual rights and majority rule—the essence of the democratic process—are singularly lacking in the Japanese political tradition.

In the West, the spread of constitutionalism following the American Revolution went hand-in-glove with the rise of industrialism and the overseas expansion of European power. One of the embellishments of the western nations, when they intruded into East Asia in the middle decades of the nineteenth century was the device of constitutional government. It was only natural, therefore, that Japan's leaders in their drive to modernize the nation should have adopted the external trappings of western constitutionalism together with its technology; it was unfortunate but understandable that they found so much that was congenial in the more conservative types of constitutional monarchy still prevalent in much of nineteenth-century Europe rather than in the republicanism of the American experiment or in the attenuated monarchy of Victorian England.

Commodore Perry's four warships steaming into Edo Bay in 1853 revealed Japan's weakness, and it soon became apparent that Japan could not hope to preserve her independence without a radical buildup of her national strength. Japanese leaders could see that British power expanding from a base in the Indian subcontinent had reached into central China following the Opium Wars in the 1840s. And native regimes had succumbed to Dutch power in the East Indies, Spanish power in the Philippines, and French power in Indochina; while in the North, Russia whittled away at the maritime provinces of Siberia.

Partly because the Tokugawa *bakufu* was unable to adapt to meet the threat posed by foreign powers and partly because it was no longer able to secure the allegiance of its vassals, it was overthrown by forces rallying around the throne, and in late 1867 the last of the shoguns surrendered his political power to the Emperor. Soon thereafter the young Emperor Meiji issued his Restoration Rescript, and in the following decades a new sense of identity as Japanese and a new nationalism were to be brought to focus brilliantly in the imperial institution.

In order to ensure her independence and security, threatened by western aggrandizement, Japan's leaders felt it necessary to establish a strong central government which would take the lead in the gigantic task of building up her economic strength and her military power. These twin objectives were popularized in the slogan "Prosperity and Arms."

It is therefore not surprising that the impulse toward constitutionalism tended to increase the power of the throne rather than to restrain the sovereign. In any case, no Emperor of Japan had exercised real power for over a millennium. As for securing individual rights, in the pervasive ideology of the day duties and obligations weighed more heavily than theoretical notions of rights, which were still only dimly perceived.

Government leaders of the time, in particular the acknowledged architect of the Meiji Constitution, Ito Hirobumi, were more sympathetic to the conception of monarchical absolutism than to theories of English constitutionalism and French liberalism espoused by the opposition. The defeat of the French in the Franco-Prussian War of 1870 undoubtedly influenced this development. Ito, who was dispatched to the West to study constitutional developments in 1882–1883, returned after spending most of his time in Germany as an ardent admirer of Prussian bureaucracy and Bismarck.

The Constitution drafted under Ito's aegis and promulgated in 1889 was a thoroughly authoritarian one, negating the spirit of the Charter Oath of 1868 which Meiji, as a stripling of fifteen, had enunciated as a guide for his newly founded government. The Charter Oath had called for the establishment of deliberative assemblies to determne policy by public debate, opportunity to work at a calling of one's choice, the discarding of outmoded customs and usages, the reign of law, the seeking and importation of knowledge, and the establishment of national unity to facilitate administration. The spirit of the Charter Oath had been liberal and progressive; the new Constitution was distinctly retrogressive. Still, it satisfied the requirement that a modern nation must have a constitution as a prerequisite to admission as an equal to the family of nations.

The Constitution—the last of the nineteenth century octroyed constitutions—was bestowed on the monarch's subjects, a fact which the preamble takes care to underscore. It is granted by the Emperor and can be amended only by imperial initiative. Sovereignty belongs to the Emperor by right of inheritance from imperial ancestors in a "lineal succession unbroken for ages eternal." Present and future "subjects" are forever enjoined to "assume the duty of allegiance" to the Constitution. The Emperor is described as "sacred and inviolable" (Article 3) combining in himself all rights of sovereignty (Article 4). Nevertheless, because he is inviolable, his ministers of state advise him and are responsible for their advice (Article 55). The usual panoply of rights are secured for "subjects" (Articles 18–32), but they are severely circumscribed by "duties" and by subsequent legislation and ideological strictures.

The theoretical absolutism of the Constitution was attenuated to some degree by the establishment of a parliament in 1890 and the steady expansion of suffrage as well as the gradual development of party government in the 1920s. Yet the prevailing ethos smothered the healthy development of those democratic attitudes and values which undergird the visible structure of government; and when the military reaction came in the 1930s, it was fatal to democracy.

In her arms buildup, Japan had been extraordinarily successful, startling the world first with her defeat of China in the Sino-Japanese War of 1895, and then with her victory in the Russo-Japanese War of 1904–1905. Such feats not only guaranteed her independence at a time when China was in danger of dismember-

ment—with Japan now included among the predators—it also
fired in her leaders dreams of continental expansion. At the same
time the second objective of Meiji policy— a prosperous nation—
was not fulfilled. Agriculture especially was depressed, since the
government in effect had confiscated surplus capital accumulated
by the farmers through severe land taxes, using the siphoned-off
surplus to finance Japan's industrialization and her military establishment.[4]

When worldwide depression struck in 1929, the prices of rice
(the backbone of the agricultural economy) and silk (the chief
cash crop) toppled, and agrarian discontent reached a new high.
The suffering of the rural masses directly affected the morale of
the Japanese army, which was based on peasant recruits; moreover, many of the younger officers were themselves products of
the impoverished countryside. Military activists and their rightist
civilian cohorts staged a series of assassinations and attempted
coups aimed at destroying party government and establishing an
expansionist foreign policy as a cure for economic ills. This military incursion into politics was disastrous to parliamentary
democracy.

There was in the working of the Meiji Constitution a fatal
dualism not without precedent in the western world. For example,
the duality between a sovereign executive and a sovereign legislature in the French Charter of 1830 could not be resolved and was
eventually broken by the revolution of 1848. In the case of Japan,
the central characteristic of the presurrender government was its
duality, with the military occupying a position of apparent independence, even of superiority, to the civilian government. This
state of affairs stemmed from the fact that while theoretically
the Emperor as supreme sovereign was at once the chief civil
magistrate and the supreme military commander, in actual practice
he was not and could not act as an absolute monarch. Real power
was exercised by responsible ministers and military officers who
reported to him separately. The supreme command (the Army
and Navy Chiefs of Staff) jealously guarded their prerogative of
independent access to the throne, especially in matters of military
strategy.

[4] E. H. Norman, *Japan's Emergence as a Modern State*, Institute of
Pacific Relations, 1940, pp. 208 ff.

If a difference arose between civilian and military advisers over policy, who would mediate and ensure unity? By tradition, the work of unification should have fallen to the Grand Minister of the Cabinet (*Naikaku Sori Daijin*), then as now more familiarly known as the Prime Minister. In fact, executive direction of Japan's affairs was managed by congeries of elites not all of which were necessarily subservient to the will of the Prime Minister.

The elites clustered around such executive agencies as the Cabinet, the Privy Council, Supreme Command Offices, the Imperial Household Ministry, and the informal body known as the Elder Statesmen (*Genro.*) In the tradition of strong executive dominance over politics, the legislative branch (the Imperial Diet) was completely overshadowed by the executive. To unify policy, a whole series of extraconstitutional and extralegal bodies, both formal and informal, were devised over the years. In the process, the Meiji Constitution was profoundly modified, and amended in fact if not by law.

Concurrent holding of office was one of the first such devices. In fact, this actually predated the Meiji Constitution and continued until it was superseded by the present charter in 1947. When the Cabinet was first established in 1885 after the Prussian model four years prior to the promulgation of the Constitution, Ito Hirobumi, the first Prime Minister, concurrently held the position of Imperial Household Minister. Three years later, when the Privy Council was created to deliberate on the then draft Constitution, Ito resigned the Premiership—which was in any case becoming untenable—to take over direction of the presidency of this vital center. A half a century later, General Tojo Hideki served concurrently as Prime Minister and War Minister in the critical pre-Pearl Harbor Cabinet of 1941.

Government by cronies was another device used to unify policy. The restorationists of 1867 came chiefly from an alliance of four "clans," and these early leaders of the Meiji government lasted well into the twentieth century. Once established in power, these "clan bureaucrats" worked to remain at the topmost level of government by instituting a system of rotating Premierships. During this period developed the practice of selecting Prime Ministers by Elder Statesmen meeting in council, and election to the highest office was based not on a popular majority in Parliament but on agreement among those government leaders who enjoyed the confidence of the Emperor.

As party government evolved in the second and third decades of the twentieth century, the Cabinet was able to assert its natural leadership over its competitors. But as party government fell into decay in the thirties and the power of the military elite rose, it became apparent that some sort of unifying mechanism would have to be established. From the invasion of Manchuria in 1931 to the attack on Pearl Harbor in 1941, the Cabinet and the supreme command were constantly at variance with each other, and it was only the unending succession of defeats during World War II that finally undermined the power of the military and enabled the government to gain the upper hand.

During the 1930s, however, various expedients were explored in an attempt to improve liaison between the civilian and military elites. Military men as Prime Ministers were one such expedient, and from December, 1931 to August, 1945, 8 of the 12 men designated as Premiers were generals or admirals on active service.[5] Another technique was the calling of ad hoc councils, such as the Five Ministers Conferences (the Prime Minister and the War, Navy, Foreign, and Finance Ministers), which met intermittently during the Saito (1932–1934), Okada (1934–1936), and the Konoe (1937–1939) Cabinets in attempts to unify national policy.[6]

Still another extraconstitutional and extralegal organ was the Government-Imperial General Headquarters Liaison Conference first established in December, 1937, following the outbreak of the war with China, to coordinate military and civil policy. Imperial General Headquarters, the brains of the supreme command, had

[5] This was of course a variation of the "concurrent office" tactic employed earlier. Between 1885 and 1945, 20 of the 43 governments were headed by military men. The influence of the military was further heightened by the requirement that the War and Navy Ministers be general grade officers in active service. The military could control or destroy a government simply by not certifying an officer for these posts when the supreme command opposed government policy.

[6] Harada Kumao, Saionji Ko to Seikyoku [Prince Saionji and Japanese Politics], Iwanami, 1951–56, vol. 3, pp. 153–154; vol. 4, p. 27; vol. 7, p. 8. The Paris-educated Saionji was the last of the Elder Statesmen and a close adviser to the throne.

itself been newly organized by imperial ordinance a month earlier to unify command relationships divided during peacetime between the War and Navy Ministries on the one hand and the Army and Navy Chiefs of Staff on the other. During World War II, this Liaison Conference was reorganized and renamed the Supreme Council for the Direction of the War—in effect an inner war cabinet consisting of the Prime Minister and the War, Navy, and Foreign Ministers representing the Cabinet, and the Army and Navy General Staff Chiefs speaking for the supreme military command. In such conferences questions of ultimate importance —war with the United States, for example—were debated and decided. It was here too that the question of surrender was debated during the summer of 1945 when it had become abundantly clear that Japan could no longer hope for victory against the Allied forces. But the Supreme Council could not reach a consensus, with the diehard Army and Navy Chiefs of Staff and the War Minister arguing that one final effort should be mounted before entertaining any thought of surrender. It was in this extremity during the days following the atom-bombing of Hiroshima that the Supreme Council met in the presence of Emperor Hirohito—a fact which, technically, transformed the Council into an Imperial Conference (*Gozen Kaigi*).[7] The Emperor spoke out for acceptance of the Allied surrender demands, and the resistance of the diehards collapsed. He had for once acted as the absolute monarch the Meiji Constitution described him as being.

Postwar Constitutional Reform

The military occupation of Japan under General Douglas MacArthur, Supreme Commander for the Allied Powers (SCAP),[8] brought about a revolutionary transformation of Japan's constitutional and political structure. Characteristically, the change was imposed and carried out from above, creating the paradox of a democratic revolution generated not by the common man or the street mob but by a military dictator. The renovation of the

[7] Literally, "Conference in the August Presence."
[8] The acronym denoted both MacArthur and the occupation administration.

political structure and the imposition of a new constitution in the first years of the occupation [9] were part and parcel of the U.S. effort to eliminate Japan forever as a military threat in the far Pacific. The first step in this direction was to dismantle the war machine, beginning with the demobilization of Imperial General Headquarters on September 13, 1945, about a month after the surrender. This was followed a month later by the abolition of the Army and Navy General Staffs. Next to go were the War and Navy Ministries, and such formal military advisory organs as the Supreme War Council (*Gunji Sangiin*) and the Board of Field Marshals and Fleet Admirals (*Gensuifu*), which, despite their grandiloquent names, had been without substantive function for some time.

Other elements of the crown regarded as obstacles to the democratization of Japan were also swept away. The government itself took the initiative in abolishing the office of the Lord Keeper of the Privy Seal in November, 1945. The Imperial Household Ministry, which had functioned as a non-Cabinet independent ministry under imperial ordinance, was reduced in status and finally replaced by the Imperial Household Office (later Agency) under the control of the Prime Minister's Office. The independent Privy Council, a stronghold of extreme conservatism in political life and watchdog of the Meiji Constitution, was transferred to the jurisdiction of the Prime Minister's Office and was eliminated altogether in 1947 when the new Constitution took effect. The peerage was abolished, and an elected House of Councilors replaced the House of Peers in the new National (formerly Imperial) Diet or parliament.

In addition to these changes involving the supreme military command and civilian advisers to the throne, the occupation further drastically altered the governmental structure by removing or modifying other ministries. The Ministry of Home Affairs had long been the control center of the unitary state. It was through this ministry that the government had exercised police-state con-

---

[9] For the official history of the political renovation with attendant documents, see Supreme Commander for the Allied Powers, Government Section, *Political Reorientation of Japan, September 1945–September 1948*, Government Printing Office, 1949, two vols.

trols, including those of an ideological nature, in virtually every phase of national life. Through its Police Bureau the Home Ministry had enforced all laws, rescripts, regulations, and administrative orders throughout the nation, paying particular attention to the enforcement of legislation relating to internal subversion and "dangerous thought." Through its Board of Shrines (*Jingiin*) it had administered and controlled State Shinto, the institutional backbone of the Emperor cult.

Reform, leading to eventual abolition of the Home Ministry,[10] began with the issuance by SCAP of the so-called "Civil Rights" memorandum of October 14, 1945. All laws restricting political, civil, and religious liberties were ordered repealed and all agencies of the Home Ministry as well as the Special Higher Police (popularly referred to as the Thought-Control Police) of Tokyo, Osaka, and other metropolitan areas charged with their enforcement were ordered disbanded. In a series of ordinances the government complied by reorganizing the ministry and repealing those statutes which had long been used by the police to suppress civil rights, in particular those which had made it a crime to discuss freely, much less criticize, the Emperor and the Emperor system. The second of the memoranda, dealing with "Disestablishment of State Religions," was issued by SCAP on December 15, 1945; it required the abolition of the Board of Shrines. This was accomplished on January 31, 1946, and state support of Shinto as the basis of the Emperor cult came to an end. The ministry itself was abolished one year later.

These two memoranda constitute landmarks in the history of the establishment of civil liberties in Japan. Perhaps their most important influence was indirect, in that they radically altered the ideological climate of Japanese national and political life. On January 1, 1946, Emperor Hirohito repudiated his divinity in a "Rescript on the Construction of a New Japan," and thus destroyed the rationale of the Emperor mystique, which had been at the center of the old ultranationalism, and prepared the way

---

[10] Its postwar counterpart is the Local Autonomy Ministry, charged with supervision of elections and with carrying out liaison between central and local authorities. It is now sometimes referred to in the English-language press as the Home Ministry.

for the establishment of the Japanese state on new foundations. The final ideological support of the old empire fell on June 19, 1948, when the House of Representatives and the House of Councilors in a joint resolution rescinded Emperor Meiji's Imperial Rescript on Education. This rescript had set the tone of social ethics for generations of school children—a tone pitched to a high nationalistic level with the supreme value being established as devotion to the Emperor and the Emperor system.

The government system which thus emerged form these occupation-sponsored reforms was entirely different from the pre-surrender Emperor system. In demilitarizing Japan and removing such elements of the crown as the Privy Council, the occupation destroyed the military base of power in political life, eliminated the dualism which had plagued the government for decades, and upgraded the Cabinet to a position of supremacy.

In order to consolidate these gains, and further to encourage the development of democratic institutions in accordance with the requirements of the Potsdam Declaration under which Japan had surrendered, General MacArthur determined at the outset that the overall political reform should encompass constitutional revision.

The Japanese government, on the other hand, apparently felt that a token amendment of the Meiji Charter coupled with fundamental political reform would satisfy SCAP requirements; it acted accordingly, submitting draft changes that were more stylistic than substantive. When the footdragging of the ultraconservatives given the task of revision became clear to SCAP, MacArthur directed the Government Section of SCAP to draft a model constitution for the purpose of instructing the Japanese government on the basic requirements. The Government Section immediately took up the job of constitution drafting, beginning on February 4, 1946, and aiming for an initial completion date of February 12, so that the new charter—one is tempted to call it Japan's Emancipation Proclamation—would be ready in time for Lincoln's birthday. The deadline was met: the draft Constitution was completed in eight days.

Under severe pressure by SCAP to accept this exemplary Constitution, the governments of Shidehara and his successor Yoshida bowed to the inevitable and agreed to wholesale revision. The government produced in short order a Japanese draft—there are some who complain that it reads too much like a direct translation from the English—and this was the Constitution debated by the 90th (Special) Imperial Diet sitting as a quasiconstituent assembly during the summer of 1946. Debated at length but changed in no substantive manner, it was approved by the House of Representatives on October 7 by a vote of 342 to 5 and promulgated on November 3, the birthday of Emperor Meiji, to go into effect six months later on May 3, 1947.

Government under the New Constitution

In constitutional theory, the most important difference between the Meiji Charter of 1889 and the MacArthur Constitution of 1946 is the locus of sovereignty. Previously the Emperor was theoretically supreme and ruled by divine right—a right inherited from his forebears "of a lineal succession unbroken for ages eternal."

In contrast, under the new Constitution the Emperor is reduced to the status of a "symbol of the State and of the unity of the people," deriving his position "from the will of the people with whom resides sovereign power" (Article 1). Whereas Emperor Meiji had granted the Constitution to his subjects, in 1946 the Japanese people, acting through their duly elected representatives in the Imperial Diet, proclaimed the doctrine of popular sovereignty and established their own constitution.

From the point of view of practical politics, the most important change has been the elevation of the Cabinet to a position of supremacy not only in the administration of the state but also in legislative matters. Although the principle of legislative supremacy is enunciated (Article 41) to accord with the conception of popular sovereignty, in actual operation it is fairly obvious that the Cabinet and the permanent bureaucracy are the superior force. There are good reasons for this, not the least important being the long tradition of bureaucratic rule and the succession of strong conservative cabinets in postwar Japan.

Another striking difference is the attempted negation of militarism in the famous article renouncing war "forever . . . as a sovereign right" and asserting that "land, sea, and air forces . . . will never be maintained" and that "the right of belligerency of the state will not be recognized" (Article 9). In fact, Japan maintains an army, navy, and air force (euphemistically referred to as Land, Maritime, and Air Self-Defense Forces), and this wide gap between constitutional terminology and reality is the source of increasing concern. The no-war article is a dead letter and has been the primary target of constitutional amendment by the conservatives, but no government to date has been able to muster the two-thirds majority in the lower houses required for amendment.[11]

The declaration of rights (Articles 10–40), which is long and extensive, includes some that are foreign to western constitutions, e.g., academic freedom (Article 23). The fundamental human rights are guaranteed as "eternal and inviolate." Respect for the people as individuals is assured, and the supreme goal of legislation is asserted to be the securing of life, liberty, and the pursuit of happiness "to the extent that it does not interefere with the public welfare" (Article 13). Equality under the law, the right to vote, freedom of thought, conscience, religion, assembly, speech, press, and all other forms of expression are assured, as is the right for labor to organize collectively and for individuals to own property. Legal safeguards, including the new (for Japan) right of habeas corpus and the right not to incriminate oneself, are introduced into the Constitution.

In a nation where the spirit of individualism is still underdeveloped and where the "public welfare" tends to take precedence over individual rights, a mere cataloging of "eternal and inviolate" rights will of course not necessarily guarantee their application or viability. But the Japanese citizen has been undergoing an intensive period—now entering its third decade—of social indoctrination in democratic values, and when these values become unshakably imprinted in the individual mind and are accepted by public official and citizen alike, the letter of the written code will gain life, spirit, and substance. The full enjoyment of

---

[11] For further discussion see Chapter Nine.

civil rights, as is the case in even the most advanced democracies, is both a goal and an existing reality.

One final aspect of the new Constitution should be noted. As a check to executive tyranny, the judicial power is vested in an independent Supreme Court and inferior courts (Article 76), in sharp contrast to the previous system where the courts were virtually an arm of the administration. As a further check, the constitutionality of all legislative and official acts is made subject to judicial review.

CHAPTER THREE

Executive Style:
the Governing Process

Parliamentary-Cabinet Government

ACCORDING TO the Constitution, the Diet (Parliament) is the "highest organ of state power" and "sole law-making" body, deriving its power as a trust from the sovereign people. Executive power is vested in a Cabinet designated by the Diet and collectively responsible to it. The Cabinet, on the other hand, has the power to dissolve the lower house and call for general elections. An independent system of courts, in which the "whole judicial power" reposes, is empowered to review the constitutionality of all statutes and administrative acts, but the Cabinet designates the Chief Justice of the Supreme Court and appoints all judges of the inferior courts.

In this apparent system of checks and balances, there exists a bicameral legislature consisting of the House of Representatives (467 members) and a House of Councilors (250 members). The Prime Minister is elected by the House of Representatives—in normal times the office goes automatically to the leader of the majority party—and he forms his government of 16 Cabinet ministers from the membership of his parliamentary party. In postwar Japan, except for a short-lived Socialist administration in 1947–1948, all governments have been conservative, headed by the Liberal-Democratic Party and its predecessors. The judicial system embraces a Supreme Court sitting in Tokyo, 8 high courts, 49 district courts, 570 summary courts, and 49 family courts.

The Constitution and the mechanisms it provides for government represent a hybrid, the prototypes of which are to be found in Great Britain, France, and the United States. Theoretically, it should operate only with the greatest difficulty, but the Japanese have made it work—just as they earlier devised means to make the Meiji Constitution a viable basis of government. In its insistence on legislative supremacy, the Constitution echoes the organic laws of the Third and Fourth Republics of France that find their ultimate rationale in the revolutionary tradition and Rousseau's concept of popular sovereignty. But it should be noted that this anomalous provision has been virtually disregarded from the beginning because of the domination of Parliament by a succession of autocratic Prime Ministers, beginning with the rule of "One Man" Yoshida Shigeru in 1946. Again, in providing for political responsibility of ministers to Parliament by rooting the Cabinet in the legislature, the Constitution borrowed from the English experience; in the ascendancy of the executive over the legislature, Japan has followed a pattern observable in Great Britain and in Commonwealth nations during the twentieth century. Finally, the system of divided powers and checks and balances finds inspiration in the American presidential model. In its essential foundations, therefore, it is patterned after the classic British model, but it betrays its recent American accretions in its stress on the division of powers and its provision for judicial review.

The English parliamentary system represents a fusion of the executive and legislative powers (as denoted by the expression "the King [or Crown]-in-Parliament"), and the enormous concentration of power represented by such a corporate entity always raises the fear of dictatorship. As Professor C. J. Friedrich has pointed out, the traditional tripartite division of powers is not the only way to avoid excessive concentration of power. Where legislative and executive powers are fused, as in Great Britain, the periodic alternation of two large political parties permits Parliament and ultimately the people to exercise continuous control over policy; it also provides for regularized restraint of government power.[1] If the people disagree with government policy, they can change it without resort to violence or overthrow of the Constitution. In Japan, however, this periodic alternation has not devel-

[1] *Constitutional Government and Democracy*, pp. 178–179.

oped because the opposition party—the Socialists—have become a more or less permanent minority faction unable to muster much more than one-third of the total votes cast in any general election.

From this strange mixture of parliamentary and presidential types of government has emerged a unique polity characterized by the ascendancy of the executive and the relative weakness of the legislature in spite of the constitutional supremacy of the legislature. Some of the regularized restraints which mark the British constitution, notably a vigorous two-party system, are missing. British ministers, moreover, are never permitted to forget their parliamentary origins, and they must constantly defend their policies in debate on the floor of Commons and in regularly scheduled question hours. In Japan, once a Diet member has reached the ministerial level, he is inclined to downgrade his obligations to the Diet and to his constituency. When Japanese ministers appear in the Diet, they are usually there for the purpose of making speeches or answering formal interpellations. The practice of extended debate between government and opposition spokesmen on the floor of the House of Representatives has shown little development.

The Diet, for all of its weaknesses, is not a nullity, and with the exception of a period in the late 1930s and during World War II, no Japanese Parliament has been a rubber stamp acquiescent to every whim of the executive. The Japanese, nevertheless, have not yet been able to attain that special equilibrium between Cabinet and Parliament that marks the operation of the British government, in which the Cabinet is able to act vigorously and effectively and yet remain firmly under the ultimate control of Commons. A significant shift toward a better balance appeared in 1960 and, if continued, should substantially modify the excessive power of the executive. When Prime Minister Kishi's government fell, partly because of his high-handed tactics in ramming through the Diet the revised United States-Japan Security Treaty, his successor Ikeda Hayato adopted as the keynote of his new administration a "low posture" policy toward the opposition. The "tyranny of the majority" was softened by this conciliatory attitude toward the minority. The new approach has been continued by Sato Eisaku, who became Prime Minister in 1964.

Legislative Supremacy vs. Cabinet Domination

The Cabinet does not merely execute and administer a program of legislative action determined by the Diet. Instead, it plans legislation, initiates bills, organizes support in the Diet, and puts through a legislative program, which it then administers. How has it managed to reach such an ascendant position in the face of the constitutional provision making the Diet the "sole" legislative organ of the state?

One reason is that the Constitution itself appears to contradict the principle of legislative supremacy by providing the executive with a variety of powers which, in the end, permit the emergence of the Cabinet as the dominant force in the government. These provisions for Cabinet action, scattered throughout the various chapters of the Constitution, may be conveniently enumerated under executive, legislative, and judicial functions, as follows:

Executive

Supervise the administration of the state (72),[2] administer the law, conduct affairs of state, administer the civil service, and enact Cabinet (administrative) orders (73).

Manage foreign affairs and conclude treaties with prior or subsequent approval of the Diet (73).

Administer national finances (83) and expend monies from the reserve fund (87).

Legislative

Submit bills, report on national affairs and foreign relations to the Diet (72).

Prepare and submit the budget bill to the Diet (73, 86), submit final accounts of state expenditures and revenues to the Diet (90), report annually to the Diet on the state of national finances (91).

Advise the Emperor * to convoke regular sessions of the Diet, dissolve the House of Representatives, and proclaim general elections (7); determine the convocation of extraordinary sessions of the Diet

* Refer to footnote on p. 43.
2 Numerals refer to numbered articles of the Constitution.

(53) and the calling of emergency sessions of the House of Councilors (54).

Sign and countersign all laws and Cabinet orders (74).

Advise the Emperor * to promulgate amendments of the Constitution, laws, cabinet orders, and treaties (7).

Judicial

Designate the Chief Justice of the Supreme Court (6).

Appoint all judges (79–80).

Determine amnesty, commutation of punishment, reprieve, and restoration of rights (73).

How formidable the powers of the Cabinet are should be obvious from this simple catalogue of functions. It administers the affairs of state through a vast bureaucracy embracing some 1,852,-000 employees (in 1963) in 53 primary ministries and agencies.[3] Although the judiciary is now independent, the Cabinet retains a measure of influence over the judicial process, not only in the appointment of judges, but also in the administration especially of criminal justice. All public procurators (prosecutors) are civil service employees of the Ministry of Justice.

Above all, the Cabinet has the right to initiate both ordinary legislation and amendments to the Constitution. Some interpreters of the Constitution deny that the Cabinet has these rights, arguing that these functions belong solely to the Diet. But as long as the Prime Minister and a majority of his ministers are required to be members of the Diet, the logic of parliamentary government demands that the Cabinet share with the Diet the right to propose legislation. Not only does it share the right: the Cabinet in fact initiates the bulk of legislation. Of the bills that are introduced into any given session of the Diet, the overwhelming majority—and the most important ones—are government sponsored.[4] Japanese officialdom has become so habituated to the

* The Emperor, of course, has no discretion in these matters and must invariably follow the advice rendered.

[3] *Japan Statistical Yearbook*, 1963, pp. 452–455.

[4] According to one study, only 270 out of 3126 bills introduced during the period 1890–1920 were private member bills; the rest were government drafts. The ratio has not noticeably changed in recent years. See K. Tsuji, "The Cabinet, Administrative Organization, and the Bureaucracy," in *Annals of the American Academy of Political and Social Science*, vol. 308 (Nov. 1956), p. 13.

practice of drafting legislation, and legislators have become so accustomed to deferring to the technical superiority of the bureaucrats, that the primary role of the Diet has been reduced to studying, questioning, modifying, and passing bills sponsored by the government.

One reason the initiative has moved from Parliament to ministerial bureaus is that the complexity of modern legislation requires technical and legal competence of the highest order, and such competence, especially as it relates to financial and economic policy, is much more likely to be found among members of the permanent bureaucracy than among Diet members. This appears to be a universal phenomenon, as is evident in the predominant number of government bills submitted to legislatures in Great Britain, the United States, and elsewhere. In the case of Japan, the deference to bureaucratic expertise finds support in basic attitudes and traditions that exalt the government official and demean the people. Moreover, the Diet in its evolution lacks a strong tradition of opposition to autocratic rule by the government.

There are additional reasons. Since virtually all legislation requires financing, and the planning of financing through the national budget and programs drafted by such bodies as the Economic Planning Agency is in government hands, it becomes easier for the executive than for any single Diet member or group to plan and coordinate the legislative program. The government, furthermore, through party controls, organizes the Diet, placing its men in key committee posts. Finally, while the legislative and judicial functions tend to be fairly narrow because of intrinsic delimitations, the same is not true of the executive. The administrative arm tends to become a catch-all for a variety of miscellaneous functions, as the proliferation of agencies and commissions attached to the Prime Minister's Office and Cabinet ministries attests. Again, this is a worldwide phenomenon: the administrative state has grown everywhere. In short, it is a combination of factors—Constitutional provisions, complexity of legislation, tradition of bureaucratic supremacy, etc.—that assures the dominance of the Cabinet in the political arena.

Cabinet Formation

Under the Meiji Constitution, the Cabinet shared executive powers with such formal and informal groups as the Elder (later Senior) Statesmen, the supreme command, the Privy Council, and the Privy Seal. Governments were formed not on the basis of popular majorities in the Diet but by imperial command. Since ministers were theoretically also appointed by the Emperor and answerable to him, the Prime Minister was merely the first among equals.

In contrast, under the present Constitution the Cabinet virtually monopolizes executive power, and it does not derive its authority by grant from the Emperor. Rather, as has been previously noted, governments are formed by that politcal party or coalition which can command a majority or plurality in the House of Representatives, and hence Cabinets today derive their authority ultimately from the people. Finally, the Prime Minister is constitutionally the head of the Cabinet with power to appoint his ministers.

While the rationale for a government responsible to the people through the Diet requires that the Cabinet be the sole repository of executive power (just as the Diet is made the "sole" legislative organ and the courts are vested with the "whole judicial power"), there are at least two organs which are virtually independent, and which perform functions normally assigned to the executive. These are the Board of Audit, constitutionally charged with preparing an audit of final accounts of expenditures and revenues for submission by the Cabinet to the Diet,[5] and the National Personnel Authority, whose functions are somewhat analogous to those of the U.S. Civil Service Commission. Though the National Personnel Authority is formally placed under the Cabinet, it is a virtually independent agency, especially in its budgeting.

Under the Meiji Constitution of 1889, the appointment of

[5] Article 1 of the law establishing the Audit Board specifies that it shall stand independent of the Cabinet.

ministers of state, including the Premier, belonged to the imperial prerogative. In actual practice, Prime Ministers were selected by the Elder Statesmen, and when these founders of the modern Japanese state passed from the political scene, their function of nominating the head of government was taken over by the Privy Seal in consultation with the Senior Statesmen (former Premiers). There was no direct relationship between the Cabinet and the Imperial Diet other than the provision that ministers of state could "at any time take seats and speak in either House" (Article 54).[6] The Cabinet theoretically was therefore not responsible to the Diet, but in the actual working of the Meiji Constitution, the government could not ignore the wishes of the Diet, and as early as 1898 a party Cabinet rooted in the Parliament was established, In the period from 1918–1932, and especially after 1925 as the two major political parties vied for power, party government was the general rule.

Today, ministerial responsibility to parliament—the foundation of cabinet government—is written into the Constitution. Thus the Prime Minister is designated by the Diet, and if the two houses disagree the will of the lower house prevails (Article 67).[7] This practice gives primacy to the House of Representatives, and it is from among members of the lower house that, according to the Constitution, Prime Ministers are designated by "a resolution of the Diet." Since all business of the legislature is decided by a majority vote of those present (Article 56), any group that can organize a majority or plurality of the Representatives is assured of gaining the most coveted prize in Japanese politics. Such majorities are normally organized by political parties, and in postwar Japan the conservatives (or conservative coalitions) have consistently managed to obtain the necessary majority and nominate their leader for the Premiership. The only exception has been the Socialist coalition headed by Katayama Tetsu in 1947. The

[6] The same provision is retained in Article 63 of the present Constitution.
[7] In 1948, the Representatives designated Ashida Hitoshi, president of the Democratic Party, as the Prime Minister, while the Councilors nominated Yoshida Shigeru, president of the Liberal Party. When a joint conference of the two houses failed to reach agreement on a candidate acceptable to both, the constitutional provision was invoked and Ashida was nominated.

successive Cabinets and their party affiliations following the first postwar general election of April, 1946, have been as follows:

Cabinet of Premier	Date Formed	Party Affiliation
Yoshida Shigeru, 1st	May 22, 1946	Liberal: Progressive Coalition
Katayama Tetsu	May 24, 1947	Socialist: Democratic: Nat. Coop. Coalition
Ashida Hitoshi	March 10, 1948	Democratic: Socialist: Nat. Coop. Coalition
Yoshida Shigeru, 2nd	October 19, 1948	Liberal Democratic
Yoshida Shigeru, 3rd	February 16, 1949	Liberal Democratic *
Yoshida Shigeru, 4th	October 30, 1952	Liberal
Yoshida Shigeru, 5th	May 21, 1953	Liberal
Hatoyama Ichiro, 1st	December 10, 1954	Japan Democratic
Hatoyama Ichiro, 2nd	March 19, 1955	Japan Democratic
Hatoyama Ichiro, 3rd	November 22, 1955	Liberal-Democratic **
Ishibashi Tanzan	December 23, 1956	Liberal-Democratic
Kishi Nobusuke, 1st	February 25, 1957	Liberal-Democratic
Kishi Nobusuke, 2nd	June 12, 1958	Liberal-Democratic
Ikeda Hayato, 1st	July 19, 1960	Liberal-Democratic
Ikeda Hayato, 2nd	December 18, 1960	Liberal-Democratic
Ikeda Hayato, 3rd	December 9, 1963	Liberal-Democratic
Sato Eisaku	November 9, 1964	Liberal-Democratic

* Renamed the Liberal Party in 1950.
** Formed by a merger of the Japan Democratic and the Liberal Parties.

The designation of the Prime Minister by the Diet is the initial order of business after the Diet is organized following a general election. The office normally goes to the president of the majority party, and in the last decade this has meant that the real political struggle for determination of the Prime Ministership has been carried out in biennial conventions of the Liberal-Democratic Party which meet to elect the party president.[8] Thus, in the general elections of November, 1963, the Liberal-Democrats won a majority of the seats in the Diet and automatically installed as Prime Minister the incumbent, Ikeda Hayato, who had won the party presidency for a two-year term the previous year in a con-

[8] For further discussion, see Chapter Seven.

vention marked by fierce intraparty factional struggles and the profligate spending of money to buy the votes of delegates. By 1964 Ikeda had been in office for four years, and there were many in his party who felt that he should step down and permit someone else to assume the Premiership. In the July convention of that year, five of the eight factions sided with Ikeda while three went over to his rivals of the Sato-Fujiyama factional coalition. Ikeda emerged with a slim majority of four votes (out of 475 valid votes cast) and thereby ensured for himself an additional two-year term as Prime Minister. Illness forced his resignation a scant four months later, however, and after a round of consultations with party leaders, Ikeda's chief rival, Sato Eisaku, was designated his successor by a parliamentary caucus of conservative party members. Sato was subsequently elected Prime Minister by plenary sessions of both Houses, and an extraordinary party congress was later convened to ratify the caucus' decision.

The election of the Prime Minister by the Diet is followed by the appointment of the Cabinet. Ministerial appointments do not require subsequent ratification by the Diet, the Constitution merely providing that a majority of the ministers be Diet members. Politics adds the further condition that all ministers be Dietmen and that most be members of the lower house and, of course, members of the political party in power. The Prime Minister is empowered to appoint and dismiss his Cabinet ministers at will. All must be civilians.[9]

While Prime Minister Yoshida had the reputation of arbitrarily appointing his favorites, in recent years a kind of priority system has been evolved by the conservatives to allocate available ministerial posts. Such posts are greatly sought after not only because they confer high honor on the recipient—honor immediately and permanently translatable into votes—but also because they can lead ultimately to the Prime Ministership itself. In the scramble for positions following every change and reshuffle of the Cabinet, the following criteria have come to be used to separate the eligibles from those who will have to be content with lesser positions:

[9] Previously War and Navy Ministry posts were filled by generals or admirals in active service. In addition, 20 of the 43 presurrender Cabinets were headed by military men.

number of times elected to the Diet, loyalty in supporting factional leaders, past experience (for example, as a former bureaucrat who has risen to the top of the bureaucracy), and administrative ability. Of the four criteria, the first is the most important, and in recent years it has been the rule that Dietmen must generally serve at least five terms before they are considered for Cabinet posts.[10] The appointment of such outsiders as financiers Ichimada Hisato and Fujiyama Aiichiro in the early 1950s constituted exceptions, and even these favorites of the autocratic Yoshida were expected to stand for election at the first opportunity.

The composition of the Sato Cabinet illustrates the political factors which must be considered by the Liberal-Democrats when forming a new government. When Sato took office as Premier, he retained the Cabinet of his predecessor [11] although it was soon being predicted that he would dissolve the lower house and call for general elections so that he could form a government of his own choosing. The holdover regime consisted of the following Liberal-Democrats first brought together (except for Sato himself) in July, 1964, when Ikeda had formed his fourth reconstructed Cabinet: [12]

Prime Minister Sato Eisaku, 63, Yamaguchi Prefecture, Tokyo University, bureaucrat, 7th-term Representative, Sato faction.

[10] Watanabe Tsuneo, *Habatsu: Hoshuto no Kaibo* [*Factions: an Analysis of the Conservative Party*], Kobundo, 1958, pp. 41, 227–231. The rule does not apply to the two or three posts filled by members of the House of Councilors whose fixed term of office (6 years) reduces the number of times one is elected.

[11] While the Ikeda Cabinet was retained intact, two vital changes were made at the subcabinet level: the replacement of Suzuki Zenko as Chief Cabinet Secretary by Hashimoto Tomisaburo, 72, a former newspaperman in his seventh term as a Representative and a close confidant of the incoming Premier and member of the Sato faction; and the retirement of the Director of the Cabinet Bureau of Legislation and his replacement by his deputy, Takatsuji Masami, a career civil servant.

[12] For each minister of state, the following information is given in this sequence: Position, name, age, Prefecture represented, college of graduation, prior career, number of times elected either as a Representative or as a Councilor, and factional affiliation: The data derives from a number of sources. See especially H. H. Baerwald, "Japan: the Politics of Transition," in *Asian Survey* (January 1965), pp. 33–42.

Foreign Minister Shiina Etsusaburo, 66, Iwate Prefecture, Tokyo University, bureaucrat, 4th-term Representative, Kawashima faction.

Justice Minister Takahashi Hitoshi, 61, Hiroshima Prefecture, Tokyo University, bureaucrat, 6th-term Representative, Ikeda faction.

Finance Minister Tanaka Kakuei, 45, Niigata Prefecture, Chuo Technological Institute, politician, 8th-term Representative, Sato faction.

Education Minister Aichi Kiichi, 56, Miyagi Prefecture, Tokyo University, bureaucrat, 7th-term Representative, Sato faction.

Health and Welfare Minister Kanda Hiroshi, 60, Shizuoka Prefecture, Hosei University, bureaucrat-industrialist, 6th-term Representative, Funada faction.[13]

Agriculture-Forestry Minister Akagi Munenori, 58, Ibaraki Prefecture, Tokyo University, bureaucrat-politician, 8th-term Representative, Kawashima faction.

International Trade and Industry Minister Sakurauchi Yoshio, 52, Shimane Prefecture, Keio University, businessman-politician, 7th-term Representative, Kono faction.

Transportation Minister Matsuura Shutaro, 68, Hokkaido, self-educated, politician, 9th-term Representative, Miki faction.

Postal Services Minister Tokuyasu Jitsuzo, 64, Shimane Prefecture, Aotani Jitsugyo Hoshu School, journalist-politician, 6th-term Representative, Funada faction.

Labor Minister Ishida Hirohide, 49, Akita Prefecture, Waseda University, journalist, 8th-term Representative, Independent.

Construction Minister Koyama Osanori, 59, Miyazaki Prefecture, Tokyo University, banker, 6th-term Representative, Ikeda faction.

Autonomy Minister Yoshitake Eichi, 61, Yamaguchi Prefecture, Tokyo University, bureaucrat, 2nd-term Councilor (previously elected to three terms in the House of Representatives), Sato faction.

State Minister and Director, Administrative Management Agency and Hokkaido Development Agency, Masuhara Keikichi, 61, Ehime Prefecture, Tokyo University, bureaucrat, 2nd-term Councilor, Fujiyama faction.

Minister without Portfolio (previously State Minister for Olympic Games) Kono Ichiro, 65, Kanagawa Prefecture, Waseda University, bureaucrat, 11th-term Representative, Kono faction.

[13] Formerly the Ono faction led by Ono Bamboku until his death in the spring of 1964.

State Minister and Director, Defense Agency, Koizumi Jun'ya, 60, Kanagawa Prefecture, Nihon University, bureaucrat, 8th-term Representative, Fujiyama faction.

State Minister and Director, Economic Planning Agency, Takahashi Mamoru, 61, Fukui Prefecture, Tokyo University, bureaucrat, 2nd-term Councilor, Ikeda faction.

The Sato administration is fairly typical of conservative governments in recent years and may be said to represent a judicious balance among the various factions which comprise the Liberal-Democratic Party in the Diet. Included are four members of the Sato faction, four members of the Ikeda faction, two each from the Funada, Kawashima, Kono, and Fujiyama factions, one from the Miki faction, and one independent. The distribution generally reflects factional strength; only the small Ishii faction is not represented.[14]

Fourteen of the ministers of state hold seats in the House of Representatives, to which they have been repeatedly elected— from a low of four terms (the Education Minister) to a high of 11 (Kono, Minister without Portfolio). This confirms the general rule that Dietmen usually must be re-elected five times or more before they are considered eligible for ministerial posts. Three of the lesser posts (Autonomy, Administrative Management, and Economic Planning) went to Councilors, who are tied to lower house factions through the party.

By profession, 11 of the 17, including the Prime Minister, began their adult careers in the central government bureaucracy, while only three may be described as professional politicians. The predominance of former bureaucrats at the top levels of government is a phenomenon perhaps unique to Japan among modern states and will be treated in greater detail in the next chapter.

[14] A "low posture" (conciliatory) attitude characterized Ikeda's attitudes toward his opponents both within and without his party. Ikeda sought to harmonize conflicting intraparty differences by a balanced distribution of available posts, but it is clear that in the process he did not reduce conflict but merely managed to undermine his own power position. In the mid-1964 Cabinet reshuffle, the Miki faction actually counted 1.5 positions as gained, since a Miki adherent had been named to the important subcabinet post of director of the Prime Minister's Office. For a detailed discussion of party factions, see Chapter Seven.

More than half (nine) are graduates of Tokyo University, which, since its establishment as a training school for public servants in the latter half of the nineteenth century, has contributed a disproportionate number of alumni to the service of the state.

The traditional respect for age is reflected in the make-up of the Cabinet, with the majority of members being 60 or more. Only Finance Minister Tanaka, at 45, is "middle-aged." Finally, geographical representation is unimportant; there are two each from election districts in Yamaguchi (Sato's constituency), Shimane and Kanagawa Prefectures, and the others come from all over Japan.

Duration of Cabinets

A Cabinet theoretically may last as long as four years—the Constitutional term of office for members of the House of Representatives. A glance at the table showing the 17 governments organized during the period 1946–1964 reveals, however, that they do not normally endure much more than one year. According to Professor Chitoshi Yanaga, the average life span of the 51 Cabinets formed during the period 1885–1954 was one year, 4 months, and 7 days.[15] And this is not the whole story. Prime Minister Ikeda is credited with three different Cabinets during his four-year tenure in office, from July, 1960, to November, 1964, but actually he formed no less than seven Cabinets during this period. These may be tabulated as follows:

First Official Cabinet, formed July 18, 1960, following the resignation of Prime Minister Kishi and the subsequent election of Ikeda to the party presidency at an extraordinary convention.

Second Official Cabinet, formed December 8, 1960, following the general elections of November in which the Liberal-Democrats obtained a majority of the seats in the Diet.

First Reconstructed Cabinet, July 18, 1961, formed by bringing in principal factional leaders: Sato, Kono, Miki, and others.

Second Reconstructed Cabinet, July 18, 1962, formed following the

15 Chitoshi Yanaga, *Japanese People and Politics*, Wiley, 1956, p. 168.

party convention at which Ikeda was elected to his second term as president.

Third Reconstructed Cabinet, July 18, 1963, formed to restore factional balance.

Third Official Cabinet, formed December 9, 1963, following the general elections of November.

Fourth Reconstructed Cabinet, July 18, 1964, formed following Ikeda's third term re-election to the party presidency.

This constant turnover, incidentally, has one unfortunate effect: it decreases the control exercised by the Diet (through the ministers of state) over the permanent bureaucracy.[16]

Governments are changed for a variety of reasons, some of which have already been indicated. Constitutionally, a Cabinet must resign en masse when it loses the confidence of the House of Representatives—or it must dissolve the House within 10 days of a vote of nonconfidence and call for general elections (Article 69). The House has passed a vote of no confidence only twice in the postwar period, both times under unusual circumstances. In 1948, Prime Minister Yoshida, heading a minority Cabinet, insisted that he was empowered to dissolve the House without a prior vote of no confidence in accordance with Article 7 of the Constitution, which requires the Emperor to dissolve the House on the advice of the Cabinet. The opposition parties, fearful of going to the people at a time when their popularity was waning, objected and were supported by occupation authorities who felt that dissolutions of the House should originate in the Diet and not in the Cabinet. A compromise solution was worked out, with the Socialists obtaining a desired piece of legislation in return for passage of a vote of no confidence. In the ensuing general elections, Socialist fears were confirmed as Yoshida's Democratic Liberal Party won a majority of the seats.[17]

The second vote of no confidence, again directed at a government headed by Yoshida, occurred in 1953 and was followed by an immediate dissolution of the House. The vote had been preceded by the disclosure of irregularities by members of Yoshida's

[16] To be discussed in greater detail in Chapter Four.
[17] Watanabe Tsuneo, *Toshu to Seito* [Party Presidents and Parties], Kobundo, 1961, p. 180.

Cabinet which had drawn censure upon the offending ministers. The vote itself was triggered by a vitriolic outburst by the Prime Minister in a Budget Committee hearing when he called a member of the opposition a "stupid idiot." It was made possible by the defection of various factions of the government party, but it is likely that Yoshida would have dissolved the House regardless of the outcome of the vote.[18] In neither of these cases was the vote actually forced by the opposition—the "normal" mode of operation of the no confidence resolution.

It is true that a threatened no confidence vote resulted in the downfall of Yoshida's fifth and last government in 1954, but since the bipolarization of Japan's parties into two major groupings in 1955, opposition forces have never been able to muster the necessary votes to bring down a government in the Diet.

Cabinet changes are also called for constitutionally when a vacancy occurs in the post of Prime Minister—whether by death, illness, or resignation. Illness in office has caused three Premiers to step down: Hatoyama in 1955, his successor Ishibashi in 1956, and Ikeda in 1964.

In a technical sense, new Cabinets are most frequently formed because of the constitutional provision that the government must resign during the first sitting of the Diet following a general election. General elections are constitutionally required only once every four years, but political pressures have prompted nine such elections in the postwar period, each preceded by dissolutions of the House of Representatives. No Diet has lasted its full life span of four years. The pressures have come not so much from the opposition Socialists as from the internal dynamics of the conservative coalition in the early 1950s and the factionalism of the Liberal-Democrats in the last decade. Thus, Yoshida's dissolution of the House of Representatives during his fourth government in 1953 was aimed at punishing dissidents within his own party, and Ikeda's call for general elections in November, 1960— only months after he had taken office as a successor to Kishi— was aimed at replacing Kishi holdovers and strengthening his own hold on the conservative party.[19]

18 *Ibid.*, p. 182.
19 *Ibid.*, pp. 179–185.

Similarly, Cabinets are often reconstituted when an incumbent wishes to consolidate his position or to mollify his internal opposition, i.e., factions within his own party. Prime Minister Ikeda's annual reshuffling of Cabinet posts during the summer months of 1961–1964 fell into this category of maneuverings to consolidate and harmonize party differences. Japanese political parties, both conservative and reformist, are characterized by strong factional divisions.[20] All conservative Premiers, if they stay in office long enough, sooner or later reconstruct their Cabinets, and though they may wish thereby to strengthen their own power position, the very act of rewarding factional supporters by the distribution of available ministerial and high party posts often has the effect of invigorating the power base of factional leaders. Observers of Japanese politics usually criticize the excessive factionalism of the parties, and the practice certainly does lend itself to abuse and corruption. Yet it has redeeming features which have gone unnoticed. One of the most important is that in the absence of the periodic alternation of government and opposition parties because of the overwhelming dominance of the conservatives, the factions work to limit the authority of any would-be autocrat. If a Kishi reaches too greedily for excessive power, there is always an Ikeda to take his place. This is no small blessing in a nation whose political history has been dominated by authoritarian regimes.

Constitutional and Political Role of the Emperor Institution

Emperor Hirohito is officially held to be the 124th monarch of Japan descended in a direct line from the legendary Emperor Jimmu, who supposedly founded the dynasty in 660 B.C. When Hirohito ascended the throne in 1926, he styled his reign Showa, and in the Japanese chronology (still almost universally used) the year 1965 is the 40th year of the Showa era.[21] The name

[20] See Chapter Seven.

[21] Both western and native chronological systems are commonly employed, the western calendar having been adopted in 1870. A third system of counting years, in which 660 B.C. was the year one, was in use until the end of the war.

Hirohito, bestowed by his grandfather, Meiji, is more or less taboo. In Japan, it is almost never seen in print nor is it heard in conversation except among uncouth foreigners. He will be known posthumously as the Emperor Showa; meanwhile, he is referred to politely as *Tenno* (Emperor), or Heika (His Majesty), or as *Tenno Heika*. There is no dynastic or family name.

In his private life, Emperor Hirohito is a marine biologist of some renown. His public life is taken up with the various ceremonial functions of state to which the new Constitution now relegates him. Thus, the year 1964 began for him with the annual Imperial New Year's Poetry ceremony at which 12 winning *tanka* (the ancient 31-syllable verse form) from among 46,886 entries were read to an invited audience of poetasters at the Imperial Palace. During the course of the year, he appeared twice at Tokyo International Airport, the first time to great King Baudoin and Queen Fabiola of Belgium, making the first state visit of a ruling monarch to Japan since the war, and the second time to welcome the King and Queen of Malaysia. He also received Anastas Mikoyan at the Imperial Palace, the first high ranking Soviet official ever to meet an Emperor of Japan.

The custom of presenting honors and decorations to living individuals, suspended since the end of the war, was revived by the government just before the Emperor's birthday—April 29, a national holiday. About a week later, in the actual presentation ceremonies, the Emperor awarded honors to some 187 statesmen and scholars who had been nominated by the Cabinet. The illustrious list was headed by former Prime Minister Yoshida Shigeru, awarded the First Class Order of the Rising Sun. Additional honors were bestowed on November 3, Cultural Day, another national holiday.

At the opening ceremonies for the XVIII Olympiad, the Emperor stood with his fellow citizens (previously his subjects) as the teams paraded into the National Stadium. The crowd cheered especially loudly as the Japanese Olympic team, holding aloft the national flag, marched into the arena and passed the reviewing stand. For perhaps the first time since the end of the war, a public event had brought together a stirring conjunction of flag, Emperor, and the people. Later, summing up the special quality of the Games, news observers interpreted the Olympiad as much more than a mere sporting event. A vast amount of energy and a stupendous sum of money had been expended in preparations; a special State Minister for the Olympic Games had even been appointed to direct the national effort. The Games, it seemed to many, marked the end of the postwar period, and the emotion-stirring appearance of the Rising Sun Flag, and the Emperor in the reviewing stand, seemed to symbolize the beginning of a new era and the rekindling of a sense of national purpose dormant for too long.

Shortly after the conclusion of the Olympiad, the conservative government of Ikeda Hayato announced its resignation. Sato Eisaku was eventually designated the new leader of the conservative Liberal-Democratic Party and he was then elected to the Premiership against Socialist, Democratic Socialist, and Communist opposition by the 47th Extraordinary Diet on November 9. After the party and the Diet had made their selection, one final step remained to formalize the transfer of power, and this took place at the Imperial Palace, where, in attestation ceremonies, Emperor Hirohito officially appointed Sato Premier and accepted his Cabinet.

When the 48th Diet reconvened on January 21, 1965, following the customary New Year's recess, the Emperor attended the opening ceremonies held in the House of Councilors chamber and read a message exhorting the Diet members to exert their utmost in the service of the nation. He then retired to his throne located behind and above the presiding officer's rostrum and sat there with his characteristic stiffness while the Speaker accepted the imperial message.

The ceremonial and ritualistic nature of the Emperor's functions in the life and government of the nation is clearly evident from these and similar activities which are regularly reported in the popular press. Under the Constitution granted by his illustrious grandfather, Emperor Hirohito had been theoretically supreme combining in himself all rights of sovereignty. Today, he is no longer the absolute monarch, and his activities in matters of state are strictly ceremonial.[22] He acts in the name of the

[22] Even under the old Constitution, Emperor Hirohito was powerless in fact if not in theory. By training and probably by personality, he never acted as an absolute monarch. He reached his majority and received his education

sovereign people, from whom he derives his position, and in both theory and in practice he is powerless. He does not even have the traditional "right to be consulted, the right to encourage, the right to warn" which Bagehot ascribed to British monarchs. He is, according to the very first article of the new Constitution, "the symbol of the State and of the unity of the people." In attending to ceremonial state functions, he acts under the direction of the Cabinet, and he does not have "powers related to government." He appoints the Prime Minister as designated by the Diet—in this act he does not retain even the theoretical discretion that the Queen of England still enjoys—and the Chief Justice of the Supreme Court as recommended by the Cabinet. Under instruction from the Cabinet, he promulgates all laws, convokes the Diet, dissolves the House of Representatives, proclaims elections, attests the appointment and dismissal of state ministers, awards honors, receives foreign ambassadors and dignitaries, and performs other ceremonial functions. In short, the constitutional role of the Emperor is to clothe the everyday acts of the government with the dignity and majesty of the throne.

Once the wealthiest individual in all Japan with properties estimated at over $1 billion, he was stripped of his wealth by postwar reforms and by 1950 he ranked, according to income taxes paid during that year, about halfway down the list of those with sufficient income (about 70,000 taxpayers in all Japan) to pay a surtax.[23] Occupation reformers destroyed the economic foundations of imperial power, no less than the constitutional and political, by nationalizing all properties of the imperial house and making the family dependent upon Diet appropriations for funds. Administrative control over the Emperor's affairs, once the province of the independent Ministry of Imperial Household Affairs, is now the business of the Imperial Household Agency, an organ of the Prime Minister's Office. The old Imperial House

during the heyday of party government; accordingly he acted in the style of limited monarchs of the modern British type. In fact, it may well be concluded that the occupation-enforced change in status from autocrat to symbol constituted a mere formalization and codification of the actual role played by modern Japanese Emperors.

[23] "The Human Emperor," in *This is Japan*, vol. 4 (1956), pp. 64–65.

Law, enacted as an imperial ordinance, which regulated such matters as the succession, has been replaced by a statute enacted by the Diet, and even the Emperor's status as patriarch of the Imperial House has been eliminated. He no longer sits as head of the Imperial Family Council, his place as presiding officer having been taken by the Prime Minister. Finally, the elimination of lese majesty provisions from the Criminal Code has removed the legal sanctions previously used to ensure proper respect and awe for the throne.

Although the Emperor as symbol has little or no legal meaning, the political effectiveness of the throne as a unifying force cannot be underestimated. Without question, the Emperor institution remains popular with the people and continues as a force for stability in political life. Opinion polls from 1946 to the present show 60 to 90 percent of respondents agreeing with statements favorable to the throne. A nationwide poll conducted by the Office of the Prime Minister in late 1962 revealed the following distribution of basic attitudes toward the Emperor:

Reverence	24%
Friendliness	41
Neither friendliness nor antagonism	30
Antagonism	1
Hatred	0
Don't know	4

Feelings of reverence were found to be inversely proportional to age and degree of education: 7 percent of the 20–24 age group as against 50 percent of the 60 or more age group chose "reverence," as did only 15 percent of college graduates as against 46 percent of those with minimal education. In terms of occupation, students were lowest in reverential feelings (5 percent) while farmers were highest (35 percent). Seven percent of polled Communists admitted feelings of reverence, as against 31 percent of Liberal-Democrats.[24]

[24] Japan, Naikaku Sori Daijin Kambo, Kohoshitsu [Prime Minister's Office, Secretariat, Public Relations Office], *Kempo ni Kansuru Seron Chosa* [Public Opinion Surveys Relating to the Constitution], no. 8 (Jan. 1963), pp. 14–16.

The young people and the educated drift into indifference rather than hostility to the throne, and eventually lack of popular support or interest may lead to the withering away of the Emperor institution. Meanwhile, the throne continues to mirror the unity of the Japanese people on the question of regime, and thus far there has appeared little support for alternative forms of government—for either republican or Communist types of regime, for example. Questions of regime can be fundamentally divisive and injurious to stable government, as the example of post-Revolutionary France has shown. The Japanese were fortunate in having avoided such a destructive issue at a time when it was necessary to concentrate all their energy on the reconstruction of a war-devastated economy.

CHAPTER FOUR

Executive Style:
Administration

ALL MAJOR national government offices are squeezed into the
capital city of Tokyo, which serves simultaneously as the commercial, financial, educational, and mass media center of the
nation. Tokyo is Washington, New York, and Boston all rolled
into one, and if there is a Japanese Establishment, it exists
largely because the top leaders of government, business, and education live and work virtually within hailing distance of one
another. Physical proximity itself makes for almost instantaneous
communication and constant contact, and increases the already
enormous power wielded by the political, economic, and intellectual leaders of the nation. The megalopolis of 10 million
souls also houses and generates the vast quantities of information
needed to run today's technological and scientific society; it is
no wonder that Tokyo is described as the nerve center of the
country. Nor is it any wonder that the government owns or
controls the major means of communication and traffic—the
Japan Telephone and Telegraph Public Corporation, the Japan
Broadcasting Corporation,[1] and the Japan National Railways;
control of the communications network is regarded as absolutely
essential to the effective administration of the unitary state.

[1] Formerly a government monopoly, the Japan Broadcasting Corporation
now operates under indirect government control and in competition with
commercial networks.

Cabinet Organization and Functions

The administration of the state is in the hands of the Cabinet, which is organized into one office, 12 ministries, and 5 agencies (at least 2 of which have near departmental status). They are the Office of the Prime Minister; the Ministries of Foreign Affairs, Finance, Education, Justice, Health and Welfare, Agriculture and Forestry, International Trade and Industry, Transportation, Postal Services, Labor, Construction, and Local Autonomy (Home Affairs); the Defense and Economic Planning Agencies; and the Agencies for Administrative Management, Hokkaido Development, and Science and Technology. Rounding out the top executive agencies are the independent Board of Audit and the semi-autonomous National Personnel Authority.

The Cabinet members customarily meet each Wednesday and Friday, beginning their deliberations punctually at 10 A.M. in the Official Residence of the Prime Minister or, when the Diet is in session, in a special office in the Diet building. The Prime Minister may call extraordinary meetings when the pressure of business requires it. On occasion, if a measure must be approved when time or other circumstances do not permit an actual gathering of ministers, runners are dispatched with documents in hand to obtain the signatures (actually seals) of the various ministers. In 1958, Prime Minister Kishi resorted to this shortcut to introduce a bill amending the existing Police Duties Law. The unpopular revision, designed to strengthen police powers, stirred up strong opposition in the Diet among the Socialists—who had been the victims of police oppression in prewar days— and enhanced Kishi's reputation as a heavy-handed autocrat.

Discussions in Cabinet meetings are kept secret and no stenographic notes are taken in order to promote the freest possible discussion and the airing of different points of view. Moreover, since the Cabinet is collectively responsible for its decisions, it must maintain secrecy over its deliberations so that it will be able to present a façade of unity to the public. During meetings, a bill to be introduced into the Diet will be explained by the appropriate minister, although in recent years the custom has arisen for the Chief Cabinet Secretary or his deputy to explain general legislative proposals. Normally, the Prime Minister summarizes the discussion and announces a consensus. There is no vote taken. Where differences cannot be harmonized, no decision is reached. Theoretically, when an important matter must be pushed to a decision, and a minister of state remains in disagreement, he must resign or be dismissed; but such cases are rare.

Cabinet meetings are not bound by many of the parliamentary procedures applicable to deliberative bodies. The lack of a vote and decision by consensus rather than by majority rule have already been mentioned. There is no quorum and of course no publication of proceedings, although as a general rule the Chief Cabinet Secretary issues a public pronouncement on important policy issues decided by a Cabinet meeting. Special rules of order provide for prompt openings of discussion as scheduled at 10 A.M., for not interrupting when a colleague has the floor, and for maintaining general decorum during the proceedings. Secretarial functions are provided by the Chief Cabinet Secretary, the director of the Legislative Bureau, and the Deputy Cabinet Secretary. The only other nonminister of state normally present is the Director of the Prime Minister's Office.

Two offices are attached to the Cabinet to render assistance: the Cabinet Secretariat and the Legislative Bureau. In addition, there are a number of interdepartmental committees and advisory groups functioning under Cabinet control.

CABINET SECRETARIAT

The function of the Cabinet Secretariat, located in the Official Residence of the Prime Minister, is to handle the ordinary business affairs of the Cabinet. It acts as a clearinghouse for meetings of the Cabinet, sets the agenda for meetings, assembles information and conducts studies relative to important policy matters, and adjusts differences between departments in order that the government may speak out with a unified voice. The Chief Cabinet Secretary [2] is one of the closest and most trusted advisers

[2] The technically correct title is Secretary-General of the Cabinet, but in the English language press he is invariably referred to as the Chief Cabinet Secretary.

to the Prime Minister. It is his business to keep his finger on the political pulse of the Diet and the executive branch and to act as the administration spokesman (press secretary) when important policy decisions have been reached by the Cabinet. (He attends Cabinet meetings as a nonvoting member.)

LEGISLATIVE BUREAU

When legislative business is on the agenda, the Director of the Legislative Bureau also attends the semiweekly meetings of the Cabinet. This office is responsible for studying and drafting bills, considering drafts of Cabinet ordinances and treaties, and submitting these documents together with recommendations to Cabinet meetings. It also advises the Cabinet and the individual ministries on legal matters, and engages in basic studies of domestic, foreign, and international law.

The actual drafting of most government-sponsored bills—which constitute the majority of bills introduced into any session of the Diet—is the joint undertaking of the administrative departments and the Bureau of Legislation. The civil servants of the various ministries normally provide the subject expertise while the officials of the Legislative Bureau (who numbered a scant 68 in 1963) supply the legal knowledge, phraseology, and constitutional interpretations if required. Bills of a general nature may be drafted in toto by the Legislative Bureau. Regardless of origin, all bills are submitted for final examination to the Legislative Bureau, after which they are studied at regularly scheduled meetings by administrative vice ministers. If approved by the vice-ministers, the bills then go to the Cabinet where, under normal conditions, they are routinely approved and finally submitted to the Diet for deliberation. The Director of the Legislative Bureau usually accompanies the Prime Minister when he faces interpellation in the Diet on a specific measure.

INTERDEPARTMENTAL COMMITTEES

The Cabinet has under its jurisdiction a number of interdepartmental committees, conferences, and consultative commissions, both of a legal and an informal variety. These include:

The Ministerial Council, whose chief function is the formulation and revision of the foreign exchange budget. Its members are the

Prime Minister and the Foreign, Finance, Agriculture-Forestry, International Trade and Industry, and Transportation Ministers, as well as the Director-General of the Economic Planning Agency.

The Defense Council, charged with basic defense policy and planning, has the Prime Minister, the Foreign and Finance Ministers, and the directors of the Defense and Economic Planning Agencies as members.

The Commission on the Constitution, established with a membership of 50 (30 from the Diet, 20 scholars), to study questions of constitutional revision. Its final report after a decade of study was submitted in July, 1964.[3]

The Conference of Parliamentary Vice-Ministers. The Parliamentary Vice-Ministers assist their chiefs in political matters and departmental planning. Since they are appointed from the Diet, they are useful not only for interdepartmental liaison but also for keeping close contact with legislative opinion. Each ministry and the 5 major agencies are represented in the weekly meetings (bimonthly when the Diet is in recess).

The Conference of Administrative Vice-Ministers. This group of the highest ranking civil servants, which meets regularly on Tuesday and Thursday of every week that the Diet is in session, discusses legislative and other matters for later consideration by the Cabinet meetings held on Wednesdays and Fridays. It also functions as a high level liaison council on administrative matters. Its membership includes not only the Vice-Ministers but the deputy directors of the Cabinet Secretariat, the Legislative Bureau, and the Prime Minister's Office, as well as the Chief Cabinet Secretary, who functions as its chairman.

In addition, there are numerous other interministry conferences, both formal and informal, set up to study and coordinate basic policy on such matters as exports, labor, military bases, and foreign policy. To date, a committee to coordinate coordinating committees has not yet been appointed, but that day will surely come.

The Prime Minister and his Office

The presurrender Prime Ministers of Japan were not in fact the first ministers of His Majesty the Emperor. The Emperor

[3] For further discussion, see Chapter Nine.

himself was theoretically the executive head, and the Prime Minister contended for executive power with the military high command, the Privy Seal, and the Privy Council. Under the present Constitution the Prime Minister virtually monopolizes the executive power as head of the Cabinet and presiding officer at Cabinet meetings. He is also, as president of the ruling party in the Diet, the chief political leader of that body. At the same time, he is legally the chief of the Prime Minister's Office, a catchall agency which by law is designated to absorb all those functions not readily assignable to the 12 other ministries. As administrative head of state, he rules over a bewildering complex of ministries, agencies, offices, and advisory and supervisory commissions. The work of liaison and coordination is attempted by various cabinet-level bodies, but recurrent interdepartmental squabbles perennially raise the issue of administrative reform. At the beginning of 1965, one of the major programs of the new Sato Cabinet was a reform bill to be pushed through the Diet aimed at consolidation of multiple agencies whose authorities often conflicted.

The Cabinet Law provides for the temporary filling of the Office of the Prime Minister if it is vacant or if the Prime Minister is unable to act for any reason by stipulating that one of the ministers of state shall be designated in advance as a substitute. During the 1950s, the post of Deputy Premier,[4] announced at the time a new government was formed, was of considerable importance and was filled by a high ranking minister (e.g., the Foreign Minister) regarded as the Premier's chief confidant and successor. With the advent of the Ikeda ministry in 1960, the practice of formally designating a Deputy Premier was apparently dropped, and instead, an Acting Prime Minister has been appointed for brief periods of time as the need has arisen. On the other hand, the appointment of Kono Ichiro as Minister of State for the Olympics in the July, 1964, Cabinet reshuffle by Prime Minister Ikeda [5] was widely regarded as a de facto recognition of this leading factional leader as Deputy Premier.

[4] An unofficial designation used by the press; there is no official office of Deputy Premier.
[5] Death claimed both Kono and Ikeda in 1965.

PRIME MINISTER'S OFFICE

The legal head of this office is the Prime Minister himself, but effective management is in the hands of the Director-General assisted by a deputy. The office of the Director, one of the most important political posts, may be filled by a state minister, and when new Cabinets are formed, the Director-General's name is listed together with the Chief Cabinet Secretary's alongside the names of the incoming ministers of state.[6] Until the law establishing the office was amended in 1957, the Chief Cabinet Secretary concurrently managed the office, but the functions were split in that year in an attempt to increase administrative efficiency. Even today there is considerable overlap in the membership of the Prime Minister's Office Secretariat and the Cabinet Secretariat (the two offices are located across the street from one another).

Administratively, the Prime Minister's Office is divided into the office proper and external organs (see Table 2). The office proper includes such internal administrative divisions as the Secretariat and the Pension, Statistics, and Special Regional Liaison Bureaus, as well as numerous advisory councils. Japanese ministries are all similarly organized into bureaus, sections, subsections, and external organs (committees, commissions, or governmental institutions), but the Prime Minister's Office includes also a number of autonomous agencies, two of which have virtual departmental status. These two are the National Defense Agency and the Economic Planning Agency.

Of considerable importance is a small group of councilors (*shingikan*) who work with their counterparts in the Cabinet Secretariat in conducting general studies on major policies and in providing high level liaison between the various ministries. For this purpose the councilors are grouped into such functional committees as Foreign Affairs, Education, and Finance. This subsection of councilors in addition provides a public opinion

---

[6] In the factional distribution of high posts, ministerial appointments count as one point, the director-generalship as half a point.

survey service which periodically conducts national polls on such
questions as constitutional revision, tax policy, and election reform. One reason the government has not pushed too hard for
immediate constitutional revision is the consistent popular opposition to such changes as reflected in the polls.

The Special Regional Liaison Bureau handles questions arising out of the continued occupation of Japanese territories by
U.S. (Okinawa, Bonin Islands) and Soviet (islands in the Kurile
chain) forces. The auxiliary organs include a whole host of coordinating (e.g., disaster relief), investigative (e.g., juvenile problems),

TABLE 2.   Prime Minister's Office

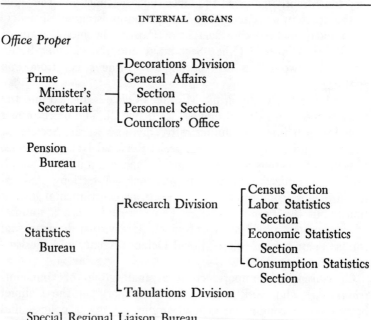

INTERNAL ORGANS

Office Proper

Prime   ┌Decorations Division
Minister's   │General Affairs
Secretariat ─┤   Section
             │Personnel Section
             └Councilors' Office

Pension
Bureau

                                        ┌Census Section
                ┌Research Division   │Labor Statistics
                │   │   Section
Statistics   │   ─┤Economic Statistics
Bureau   ─┤   │   Section
                │   └Consumption Statistics
                │   Section
                └Tabulations Division

Special Regional Liaison Bureau

Auxiliary Organs

   47 Advisory Councils, 1 Office, 1 Training Institute

Organ

   Science Council of Japan

Table 2 (*Continued*)

EXTERNAL ORGANS

Fair Trade Commission
National Public Safety Commission
  Police Agency
Land Coordination Commission
National Capital Regional Development Commission
Imperial Household Agency
Administrative Management Agency
Hokkaido Development Agency
Defense Agency
Economic Planning Agency
Science and Technology Agency

---

and advisory (e.g., taxation) committees. The Science Council of Japan functions as the top representative body for Japanese scientists.

EXTERNAL ORGANS OF THE PRIME MINISTER'S OFFICE

These external organs include 4 regulatory or planning commissions and 6 administrative agencies. The Fair Trade Commission, charged with administering the antimonopoly and fair trade laws introduced by occupation reformers to "democratize" the economy dominated then as now by giant trusts (*zaibatsu*), has a chief commissioner, 4 commissioners, and an investigative and advisory staff (of some 242 members in 1963). The Land Coordination Commission of 5 commissioners and a small staff of 18 attempts to regulate the use of available land among such competing interests as mining, agricultural, forestry, and industrial users, always keeping the public interest in mind. The National Capital Region Development Commission engages in large-scale city planning for Tokyo and environs. The National Public Safety Commission, which supervises the national police through the Police Agency, has been the center of controversy for a number of years. When it became evident that occupation-sponsored reforms decentralizing the system had overly weakened the police, the law was amended to give greater authority to central authorities over the strong resistance of those who saw in the revision an attempted revival of prewar police state controls.

The National Defense Agency, headed by a civilian minister of state, controls the Land, Sea, and Air Self-Defense Forces in accordance with basic policy set by the Cabinet Defense Council. Japan's armed forces, originally organized in 1950 as a paramilitary Police Reserve, have the dual function of defending Japan against aggression and maintaining public order. Recent efforts to raise the agency to ministry status have met with strenuous objections from preservers of the Constitution who regard any buildup of the armed forces as unconstitutional.

The important Economic Planning Agency, also headed by a minister of state, is responsible for short-range forecasts and long-range planning of the economy. Basically it is a research and policy-study organization which sets general and specific targets for the nation's economy. The famous 10-year "income-doubling plan" of 1960 associated with Prime Minister Ikeda was a product of this agency. Administration of economic plans developed by the agency is left to the various ministries, who work either through direct controls or through cooperation with private enterprise. The agency's annual forecasts issued at the end of the year are timed to coincide with the final stages in the drafting of the national budget.

The Administrative Management Agency, originally established to safeguard gains made in the democratization and modernization of the bureaucracy, studies the administrative system, coordinates agency reorganizations, and inspects the work of government offices. During 1962, for example, it investigated the work of 13 agencies and advised 21 others on managerial problems. Personnel and fiscal management are not within its scope; these fall under the jurisdiction of the National Personnel Authority and the Finance Ministry.

The mission of the Hokkaido Development Agency is to open up and exploit the relatively sparsely settled land of Japan's northernmost "frontier." The Imperial Household Agency, which manages the ceremonial and personal affairs of the Emperor and his family, has custody of the Imperial Seal and the Great Seal of State used to promulgate all statutes enacted by the National Diet. Government planning in atomic energy, air-space technology, and natural resources is the work of the Science and Technology Agency.

Cabinet Ministries

Some of the flavor of the state administration is conveyed in the following capsule summaries of the primary functions of the 12 ministries, each headed by a minister of state who is assisted in political matters by one or two parliamentary vice ministers and in administrative matters by permanent vice-ministers.

Ministry of Finance (86,204 civil servants in 1963[7]). Traditionally the center of power in the executive mechanism and the first choice of the top graduates of Tokyo University, this large-sized ministry exerts a strong influence over the economy through its budgetary and tax policies. Its Budget Bureau sets the economic tone for the year when it prepares the annual budget bill for the Diet, and its Tax Bureau controls revenues through its power to initiate tax bills. The Ministry works closely with the central Bank of Japan in establishing monetary controls, one of the most important levers in government hands for the control of the economy.

Ministry of Justice (47,139 employees). The Justice Ministry is responsible for the investigation of crime and prosecution of criminals through public procurators (organized into Supreme, High, Regional, and Local Public Procurators' Offices), the administration of penal institutions, and the rehabilitation of criminals. It is also charged with the protection of human rights and the drafting of legislation relating to the judicial system, as well as amendments to the Civil and Criminal codes.

Ministry of Foreign Affairs (2,517 employees). Revived in 1951 with the recovery of independence, the Foreign Ministry is responsible for the overall planning and administration of foreign policy, conducting diplomatic negotiations, concluding treaties, and carrying out basic research on foreign countries. Its important Bureau of Economics determines trade policy and is responsible

[7] All government employment figures cited in this section are from *Japan Statistical Yearbook*, 1963, p. 452.

for treaties of commerce and navigation. Its Economic Cooperation Bureau is in charge of economic aid and technical exchange.
Its small size reflects in part the still passive role played by
Japan in international politics and also assignment of foreign
economic relations to other departments, such as the Ministry
of International Trade and Industry.

Ministry of Education (86,469 employees). Japan boasts the
highest literacy rate in the world, and more than 99 percent of
her children undergo the full nine years of compulsory education,
with the percentage of those going on to higher education second
only to the United States. Her best universities, all state operated,
are administered by the Ministry of Education though with considerable local autonomy. The Ministry also studies, advises,
coordinates, and exercises leadership over local education, administers the Cultural Properties Commission and national mu-
seums, and of course drafts educational legislation.

Ministry of Health and Welfare (90,734 employees). "In all
spheres of life," reads Article 25 of the Constitution, "the State
shall use its endeavors for the promotion and extension of social
welfare and security, and of public health." To these ends the
Welfare Ministry plays a leading role in public health, operates
national hospitals, regulates drugs and medicines, leads in social
welfare work, promotes the welfare of children and mothers,
and plans health and welfare legislation. A major objective of
the new Sato administration in 1965, it was announced, was
to be "social planning," and this priority was reflected in increased spending on social security and welfare benefits.

Ministry of Agriculture and Forestry (175,709 employees). In
a nation founded on agriculture, the Agriculture Ministry was one
of the power centers, and even today, with 30 percent of the population still tied directly or indirectly to the land, it is still a
major department. Its Bureau of Agricultural Economics and
Bureau of Farm Lands are currently deeply involved in the rationalization of farm practices and the consolidation of land into
larger, more efficient holdings (present average: 2.5 acres per
family), and the planning and drafting of legislation to fulfill
these objectives. Through its Fisheries Agency, the Ministry provides leadership to Japan's important sea food industry which

supplies the bulk of the animal protein in the diet. It has long administered agricultural and marine experiment stations which not only engage in basic research (a current project is the cultivation of salt-water fish) but also serve as centers for the quick dissemination of the latest agricultural techniques, seeds, and fertilizers.

Ministry of International Trade and Industry (15,449 employees). Japan has long rejected all notions of economic self-sufficiency and is now committed to a trade-or-die policy. Her major industries—steel, machinery, automobiles, and electronics —are overwhelmingly export-minded, while, at the same time, they continue to be heavily dependent on foreign capital and raw materials. Accordingly, the International Trade Ministry has become a major power center: it not only provides the basic legislation that controls foreign trade, it also contains the offices that control foreign trade through licensing, regulation of patent agreements, administration of the Import-Export Law, and supervision of economic and trade agreements. The ministry also influences domestic industry through such offices as the Agency for Medium and Small Enterprises, which seeks to modernize and rationalize this underdeveloped sector of the economy through legislation if necessary.

Ministry of Transportation (88,534 employees). The Ministry of Transportation plans basic land, sea, and air transportation policy. As an offshoot of its close supervision of the shipping industry, it prepares the foreign exchange budget bill and administers the induction of foreign capital—absolutely essential in a perennially capital-starved economy. It subsidizes the construction of ships (Japan still registers substantial losses in invisible trade because of insufficient shipping), promotes the development of the rolling stock industry useful in the Asian trade, and conducts the economic and technical planning for the government-owned Japan National Railways. Prime Minister Sato Eisaku began his public career in this ministry and still retains a power base there.

Ministry of Postal Services (303,387 employees). The largest of the departments, it is responsible for the mail and for postal savings, still an important institution in the Japanese economy.

Ministry of Labor (26,568 employees). Established in 1947 as the first independent agency responsible for labor problems, its primary missions are to safeguard the rights of the working man, provide job stability, and draft and administer labor laws.

Ministry of Construction (35,723 employees). An increasingly important department as the government allots a greater and greater share of the budget to improving the "infrastructure" of the economy, the Construction Ministry is responsible for long- and short-term national, regional, and urban planning; planning for highway construction; and the administration of the Public Housing Act and other legislation relating to housing.

Autonomy (Home Affairs) Ministry (671 employees). Originally established to guarantee local autonomy, the primary functions of this small agency are to supervise national and local elections, maintain liaison between national and local governments, and administer the Local Grants-in-Aid Tax Law.

The Public Service and the Bureaucracy

The number of budgeted positions in the national government in 1963 stood at 1,851,777, while the figure for local government (prefectural, city, town, and village) employees was 1,217,429, giving a total of 3,069,206 individuals engaged in the public service out of an employed work force of approximately 47 million.[8]

National government employees, from the lowliest laborer to the Prime Minister himself, are grouped under one of two services: the regular or the special. Technically, even the Emperor is a civil servant, a fact which was made explicit at one point in an early draft of the basic law governing public officials. Broadly speaking, the regular (i.e., classified) service includes all those who enter government employment through competitive examinations whereas the special service includes elected officials and political appointees—although there are exceptions in both categories. The Public Service Law of 1947, administered by the nominally independent National Personnel Authority, regulates

[8] *Japan Statistical Yearbook,* 1963, p. 452–453.

such matters as recruitment through competitive examination, promotions, conditions of employment, compensation, separation, standards of performance, and position classification. The chief objective of the law, adopted at the insistence of occupation authorities, was the democratization and modernization of the civil service in keeping with the spirit of the Constitution which declared that all public officials are the servants and not the masters of the sovereign people. The law bans collective bargaining and strikes by all government employees in the regular service.

The regular service enrolls the majority of government employees and includes the administrative and clerical staff of all ministries and agencies—from permanent vice-ministers to bureau directors to section chiefs to unit heads and finally to the individual official. These public servants form the heart of the "bureaucracy." Teachers and administrative personnel of national (government) schools and universities, employees of public corporations (Monopoly, Telephone and Telegraph, National Railway), and technicians of such government enterprises as the Printing Bureau and the Mint also come under the regular service.

The special service, covered by a series of statutes such as the Diet Law, includes members of the Diet (from the Prime Minister to administrative employees), judges and other officers of the judiciary, high appointive officials such as members of the Audit Board, ambassadors, court attendants, officials and personnel of the Defense Agency, and individuals who receive employment through government relief projects.

Local officials are also divided into the regular and special services, and include public school teachers, police, firemen, and administrative and technical employees of local governments and public enterprises.

Nature of the Japanese Bureaucracy

Like all formal human institutions of any size, the government of Japan bears the stamp of bureaucratic organization: differentiation of function by ministry, hierarchical controls within the ministries, formal qualifications for entry into and advance in the system, impersonality, and regularized methods of discipline. It is all too obvious that the system suffers from such characteristic drawbacks as the proliferation of rules governing all steps in the decision-making process—"red tape"; reluctance to render a decision—"passing the buck"; and eternal slowness in obtaining an answer or a decision from the government.

In what way, then, does Japanese bureaucracy differ from its counterparts in, for example, Great Britain and the United States? Perhaps the most striking difference, which has caught the attention of both foreign and native observers, is the greater prestige and power of Japanese officialdom in the affairs of state. Though there is evidence that the efflorescence of the bureaucratic spirit has been checked in recent years by constant democratic propaganda, there can be little question that the Japanese bureaucracy today occupies a position that would be unacceptable if not entirely unthinkable in London or Washington. As such, the bureaucracy is commonly regarded as a source of danger to the further development of a democratic state.

Although the administration of the state, to be sure, is ostensibly under the control of elected political leaders comprising the Cabinet, the permanent bureaucracy has managed to a surprising degree to persist as a quasi-independent power source. The exaltation of the scholar-bureaucrat in the Confucian tradition forms the historical and ideological base—now being eroded by the influence of the democratic tradition—for the power of the bureaucracy. The idea that the official can do no wrong was enhanced by the fact that under the old system appointments to the civil service were part of the imperial prerogative, and hence officials were regarded as servants of the infallible Emperor, not of the people. Moreover, while the occupation destroyed the military base in government and attempted to weaken the power of the large financial combines, it left virtually untouched the bureaucracy through which it governed Japan in the immediate postwar period.

History has not been the sole ally of the Japanese official in maintaining his power; existing political practices work toward the same end. The ephemeral nature of Japan's constantly recon structed administrations means that state ministers do not serve much longer than one year before being replaced. As a result, they naturally find it difficult to assert administrative control over the departments; the actual control tends to fall into the hands of the permanent vice-ministers and bureau directors. This tendency has been accelerated by the growth of the administrative state, which works to strengthen the role of the government expert backed by an experienced staff as against the political neophyte whose only power base may be a small group of factional adherents in the Diet. It is the bureaucracy, moreover, which supplies the expertise in the drafting of legislation and the budget, and which oversees the spending of appropriated funds and the administration of the law.

The Diet member, in addition, is always subject to popular control through periodic elections, and business leaders, who often have an important influence in the councils of government, are checked by competition in the market place. Only the bureaucrat, firmly ensconced in his organization and protected by complex regulations and a guaranteed status, is virtually immune from control. Such a state of affairs is not unique to the Japanese experience, but it tends to make a mockery of the constitutionally guaranteed "inalienable right" of the people to choose and dismiss all public officials, the "servants of the whole community." [9]

The Bureaucracy in Politics

The bureaucracy as a source of power in the political process manifests itself in a variety of ways. While the civil service in the United States rarely serves as an avenue of ascent to high political office, it continues to be a popular mode of advancement in Japan. In prewar days, a civil servant could aspire to the Premiership itself by climbing the bureaucratic ladder. He did not necessarily require a power base in the Imperial Diet or in a political party, because ministerial appointments could be and were made by advisers to the Emperor without regard for

[9] Article 15 of the Constitution.

party affiliation. Beginning with the first party administration of Kato Takaaki in 1924 and ending with the surrender-government of Admiral Suzuki Kantaro, some 48 bureaucrats, largely from the influential Finance, Foreign, and Home Ministries, reached the rank of ministers of state, and of these only nine were members of the Imperial Diet.[10] In the postwar period, all but one of the Prime Ministers have been former bureaucrats, but because of new constitutional requirements they have all come from the Diet.

We have noted elsewhere that constitutional and political requirements today ensure that virtually all important ministry posts are filled with members of the lower house, thus sealing off direct appointment from the higher bureaucracy to these important offices. One result has been a migration of ambitious classified civil servants from the ministries into the rough-and-tumble world of politics. For example, it was reported that the 1958 Diet contained 181 ex-bureaucrats: 96 in the 467-member House of Representatives and 85 in the 250-member House of Councilors.[11] Another study estimated that 30 percent of Liberal-Democrats in the Diet were former bureaucrats who had resigned from the regular service to stand for elections.[12]

Many of these Diet members retain their connections with the ministries which nurtured them, and indeed often find their former colleagues very useful, especially in intraparty factional struggles in which every bit of support counts. Thus, former Prime Minister Ikeda, who went from Kyoto Imperial University into the Finance Ministry and subsequently rose to high office there, retained ties with the higher bureaucracy in that ministry long after his move to the Diet. Collateral ties with the banking community developed during his days as an official dealing with finance stood him in good stead, as attested by affluent contributions to his campaign funds by the financial community. The present Prime Minister, Sato Eisaku, who rose through the Transportation Ministry, similarly retains connections both with that

[10] Watanabe Tsuneo, *Habatsu* [Factions], Kobundo, 1958, pp. 60–61.

[11] Tokyo Shimbun Sha (ed.), *Kancho Monogatari* [The Story of Government Agencies], 1962, p. 172.

[12] Fujiwara Hirotatsu, *Kanryo* [The Bureaucracy], Kodansha, 1964, p. 15.

ministry and the communications and transportation industry, and with other business groups. Sato's personal contact with the business world is his eldest son's father-in-law, Anzai Hiroshi, president of the Tokyo Gas Company, long a leading contributor to Liberal-Democratic coffers.[13]

If Diet members find support in the ministries, they in turn act with paternalistic concern toward their favored departments. Iwasawa Tadayasu, Liberal-Democrat in the House of Councilors, who began his career in the Construction Ministry, is known familiarly by his former cohorts as Emperor Iwasa (Iwasa Tenno), and they know they can count on his benevolent attention when matters affecting the ministry are brought before the house. Similarly, Hirose Hisatada is known as the Tutelary Deity (uji-gami-sama of the Welfare Ministry. Ishiguro Tadaatsu goes him one better by being known as the God of Agricultural Administration (Nosei no Kamisama) working on behalf of the Agriculture Ministry in the Diet.[14]

The Bureaucracy and Business

Aside from ordinary contacts developed in day-to-day operations—and the government is deeply involved in business affairs—there are many ways in which the bureaucracy and the business world intermesh. There is, for example, the one-way movement of high-ranking bureau directors and vice ministers into top management positions—presumably for the same reason that retired generals and admirals are hired in the United States by defense industries.

There is also the "old school tie." For almost a century, ambitious young men who aspired to high office used the great national universities to attain their goal. The training of earnest young bureaucrats was in fact largely the function of the Law Faculty of Tokyo Imperial University—perhaps even the primary function

[13] Nagasaki Yukio, "Shin Shusho o Torimaku Zaikai Gunzo" [The Business Crowd Surrounding the New Prime Minister], Ekonomisuto, Nov. 24, 1964, p. 26.
[14] Tokyo Shimbun Sha (ed.), Kancho Monogatari, pp. 75–81.

of that university. At the turn of the century, 53 percent of that university's students matriculated in the Law Faculty, and as late as 1959 the figure was a startling 38 percent.[15] A disproportionate number of all Tokyo and Kyoto Imperial University graduates entered the government service (in 1903, 1531 graduates entered the civil service as against 716 who went into business management), but with the growth of large-scale private enterprises following the Russo-Japanese war of 1904–1905, the number of those seeking a career in industry began to climb and by 1917 it had overtaken graduates entering the government. By 1959 the percentage of Tokyo University graduates taking competitive examinations for the regular service had declined to 25 percent.[16]

Because entrance into the great national universities providing both top management and government personnel is strictly according to competitive examination, the result has been the evolution of a kind of meritocracy that may be said to govern Japan's "Establishment." According to a 1959 survey, fully one-third of the 900 top management positions in Japanese industry were occupied by graduates of Tokyo University, and over one-half were from three universities: Tokyo, Kyoto, and Hitotsubashi.[17]

Tokyo University graduates similarly tend to monopolize the higher government positions. When the Japanese refer to the bureaucracy (*kanryo*, often used perjoratively as in the United States), they usually mean those top-level officials who have a considerable measure of political influence through their connections with parties and the world of business. In concrete terms, these would be the administrative vice-ministers, bureau directors, and powerful section chiefs, numbering about 1700 individuals altogether.[18] A more exclusive count of upper echelon government posts puts the number at 536 in 1958. Of this total, a full 324 were occupied by graduates of Tokyo University.[19]

---

[15] Noda Kazuo, *Nihon no Juyaku* [Big Business Executives in Japan], Daiyamondo Sha, 1960, p. 148.

[16] *Ibid.*, pp. 151–154.

[17] *Ibid.*, p. 161.

[18] Matsumoto Seicho, *Gendai Kanryo Ron* [On the Contemporary Bureaucracy], Bungei Shunju Shinsha, 1964, vol. 1, p. 8.

[19] Compiled from tables given in Tokyo Shimbun Sha, *Kancho Monogatari*, pp. 158–198.

Thus, it is not only the historical and political factors which account for the enduring power of the bureaucracy; the fact that they constitute part of a small homogeneous group of men who occupy the top positions in government, business, industry, finance, education, and the mass media adds to their influence. Living in and around Tokyo, belonging largely to the same generation, inevitably sharing a similarity in outlook and operating style as shaped by a handful of universities, possessing an elitist mentality, these men work together easily whether they are in government or in the practical world of business and constitute a kind of invisible and informal Establishment not answerable to the usual constitutionalized controls.

One important qualification needs to be added. It is easy enough to condemn bureaucrats altogether and pretend that if they were eliminated the golden age of democracy would dawn. But the bureaucracy is of course essential in a modern society, and the problem is not to eliminate it but to bring it under popular control—as it has been in Great Britain and the United States. This appears to be happening in Japan today. When we look behind the abstraction we label the bureaucracy and examine the individual official in his government office, we find after all a human being subjected to all of the social and political pressures of the ordinary citizen. And increasingly, those pressures are being applied to democratize the political process and make the official more amenable to popular control as prescribed in the Constitution. How is he responding? Let us take one example, the case of Mr. Hayashi Shuzo, until recently Director of the Cabinet Bureau of Legislation.

Born in 1910, a graduate of the Tokyo Imperial University Law Faculty in 1932, Mr. Hayashi entered the Ministry of Finance and rose over the years from Section Head to Deputy Director of the Cabinet Bureau of Legislation, and finally to the directorship. He is, in short, the Japanese bureaucrat par excellence. Shortly before his retirement in late 1964, Mr. Hayashi published a book instructing officials on the art of drafting legislation. Throughout the work Mr. Hayashi emphasizes the fact that a proposed law must not conflict with any provision of the Constitution, particularly those which guarantee fundamental human rights; that the individual personality must always be respected while attempting to promote the public welfare; and that legal terminology should be chosen with care so that all statutes accurately reflect the intent and purpose of the legislators.[20] Is Mr. Hayashi an exception in his apparent commitment to those fundamental values which ultimately determine whether an administration is democratically operated or not? The future of Japanese democracy rests in part on a negative answer.

Budget-Making by the Administration

The Cabinet is constitutionally charged with the preparation of the national budget; and the steps followed in the compilation of the 1964 budget will now be described in detail as an illustration of the administration in action. As in Great Britain, the Japanese fiscal year runs from April 1 to March 31, and preparations for the budget bill to be submitted to the Diet begin well in advance of expected passage in March. Thus, work on the fiscal 1964 budget of about $9 billion [21] began in June, 1963, with the compilation of a target budget based on the previous year's expenditures by the Budget Bureau of the Ministry of Finance.

In prewar days, the Cabinet used to adopt and announce a basic budget policy in June or July, but in the postwar period the practice has been to delay the announcement until the Finance Ministry's draft budget is ready in December—that is, about one month before formal presentation to the Diet in late January—in order to take into account the latest developments in an economy which has been characterized by rapid change. The policy announcement for the 1964 budget as determined by the government was an exception and came shortly after the formation of the second Ikeda Cabinet in late July, 1963. Finance

[20] Hayashi Shuzo, *Horei Sakusei no Joshiki* [How to Draft Legislation], Nihon Hyoron Sha, 1964.

[21] Up 14 percent from the previous year. The basic figures in this section are taken from the report on the fiscal 1964 budget compiled by the Zaimu Chosakai and published as *Kuni no Yosan* [The National Budget], Doyu Shobo, 1964.

Minister Tanaka Kakuei, having been renamed to his post, declared that Japan's international competitive position would increasingly be put to a test as she liberalized trade controls while her competitors in the world markets maintained their quotas and tariffs. Domestically, rising price and cost-of-living levels were regarded as inevitable because of the expansion of the economy, but the government planned to take measures to guard against inflationary increases. The government, Tanaka concluded, would establish a "healthy balanced fiscal policy" through a proper distribution of expenditures and capital outlays and thus provide for long term stable growth while protecting Japan's balance of payments position.

On the basis of this very broad policy statement, the ministries prepared their estimates and submitted them to the Budget Bureau by the end of July as required by law. They had been warned to keep their estimates within 5 percent of their initial requests for the previous fiscal year, and a joint conference of heads of accounts sections of the various ministries had been called to discuss estimated expenditures.

Despite the warning, the initial general accounts budget based on estimates received from the agencies was reported by the Cabinet meeting of September 17 to be 34.9 percent over the 1963 budget. Consequently, there began a series of administrative hearings and conferences with ministry spokesmen seeking to justify the additional expenditures on the one hand, and the Budget Bureau attempting to whittle them down on the other.

The budget-making process was interrupted in late October by the dissolution of the House of Representatives and the call for general elections. Inevitably, budget policy became a campaign issue. The Liberal-Democrats called for continued high growth, doubling of the national income, correction of income disparities, stable prices, modernization of the underdeveloped sector of the economy, and liberalization of trade, while the Socialists criticized the drift toward high prices and the mismanagement of the economy by the conservatives. When the conservatives were returned to power in the general election of November 21, Ikeda formed a new government and once again appointed Tanaka as Finance Minister.

In early December, the draft budget went to the Policy Committee of the Liberal-Democratic Party for study by functional subcommittees on foreign affairs, finance, etc. (corresponding to the various ministries and to the standing committees of both houses). Shortly thereafter, the Liberal-Democratic Party presented to the government its recommendations which were, in its outlines, a mere restatement of its campaign promises. In specific terms, however, the party called for a ¥20 billion tax reduction not only to provide tax relief to low income families but also to promote the modernization of smaller enterprises. At the same time, it proposed that public utility rates—a substantial factor in the cost of living—remain unchanged. While politically attractive, both recommendations called for a decrease in revenues and were bound to cause trouble in Tanaka's balanced budget policy.

In mid-December, the advisory Commission on Taxation brought in a special report on tax reform recommending a slight reduction in income and business taxes and correction of inequities in taxes collected from urban and rural inhabitants. All of the recommendations were incorporated into the government's budget policy. On December 20, the Cabinet took up the Economic Planning Agency's forecast for 1964 in which a real growth rate of 7 percent, a continuing deficit in the balance of trade, and a 3 percent rise in commodity prices were predicted. On the same day, the new government announced its budget policy for 1964—once again basically a restatement of the conservative party's campaign promises with the addition of a call for tax reduction.

In the Budget Bureau, the departure of the Finance Minister and parliamentary vice-ministers as well as of all Liberal Party members in the lower house for the election campaigns had interrupted the high level political consultations taking place and, for a time, only routine matters could be decided at the agency level. Following the elections, the Diet was called into a special session, and the necessity for resubmitting supplementary budget bills for fiscal 1963 further delayed the formation of the 1964 budget. Fortunately, there were no major changes in either the Cabinet or in the higher offices of the Liberal-Democratic Party.

On December 18 and 19, the Finance Ministry draft went through final scrutiny in the ministry itself, and then it was presented on December 20 to the Cabinet and the other ministries for final discussions. Negotiations between the ministries, the government party, and the Finance Ministry proceeded smoothly, final adjustments were made, and on the 29th the Cabinet approved the draft. It then went back to the Budget Bureau for tabulation, editing, and printing.

On January 21, 1964, Finance Minister Tanaka presented the budget to the Diet and at the same time outlined the government's budget policy in the customary address to the Diet. It was then referred to the Budget Committee of the House of Representatives where Tanaka again explained the government's policy. Deliberations, public hearings, and inquiries continued throughout the month of February, and after the Committee voted to accept the government measure without change, it was voted out on March 2 and presented to the plenary session of the House on the same day. Introduced by the chairman of the Budget Committee and seconded by a member of the Government party, it was routinely opposed by Socialist and Democratic-Socialist members but was adopted without revision. It only remained for the House of Councilors to deliberate on the measure for the remainder of the month and finally approve it in time for the beginning of a new fiscal year on April 1.

The actual compilation of the budget, then—and this is also true of the drafting of the bulk of the bills considered by the Diet—is the work of the government ministries, with policy advice and recommendations furnished from time to time by the Liberal-Democratic Party, which formally examines the budget in its final draft form. The task of the legislature in the process is essentially to approve the appropriation of funds called for by the budget.

CHAPTER FIVE

The National Diet:
Functions, Organization,
Representation

THE National Diet of Japan represents three-quarters of a century of parliamentary experience in a section of the world where popularly elected legislatures are either in their adolescence or are nonexistent. Its predecessor, the Imperial Diet, was patterned after the Prussian Diet and was subordinate to the Cabinet in accordance with German constitutional practice. The bicameral Imperial Diet consisted of an elected House of Representatives and a House of Peers comprising hereditary and life peers as well as scholars of the realm nominated by the Emperor. Ito Hirobumi, the architect of the Meiji Constitution, also set up the peerage system in 1894 after the German model. He envisioned the upper house as a conservative force to check the excesses of the popularly elected House of Representatives. Hence, under the Constitution, the Peers were able to block a measure passed by the Representatives by withholding assent.

In contrast, the Diet today is constitutionally the supreme organ of state power and the sole law-making body of the government. Previously, it had shared the legislative function with the Emperor who could, when the Diet was recessed, promulgate emergency imperial ordinances having the force of law. The lower House of Representatives, moreover, is now superior to the upper House of Councilors. The abolition of the peerage in the postwar democratic reforms instituted by the occupation actu-

86

ally destroyed the *raison d'être* for a second house: Japan is a unitary state, and there is no need, as in the United States, for dual representation on the basis of both population and geography. For this reason, the original SCAP draft of the Constitution provided for a unicameral legislature representing the sovereign people, but eventually, in the only major concession to Japanese opinion, the bicameral system was continued. By stipulating a six-year term of office for members of the House of Councilors as against a four-year maximum for members of the House of Representatives, it was hoped that greater stability would be introduced into parliamentary deliberations; and by requiring that 100 of the 250 Councilors be elected from the nation at large, it was expected that a new aristocracy of eminent scholars and statesmen of national stature would be attracted. The Councilors would act as a further stabilizing and conserving force against the presumably more volatile and radical lower house representing the masses. These hopes have never really been fulfilled, and today the conservative party advocates a reversion to the earlier system of direct appointment of part of the membership of the upper house.

The superiority of a lower house representing the people over a more conservative upper house is a universal phenomenon in the development of parliamentary democracies, and is particularly evident in the British Parliament where Commons is virtually unchecked by Lords. In Japan, a number of constitutional provisions codify the supremacy of the Representatives. Generally, in the event of an impasse, the will of the lower house prevails. Thus, the Constitution does not require that the Prime Minister be a Representative (merely that he be a member of the Diet), but as in England constitutional practice demands that he be nominated from the lower house. The reason is that in the event of a disagreement between Representatives and Councilors on the choice of a Prime Minister, the decision of the House of Representatives is final (Article 67 of the Constitution). In the selection of ministers of state, moreover, the majority are drawn from among Representatives while only a handful of the lower ranking posts are given to the Councilors. In other words, the fundamental struggle for power periodically waged by the political parties to form new governments begins and ends in the House of Representatives—it is the Representatives who are empowered to cut down a government by denying confidence—and thus ensures the political supremacy of the lower house.

The Constitution also gives priority to the House of Representatives in the passage of bills. A measure opposed by the Councilors becomes law when passed a second time by a two-thirds majority of the members present in the House of Representatives. The all-important budget bill must first be submitted to the Representatives, and if the Councilors do not concur, the budget is adopted automatically in 30 days as passed by the lower house without further action. The same procedure is also followed for ratification of treaties.

Functions

The Diet is not merely the legislative organ of the state. Its larger mission is to act as the prime mover in the political affairs of the state, organizing a majority to form a government and then sitting in judgment on the administration it creates, bringing broad policy issues to the attention of the government and publicizing them and thus informing the people, and of course enacting programs of action through legislation.

The very first function of the Diet is not the passage of legislation but the designation of a Cabinet, a topic which has been already discussed in detail in Chapter Four. The Diet also initiates constitutional amendments, ratifies treaties, and oversees administration, all powers that previously belonged to the Emperor. It is true that the old Constitution was replaced by the Imperial Diet sitting as a quasiconstituent assembly, but this was done in opposition to orthodox theory which held that only the Emperor had the right to change the fundamental law. Article 96 of the present Constitution clearly specifies that amendments are initiated by the Diet through a concurring vote of two-thirds of all members of each House, the decision then being referred to the people for ratification by a simple majority of all votes cast. As in the case of ordinary legislation, however, it is clear that the Cabinet also shares the right to initiate amendments. In point of fact, it is the Cabinet's Commission on the Constitution which has, over the past decade, taken the responsibility for studying the question of constitutional revision, and if amendments are ever voted, they will in all likelihood be based on government measures. Nevertheless, the ultimate responsibility of the Diet in the amending process is clearly recognized; for though the conservative party governments of the last decade have been anxious to introduce a number of amendments (see Chapter Nine), they have never been able to muster the necessary two-thirds majority in the Diet.

The Diet also shares responsibility for foreign affairs, for the Constitution stipulates that the Prime Minister must report on foreign relations to the Diet. In practice, it is usually the Foreign Minister who delivers the foreign policy message at session openings while the Prime Minister spells out the government's administrative policy. Treaties concluded by the government, furthermore, must obtain either prior or subsequent approval of the Diet.

The power to investigate government operations—including the right to demand testimony of witnesses and the production of records—is constitutionally recognized (Article 62). The purpose of the provision is to secure greater control over the executive by permitting the Diet not only to inquire into the need for legislative measures but also to investigate the administration of existing legislation. This objective is nullified to a certain extent by the initiative taken by the government in making its own studies. Diet investigations appear to be sporadic and seem not to touch truly vital issues, as similar inquiries occasionally do in the U.S. Congress.

The Diet, finally, functions as a public forum where the great issues of the day are publicized, analyzed, debated, and then acted upon in the form of legislative programs that commit the nation to specific courses of action. It is a kind of political market place where parties, pressure groups, and the government itself meet to propose and select from among a variety of alternative policies those deemed most urgently needed to promote the general welfare of the nation. Whether the nation should align itself with the West or adopt a neutralist course; how to ensure a steadily expanding economy while keeping imbalances to a minimum; how to provide higher education to answer the needs of an increasingly technologically advanced society; whether the Constitution, which forbids the maintenance of military forces, should be amended—these and other broad issues are grist for the parliamentary mill.

Although the government party normally exercises a virtual monopoly on measures to be deliberated on by the Diet, it still must pay attention to minority demands and needs, and it is the Diet that provides the meeting ground where compromise solutions are worked out. These solutions may take the form of modifying, rejecting, or tabling government bills. It is the function of the Diet, then, to deliberate and put its stamp of approval on those bills which it wishes to become the law of the land. A measure normally becomes law by securing passage through both houses, but there are exceptions. When the Councilors choose to oppose a measure adopted by the Representatives, the bill becomes law if passed again by the Representatives with a two-thirds majority, although normally a joint conference of both houses is called to settle differences. Furthermore, a bill may be enacted by an emergency session of the House of Councilors (convoked when the lower house is dissolved), but such a measure must be subsequently approved by the Representatives.

Sessions and Principal Officers

The first National Diet under the new Constitution convened on May 5, 1947, and by late 1964 the members were gathering for the 48th session in the series. Of these, 18 have been ordinary (annual) sessions, 22 have been extraordinary sessions, and 8 have been special sessions. In addition, 2 emergency meetings of the House of Councilors have been called.

ORDINARY SESSIONS

Constitutional and statutory provisions regulate the convocation and length of Diet sessions. Annual meetings of both houses of the Diet in ordinary session are required by the Constitution, and the

Diet Law of 1947 stipulates that each session must under normal circumstances begin in December and continue for a period of 150 days. The term may be prolonged by a concurrent resolution of both houses. The longest session to date was that of the 13th Diet, which was extended five times after its normal closing date and ran for 236 days from December 10, 1951, to July 31, 1952. This was the Diet that ratified the peace and mutual security treaties with the United States and, in addition, considered a variety of measures that were to shape the economy, then beginning to develop rapidly, for years to come.

EXTRAORDINARY SESSIONS

When unfinished business remains from an ordinary session, or when a natural or political emergency requires convocation, the Diet is called into extraordinary session. Such calls, which are quite frequent, as the total number of extraordinary meetings attests, may be initiated either by the government or from the floor of the Diet. Usually the primary objective is the approval of a supplementary budget, but often there may be a hidden political purpose. Thus, the Cabinet convened the 44th Diet (Extraordinary) on October 14, 1963, for an anticipated term of 30 days ostensibly to consider a supplementary budget measure and a total of 45 other bills representing programs which the government felt to be important. For several months, however, there had been talk of dissolving the lower house since the four-year term was approaching an end. When the government encountered opposition to its program, it promptly dissolved the lower house and called for a general election.

SPECIAL SESSIONS

A general election must be held within 40 days after dissolution of the lower house, and a special Diet must be convened within 30 days after the election. The primary function of the special session is to select a new Prime Minister and install his government. At the same time, it reorganizes the lower house by the election of the Speaker, the Vice-Speaker, the Secretary General,

and committee chairmen. Thus, the 45th Diet (Special) re-elected
Ikeda as Prime Minister and organized the lower house along
strict party lines following the general election of November,
1963, which returned the usual conservative majority to the House
of Representatives.

EMERGENCY SESSIONS OF THE HOUSE OF COUNCILORS

If, during the 70-day period following dissolution and the
formation of a new government, an emergency arises requiring
legislative action, the House of Councilors (automatically adjourned following dissolution of the House of Representatives)
may be convened by the Cabinet in emergency session. Any
action taken by the Councilors, as noted earlier, must be subsequently approved by the new House of Representatives. Two such
sessions, which are not counted in the sequence of numbered
Diets, have been held in the period 1947–1964. The first was
convened in 1952 to appoint members of the Central Election
Commission and the second, lasting only three days, was called
the following year in late March to pass a provisional budget since
the lower house had not acted upon the regular budget bill before
it had been dissolved.

OFFICERS OF THE DIET

For each house the Diet Law provides the following officers: a
president (commonly called the Speaker when referring to the
House of Representatives), a vice-president (vice-speaker), president pro tempore, chairmen of the standing committees, and an
administrative secretary–general.

The first order of business for any new session of the Diet—that
is, for the first session in the House of Representatives following
a general election or for the first session in the House of Councilors following a triennial election—is the election of presiding
officers. The role of the president is critical since he functions
as a kind of traffic controller and policeman, distributing bills
presented by the government to the proper committee, setting the

schedule of business, and enforcing discipline—by calling in parliamentary guards and city police if necessary.

Currently, the Liberal-Democratic Party monopolizes the four key posts—the presidents and vice-presidents of both houses—as well as the committee chairmanships of the lower house. As recently as 1960, however, it was the practice to allot at least the vice-presidencies to members of the opposition Socialist Party.

The Committee System

The most conspicuous illustration of the forced wedding of the presidential and parliamentary styles in the Japanese government is to be found in the standing committee system of the National Diet. Under the Imperial Constitution, the two houses of the Diet conducted most of their business while sitting as committees of the whole house after the British fashion. This system was changed under the new Constitution and most of the work of the Diet is now done, as in the U.S. Congress, by standing committees and assorted special committees which are appointed as needed. Today, each house has 16 standing committees (reduced from 22 in 1955), their areas of competence being reflected by their names: Cabinet, Local Government, Legal Affairs, Foreign Affairs, Finance, Education, Society and Labor, Agriculture, Commerce and Industry, Transportation, Communications, Construction, Budget, Audit, Diet Operations (Steering), and Discipline.

Most of the committees parallel the ministries and major agencies, and the parallel sets work closely together—so closely in fact that the standing committees are often criticized as being too subservient to the agencies which they were in part designed to control. There is a further linkage with the functionally designated subcommittees of the Policy Committee of the Liberal-Democratic Party. Thus, a measure affecting foreign relations, for example, may be studied by four separate groups: the Foreign Ministry, the Foreign Affairs committees of the two houses, and the Diplomatic Affairs subcommittee of the government party. (There is likely to be an overlap in the membership of the Diet and party committees.) Coordination and resolution of often

conflicting demands tend to be worked out at the policy level by
the functional subcommittees of the party and at the administrative level by the parliamentary vice-ministers.

In the House of Representatives, committee memberships range
from a low of 20 in the Disciplinary Committee to a high of 50 in
the powerful Budget Committee (the corresponding figures for
the House of Councilors are 10 and 45). The jurisdiction and
membership of the committees may be changed by the Diet, and
often the actual number serving is well below the legal limit. By
Diet Law, committee memberships are allocated to the various
political parties in proportion to their numerical strength. This is
the responsibility of the Steering Committee, but actual assignments are decided in advance in party councils. The top party
leadership (heads of factions) meet to determine the assignments,
and the result is that each committee tends to reflect party and
factional alignments of the Diet.

All Diet members must serve on at least one standing committee, although some individuals—the Prime Minister, other
cabinet ministers, and certain high ranking officers—may resign
their memberships. They continue to serve until the ends of their
terms as Diet members.

The powers of committee chairmen of the House of Representatives as determined by house rules are considerable. It is the
chairman who sets the agenda, maintains order, represents the
committee, calls meetings, declares recesses, and adjourns meetings. Since the opportunities for delay, obstruction, and outright
rejection of a measure in a committee controlled by the minority
party are theoretically endless, the majority party has consistently
rejected minority claims to these key posts. On the other hand,
according to the Rules of the House of Councilors, committee
chairmen have considerably reduced powers (they do not, for
example, set the agenda), and this may be why some of these
posts have often gone to opposition members.

Criticisms of the Standing Committee System

The committee system as it is now organized and operated has
been under constant attack for a number of reasons. A general

criticism is that the coupling of a parliamentary-cabinet system of the government with a U.S. congressional committee type of organization in the Diet is inherently contradictory and leads to a variety of operational problems.[1] Theoretically, it is argued, in the American presidential system based on a separation of functions and checks and balances, the committees of Congress serve to check executive tyranny and should be developed to the full. On the other hand, in the cabinet system of government in which the executive and the legislature are fused and ministers are responsible to parliament, the proliferation of standing committees is to be avoided as an obstruction to efficient government. Therefore, the argument concludes, in order to restore harmony, the British system of generalized committees should be adopted.[2]

The argument is theoretically sound, but in the upside-down world of practical everyday politics in Japan, the adoption of the British committee system could very well be disastrous to parliamentary government. Such a change would increase the influence of an already too powerful executive by permitting even stricter control of pending legislation than is the case today. Such controls are of course applied through the government party. Party discipline means that a measure desired by the Cabinet is treated with respect in the Diet; it also means that there is little possibility for disaffected members of the majority party to team with a recalcitrant minority to obstruct the smooth flow of legislative proposals. Such a defection would not merely embarrass the government—as happens occasionally in the U.S. Congress where party discipline is notably lax—it could lead to the downfall of the Cabinet, and accordingly cannot be permitted.

Party controls are tight enough at present, even with the majority party membership scattered throughout a mass of standing and special committees, so that the government is not en-

[1] See, for example, Japan, *Kempo Chosakai Hokoku Sho* [Summary Report of the Commission on the Constitution], 1964, pp. 612–613.

[2] In the House of Commons, much of the business is transacted by the Committee of the Whole House, or by standing committees which are without functional specialization and are designated merely by letters of the alphabet. Although Parliament in recent years has been under pressure to develop a more extensive committee system, the main argument against such a development has been that the Cabinet finds it much easier to control pending legislation in the Committee of the Whole House than in standing committees.

cumbered when it sends bills to the Diet for action. In fact, discipline is so rigid that the standing committees tend to automatically approve measures submitted to them by the various agencies, and in this way become captives of the powerful agencies they are supposed to control. Hence they cease to function as checks to the excessive growth of bureaucratic power.

Adoption of the British system would of course correct other defects of the existing system. For example, the standing committees are criticized as being excessively vulnerable to external pressure groups representing special interests (shipping, steel, labor, etc.) since the access points (Transportation Committee, Commerce and Industry Committee, Labor Committee) are clearly labeled and visible. The institution of a system with undifferentiated committees would partially solve this problem.

A healthy parliamentary democracy depends on the existence of a vigorous two-party system, and one of the effects of the transfer of the deliberative process from the whole house to committees is to splinter into 16 fragments an already permanently weak opposition. The voice of the minority is further debilitated by the practice of conducting discussions through interpellations rather than through free debate. This is a holdover from the days when the Diet was subordinate to the Cabinet and the usual mode of controlling the administration was the submission of written or formal questions (interpellations) to Cabinet ministers through an intermediary—the presiding officer of the legislature. The Diet has not yet developed the practice of holding periodic debates between government and opposition party spokesmen in plenary sessions—debates which might inform the public on vital issues, enliven the political scene, unite the government party, and invigorate the opposition. Sir Winston Churchill once argued forcefully that the physical arrangement of the oblong House of Commons with opposition parties facing each other in cramped quarters contributes in no small measure to the vigor of partisan politics in Great Britain.[3] No one has yet suggested that the seating arrangements in the chambers of the Japanese Diet, with seats aligned in graceful arcs and opposition forces seated side

[3] In an address supporting reconstruction of the House of Commons after it was destroyed during World War II, as quoted in H. M. Stout, *British Government*, Oxford University Press, 1953, pp. 106–107.

by side, be converted to the Commons model. But any fundamental reform of the Diet, including that of the committee
system, may well have to consider such symbolic matters as seating arrangement.

Membership

Of the 467 members of the new House of Representatives
elected in 1963, only 68 were first-termers, while the remaining 399
had previously served in the Diet. Of the 399, some 258 had been
elected five or more times, i.e., had served over a decade in the
Diet.[4] In other words, the full-time professional politician is coming into his own in the Japanese Diet. In the traditional breakdown by original occupation, however, the "party official" category
still is relatively small. The Election Bureau's official tabulation of
the 1963 election results gives this breakdown of occupational
backgrounds:[5]

Trade Associations and Labor Unions	127	members
Business	115	
Political Parties	58	
Miscellaneous	39	
Law	35	
Agriculture	31	
Writing	20	
Education	12	
No Occupation	12	
Medicine	10	
Mining and Commerce	5	
Religion	2	
Accounting	1	

Of special interest are the large numbers of representatives
coming from business and from trade associations and labor
unions—the traditional pressure groups. The heavily weighted
business representation among the Liberal-Democrats and the
orientation of the Socialists toward labor and the professional

[4] *Kokkai Benran* [National Diet Handbook], September, 1964, pp. 326–
328.
[5] Japan, Jichisho Senkyokyoku [Ministry of Autonomy Election Bureau],
Shugiin Giin . . . Kekka Shirabe [Results of 1963 General Election], p. 14.

categories continue past trends. There are only 39 lawyers, a small proportion compared to American legislatures, which are dominated by those trained in the law.

The average age of the nation's legislators has been increasing steadily in the postwar period and now stands at 56. The average conservative is three or four years older than his Socialist opponent, perhaps reflecting an influx from the younger labor ranks into the Socialist Party. Significantly, the percentage of members in the below-40 age group has steadily decreased (to about four percent of the total membership), while the above-60 category has picked up the slack and constitutes 35 percent of the house.[6]

The percentage of college graduates (about 70 percent in the 1958 House of Representatives) appears to be decreasing, but as is the case in just about every field of endeavor, graduates of Tokyo University occupy a disproportionate number of seats. About one-quarter of the Representatives attended Tokyo University, and approximately another quarter are graduates of the five top private universities in Tokyo. This particular breakdown reveals, moreover, that the government schools tend to turn out staunch conservatives, while the private schools, which in Japan are generally rated lower than the best government schools, tend to split their graduates between the two parties.

College Backgrounds of Diet Members Elected in 1958

School	Lib.-Dem.	Socialist	Communist	Un-affiliated	Total
Tokyo (G)	90	18	1	2	111
Waseda (P)	28	14		1	43
Nihon (P)	15	16			31
Kyoto (G)	23	6		2	31
Chuo (P)	11	11			22
Meiji (P)	12	1		1	14
Keio (P)	10	3			13
Hitotsubashi (G)	5	4			9

SOURCE: Fujiwara Hirotatsu, *Kokkai Giin Senkyo Yoran* [Survey of Diet Elections] 1960, p. 325. G=government university; P=private university. Figures for top eight colleges only.

[6] See also Fujiwara Hirotatsu, *Kokkai Giin Senkyo Yoran* [Survey of Diet Elections], 1960, p. 324.

Religion, ethnic origin, and regional background, all of which loom large in American politics, are unimportant in Japanese elections.

QUALIFICATIONS

Diet membership qualifications, rights, privileges, immunities, compensation, and discipline are provided for in the Constitution, the Diet Law, rules of both Houses, the Public Officials Election Law, and other statutes. The Constitution stipulates that membership qualifications are to be fixed by law but expressly forbids discrimination on the basis of race, creed, sex, social status, family origin, education, property, or income. No individual may serve in both houses simultaneously. Occupation or employment may, however, disqualify certain candidates since the Election Law specifically bans public officials from seeking elective office.[7] The same law requires only that candidates be Japanese nationals and that Representatives be 25 years of age or over and Councilors 30 or over. Residence in one's own constituency is not mandatory, on the theory that the voters should ideally be able to select from among the best candidates in the nation; in this respect the British rather than the American practice is followed. In fact, most Diet members, especially those representing rural constituencies, are locally based because of the need to maintain a strong personal following or party network (*jiban*) in order to ensure continuing re-election.

IMMUNITIES

Broad constitutional and statutory safeguards are provided against political arrests and harassment of legislators by the regime in power. The prewar experience with "thought-control" police has made Japanese legislators especially sensitive to any encroachment, real or imagined, on constitutional immunities. No

[7] Article 89 of the Public Officials Election Law. Exceptions are made of course for Cabinet ministers and others. Those judged to be incompetent and individuals serving prison terms are also denied the right to vote and to be elected.

member may be arrested while the Diet is in session, and if arrested while the Diet is recessed, he must be released upon demand of the House of which he is a member. The Diet Law permits an exception for this constitutional provision for members caught "in the very act of committing criminal offenses outside the House" (Diet Law, Article 33). In order that all measures may be freely discussed, the Constitution provides that punitive actions may not be taken against members for speeches, debates, or votes cast inside the House.

COMPENSATION

Legislative pay and other emoluments have risen steadily during the postwar period. The Diet Law stipulates that members receive compensation equivalent to that paid high government officials, with the result that the presidents (speakers) of both houses receive the same pay as the Prime Minister and the Chief Justice of the Supreme Court, while the vice-presidents are paid at the same level as Cabinet ministers. The ordinary member receives about half the income of the presidents. In 1964, monthly pay and expense allowances together with per diem allotments were as follows: [8]

President	Vice–President	Dietmen	Mail–Travel	Per Diem
¥400,000	¥300,000	¥180,000	¥100,000	¥4000
($1111)	($833)	($500)	($277)	($11)

The average Diet member therefore receives a base pay of $6000 per year, to which are added correspondence and travel expenses amounting to about $2077 and per diem allowances of about $2475 while the Diet is in session,[9] or a total of about $10,552. Although political exactions, such as party dues and entertainment of constituents, are high, this remains a handsome income in today's Japan.

[8] *Asahi Nenkan*, 1964, p. 220.
[9] Both computed on the basis of the average number of days—225—that the Diet remains in session each year.

DISCIPLINE

Not even the mother of parliaments is immune to ungentle-manly conduct on the part of the MPs, and the Japanese, who are relatively inexperienced in parliamentary procedure, have often seen their Diet become the arena for violence, name-calling, and other irregular tactics such as the slow-down,[10] the squat-in, and the boycott. The presiding officer of each house is empowered to exercise police functions and to request the dispatch of police officers to the Diet by the Cabinet. He may also warn or restrain members and force them to retract intemperate remarks. Insulting language is supposedly forbidden.

Although both government and opposition parties are publicly committed to parliamentary procedure, a party may often resort to extraparliamentary or illegal measures when emotionally charged issues are brought to the floor of the Diet for deliberation. Such tactics when used by the opposition are roundly denounced by the government party as an affront to the democratic spirit of majority rule. At the same time, they are widely supported by those who believe that the tyranny of the majority should be curbed and who find ultimate justification in the supposedly higher values of consensus and compromise—the traditional face-saving means of resolving disputes.

In 1954 the Diet passed a defense establishment bill over the bitter opposition of the Socialists, and then attempted to ram through a government bill aimed at recentralizing the police. Because the national police had been the instrument of control over "subversive" (Communist and Socialist) parties in prewar Japan, the Socialists were determined to oppose the government bill by force if necessary. A riot in the lower house resulted when the Socialists attempted to block the Speaker from entering the House chamber and thereby to close off deliberations. The police

[10] A favorite opposition tactic is the "cow-waddle." In plenary sessions of both houses, voting may take the form of individual balloting. In order to delay adoption of a measure, or to show displeasure, opposition party members individually waddle with infinite slowness to the ballot boxes located on the rostrum. The tactic appears to be perfectly legitimate.

were called in to restore order and the Socialists boycotted subsequent sessions in which the bill was adopted. The Speaker was
also forced to call in the police in 1960 and 1961 when the
United States-Japan Mutual Security Treaty and the Diet Anti-
Violence bills were being considered. The net effect of such
disorders in the Diet has been to lower the esteem of the public
for legislators of both parties and hence to damage the cause of
parliamentary democracy. There is evidence that both sides
have learned from earlier excesses: the conservative response to
the charge of majority tyranny has been the adoption of a "low
key" conciliatory attitude toward the opposition, while the Socialists have refrained from violence-inducing tactics, using only the
boycott to show their displeasure.

CHAPTER SIX

The National Diet
in Action

THE 34TH National Diet (Ordinary), which convened on December 29, 1959, and adjourned on July 15, 1960, considered some 207 legislative bills, approved 140, and held the remainder over for further deliberation. But its major task was to study the revised Treaty of Mutual Cooperation and Security which the Kishi regime had concluded with the United States and submitted to the Diet for ratification. Because public opinion over the timing of the revision was divided, Kishi's national support was fragile, and the opposition was determined to block ratification, it was questionable whether the Prime Minister would have his way. When the Kishi administration attempted to force the issue, leaving no room for compromise, the Diet erupted in violence and disorder, and a mass movement of unprecedented proportions developed throughout the country as the protest was carried to the streets.

It is the development of this parliamentary crisis that we shall now examine, focusing not so much on the events as such but rather on the underlying processes that are illustrative of the manner in which the Diet operates.[1] The 34th Diet is in many

[1] This account of the operations of the 34th Diet is based primarily on a work jointly compiled by the House of Representatives and the House of Councilors and published in 1961 by the Okurasho Insatsukyoku under the title *Gikai Seido 70-nen Shi: Kokkai Shi* [A Seventy-Year History of the Parliamentary System: History of the National Diet], vol. 2, pp. 799–877. The May-June disturbances have been analyzed by many writers. For an especially full account see R. A. Scalapino and J. Masumi, *Parties and Politics in*

ways atypical—in the outbreak of violence, for example—and there is a danger of creating the impression that the Japanese parliament normally operates in a highly irregular fashion. Actually the basic political processes, practices, routines, and accomodations (or lack of them) are essentially the same from session to session, and in these respects the 34th Diet may be regarded as fairly typical of postwar sessions.

The Security Treaty as a Political Issue

The original security treaty between the United States and Japan had been concluded as an adjunct to the San Francisco Treaty of Peace on September 8, 1951, almost six years to the day after Japan's formal surrender on September 2, 1945. One of the Allied objectives had been the elimination of Japan forever as a military threat to the peace in East Asia, but almost immediately after the termination of hostilities the Cold War began to affect American attitudes toward former allies and enemies both in Western Europe and in Asia. By the time of the Communist takeover of the Chinese mainland in the fall of 1949, the new international alignment had become quite clear: the wartime alliance of the United States, Great Britain, the Soviet Union, and China opposing the Axis powers of Germany, Italy, and Japan was now more or less reversed, with the United States, Great Britain, West Germany, Italy, and Japan in the western camp and the Sino-Soviet bloc in the "Iron Curtain" camp.

The outbreak of the Korean War in June, 1950 increased the momentum of the forces driving the two former bitter enemies into an alliance even while the military occupation was still in effect. One immediate consequence of the transfer of U.S. troops from occupation duty in Japan to combat status in Korea was the establishment, under authorization from General MacArthur, of a paramilitary National Police Reserve of 75,000 men for the

Contemporary Japan, University of California Press, 1962. Included is an extended case study of the May-June incident analyzed against the background of postwar politics and parties.

ostensible purpose of preserving domestic order. Although it is now clear that this indeed was the primary purpose, it cannot be denied that a further objective was the creation of a military establishment in Japan. In fact, the Reserve evolved within a few years into the Land, Sea, and Air Defense (Armed) Forces of today, opposed at every step by large and vocal segments of the population, in particular by the press and by the left-wing intelligentsia.

The drive to link the United States and Japan in a military alliance over the strong opposition of an antiwar-minded population has been one of the major divisive issues in Japan for the past decade and a half. On the one side have been arrayed the Liberal-Democratic Party and its adherents and on the other the Socialists, Communists, student activists, the intellegentsia, and those who generally take a neutralist stance in matters concerning international relations. In essence, the conservatives have looked to the United States to provide for Japan's national security while the opposition has stressed the need to remain neutral in a world divided into two powerful armed camps.

At the same time, economic bonds between America and Japan have been greatly strengthened in the postwar period (Japan's biggest trading partner is the United States), and a large measure of the unprecedented prosperity enjoyed by the Japanese people is directly due to the economic alliance established between the two nations. Moreover, the increasing person-to-person contacts at all levels, especially through cultural and educational exchange programs, have modified at least in part the Japanese intellectual's almost obsessional ties to Marxism. The Japanese man in the street is thus simultaneously pulled toward a commitment to the West and repulsed from closer ties with the chief representative of the West, the United States. Although in international relations the pull toward the left and neutralism is intense, if relatively weak in numerical terms, in person-to-person contacts and in economic matters the attraction of the West and especially the United States is overwhelming.

The resulting ambivalence of the Japanese attitude must be kept in mind in our discussion of treaty revision, which began to be considered seriously by the conservatives in 1957. The 1951 treaty contained certain features which were regarded as infringing on Japan's status as a sovereign nation and hence raised the ghost of the infamous unequal treaties of the nineteenth century. For example, the treaty explicitly provided that a third power could not be permitted bases in Japan without prior consultation with the United States, and furthermore, American forces were given a free hand in the use of bases. These provisions, which appeared to limit Japan's sovereignty, were widely regarded as placing Japan on an inferior footing with respect to the United States.

The Liberal-Democrats pleaded that they were attempting to eliminate the unequal provisions by revising the treaty, but the opposition forces wanted to cut all military ties with the United States. Any outbreak of hostilities, they argued, would bring a rain of firebombs onto the Japanese islands. Controversy and opposition steadily mounted against treaty revision throughout 1958 and 1959 as the government continued to negotiate with the United States.

Public suspicion of Prime Minister Kishi's high-handed methods was not allayed when he attempted in 1958 to force through a bill to revise the Police Duties Law. This measure, which would have increased the powers of the police, was introduced without warning,[2] and when opposition developed, Kishi attempted to have the Diet extended through the irregular procedure of calling for a vote while the opposition was not yet seated. Kishi's image, already tarnished by service in the wartime cabinet of General Tojo Hideki, suffered a further decline.

It was in an increasingly tense atmosphere that the Kishi administration concluded negotiations with the United States over the revised security treaty. In mid-January, 1960, Kishi led a delegation to Washington to sign the revised security treaty and the ancillary administrative agreement. President Eisenhower and Prime Minister Kishi then issued a joint declaration affirming accord on the basic principles of cooperation for mutual security and broadening of trade between the two nations. As a gesture of good will, Kishi announced that Crown Prince Akihito would

[2] The bill was introduced without previous clearance by a regular cabinet meeting although the ministers had been apprised in advance and had acceded to Kishi's wishes individually.

tour the United States and that in return Eisenhower would visit Japan later that year.

In the treaty, the controversial grant by Japan of the use of "facilities and areas" (i.e., bases) to U.S. land, sea, and air forces for the "purpose of contributing to the security of Japan and the . . . Far East" was acknowledged anew although it was made clear in an exchange of notes that any major change in troop deployment or in "equipment" (i.e., introduction of atomic bombs) would require prior consultation with the Japanese government. To soften the granting of military bases, the treaty also emphasized commitment to the United Nations Charter, the desire to seek peaceful solutions, and most important, the strengthening of "free institutions" and the encouragement of "economic collaboration" between the two nations. The treaty would remain in force until the United Nations could provide for the maintenance of peace in the "Japan area," but could be terminated unilaterally after it had been in force for 10 years. It was this treaty, then, that the 34th Diet was asked to consider and approve over the objections of an aroused opposition. But Kishi's popularity was at a low ebb, and the time seemed ripe for the opposition to set into motion efforts to check his ambitions, defeat the ratification effort, annul the treaty, and thus bring down his government, which was then entering its fourth year in office.

The 34th Diet (Ordinary), December 29, 1959–July 15, 1960

The 34th Diet began quietly on December 29 after a call for convocation had been issued in the form of an Imperial Rescript on December 8, 1959—ironically enough, the anniversary of the attack on Pearl Harbor.[3] Normally, ordinary sessions are convened early in December, around the 10th, but the extension of the 33rd Diet (Extraordinary) until December 27 had postponed the date of the convocation. The extension had been caused in part by mass demonstrations near the Diet spearheaded by militant stu-

[3] Because of the international date line, the Japanese anniversary of the attack falls on December 8 rather than on December 7.

dent groups protesting the upcoming security treaty. The demonstrations had led to debate over a bill to control such actions and an attempt to pass a vote of no confidence in the Speaker of the House of Representatives.

The Diet thus convened on the 29th and, after deciding on the date of the formal opening ceremonies,[4] immediately adjourned for the customary New Year's and post New Year's recess. The time would be spent in political fence-mending and in annual party congresses scheduled for mid-January.

Meanwhile, bitter factional struggles in the Socialist Party over ideology and political strategy (methods to be adopted in attempting to woo voters and reduce the crushing conservative majorities regularly returned to the Diet), led to a schism in the party. The precarious unity it had achieved in 1955 collapsed as the right wing split off to form the Democratic Socialist Party publicly committed to support parliamentary democracy in Japan and to reject irregular tactics. By early January, 1960, therefore, party alignment in the Diet was as follows:

House of Representatives		House of Councilors	
Liberal-Democrats	288	Liberal-Democrats	136
Socialists	128	Socialists	68
Democratic Socialists	37	Democratic Socialists	16
Unaffiliated	3	Unaffiliated Clubs [5]	14
Vacancies	11	Ryokufukai (Green	
	467	Breeze) [5]	10
		Communists	3
		Unaffiliated	1
		Vacancies	2
			250

[4] It was not necessary to elect Diet officers since they had originally been designated by the 29th Diet (Special) which convened in June, 1958, following the general elections of May. Officers thus elected are expected to serve until the expiration of their terms as Diet members, i.e., until the next general election. The Speaker and Vice-Speaker of the House of Representatives were replaced in the 31st Diet when they both resigned.

[5] Combined on January 30, 1960, to form a new group known as the Friends of the House of Councilors (Sangiin Doshikai).

The government party, therefore, possessed more than enough strength to secure Diet approval of the security treaty even though the measure lacked strong support among the people as reflected in public opinion surveys and vociferous press condemnation. The polls compiled by the Prime Minister's Office showed that while over 40 percent of the people upheld the Liberal-Democratic Party, only about 25 percent approved of the Kishi administration, and that while 45–50 percent were for alignment with the Free World and endorsed the existing security arrangements, only 20–25 percent favored immediate revision as against 35 percent or more who opposed.[6] Regardless of the lack of popular support, Kishi was as determined to secure approval for the treaty as his opponents were to stop it.

A month after convocation on January 30, the formal opening ceremony for the Diet was held in the Chamber of the House of Councilors commencing at 1 P.M. This was attended by Prime Minister Kishi and his Cabinet, the Chief Justice of the Supreme Court, the Emperor, and the assembled Representatives and Councilors. There was the usual parade of platitudes: Speaker Kato reminding the Diet that peace and prosperity were the fervent hopes of all mankind, and the Emperor thanking the members for their unremitting efforts to enhance relations with friendly nations, to attain world peace, and to accomplish their mission as the supreme organ of the state.

The Diet did not get down to business until two days later; first, an organizational matter had to be disposed of. Feeling that their effectiveness as supposedly neutral leaders had been compromised as a result of the disorders in the Diet during the preceding session, Speaker Kato of the Liberal-Democratic Party and Vice-Speaker Masaki of the Socialist Party submitted their resignations and were replaced by Kiyose Ichiro and Nakamura Koichi, respectively. Neither Kato nor Masaki asked that their names be stricken from their party rosters—a custom of recent origin. The rostrum was then turned over to government spokes-

[6] Japan, Naikaku Sori Daijin Kambo, Shingishitsu [Prime Minister's Office, Secretariat, Councilor's Room], *Zenkoku Seron Chosa no Genkyo* [Report on National Public Opinion Surveys], April 1959–March, 1960, pp. 129–137.

men for the formal policy speeches that begin each session of the Diet.[7]

Prime Minister Kishi began his administrative policy speech by defending the revised security treaty which had just been concluded in Washington. Pointing out that the "Free World" and the "Communist bloc" were seeking common grounds for co-existence while a precarious military balance was being maintained, he warned that all nations must work to promote the thaw in East-West relations within the framework of the United Nations Charter. It was with this international development in mind, he said, that he had negotiated the new treaty which swept away any intimation of Japanese inferiority and placed the nation on a footing of equal partnership with the United States. The treaty, he stressed, was strictly within the spirit of the United Nations Charter, which permitted regional collective security arrangements which would not be invoked short of invasion of the homeland by hostile forces. He declared flatly that he had placed his diplomacy squarely in support of the Free World and hence rejected the neutralist course.

Foreign Minister Fujiyama Aiichiro followed Kishi to the rostrum and spelled out in further detail the thinking behind the government's commitment to the United States in world affairs. Security through the United Nations, he pointed out, was unfortunately impossible under existing conditions; consequently, the only realistic course was to conclude collective security and economic cooperation arrangements with a nation with which Japan shared basic political and economic goals. Finance Minister Sato Eisaku then addressed the House, stating that further economic development must be founded on greater liberalization of trade. His budget policy, he averred, would be based on the maintenance of a sound fiscal system and a balanced general accounts budget without resort to deficit financing. The budget, he concluded, would give priority to long neglected sectors of the economy, beginning with conservation measures and continuing

[7] In brief extraordinary sessions, the policy speech may consist merely of a state of the nation address by the Prime Minister. In ordinary sessions, the Prime Minister and Finance and Foreign Ministers normally address both houses on successive days.

through road, port, and railway construction and ending with improvement of living and housing conditions. The Director-General of the Economic Planning Agency concluded the addresses for the government by emphasizing the need for long-range planning to accelerate the economic growth rate, especially in qualitative terms.

In two days of wide-ranging interpellations, Socialist and Democratic Socialist spokesmen—and even members of Kishi's own party—questioned the Prime Minister vigorously on every point of his proposed program. The opposition especially viewed with disfavor the timing of the treaty, coming, as it did, virtually on the eve of the East-West summit conference. The treaty, moreover, according to Socialist charges, was detrimental to the development of friendly relations with China, the Soviet Union, and other Asian countries. The opposition therefore demanded a dissolution of the House of Representatives so that the treaty and other issues could be taken to the people for a vote, a course of action which Kishi promptly rejected. Two further days of interpellation followed in the House of Councilors.

On February 4, attention shifted to the Budget Committee of the House of Representatives to which the government's budget bill had been committed. The Budget Committee is one of the first to meet, since it must approve the budget by March 1 so that a budget will be in effect at the beginning of the fiscal year, April 1. Accordingly, debate on major policy questions moves from the Diet floor to the Committee, even on questions not directly related to the budget. On this occasion also, questioning on the controversial security treaty pursued Kishi into the hearings of the Budget Committee. The opposition directed its attack initially to definitions of the "Far East" and the question of "prior consultation." The treaty granted the use of military bases in Japan to U.S. forces for the purpose of maintaining "international peace and security in the Far East" and the Socialists argued that if mainland China and the offshore islands were included in the "Far East," Japan would easily be drawn into a major conflict which it was unprepared to fight. The government at first denied that China was included in the "Far East" and then changed its approach, stating that the region could not be defined rigidly in advance but would have to be defined by developing conditions affecting the peace and security of both the United States and Japan. This nebulous response merely deepened suspicions that the government was blindly committed to a course of action fraught with the greatest danger. The "prior consultation" debate was the legal cover for another fundamentally explosive issue: whether nuclear bombs could be introduced into U.S. bases on Japanese soil without prior consultation and agreement of the Japanese government.

In the House of Councilors, furthermore, the treaty was attacked as violating the "no war" article of the Constitution, but the government maintained that the Constitution did not deny the right of self-defense. In this case, the opposition appeared to be on firm legal ground, since in December, 1959, the Tokyo District Court had held that the stationing of American troops on Japanese soil did in fact violate Article 9 of the Constitution— and this decision was not to be reversed by the Supreme Court until the political crisis caused by the treaty revision debates was long over.

After the initial arguments in the plenary session and in the Budget Committee, debate over the measure next moved to the Special Committee for the Security Treaty which was set up in the House of Representatives on March 9 with a membership of 35.[8] The deliberations began quietly enough with an examination of the fundamental question of the right of the Cabinet to conclude treaties and the right of the Diet to ratify. After public hearings, 10 of the members were dispatched to Osaka, Sendai, and Fukuoka to check the local pulse, while the remainder of the special committee continued the seemingly interminable deliberations. The following exchanges between governmental and opposition spokesmen indicate some of the issues raised: [9]

Q. What is meant by "major" changes in troop deployment and in armaments requiring prior consultation?

A. The introduction of more than one division of troops or of nu-

[8] Its counterpart in the House of Councilors was organized a month later.
[9] Summarized from the account in Gikai Seido 70-nen Shi: Kokkai Shi, vol. 2, pp. 830–832.

clear weapons by the United States would require prior consultation with the Japanese government.

Q. Assuming that, as the government argues, Japan has the right to self-defense under the Constitution, does the government now affirm that Japan also has the right under collective security agreements to dispatch troops outside the country?

A. Japan has the right to collective security under Article 51 of the U.N. Charter, but because of domestic constitutional restrictions we do not enjoy the right to dispatch troops overseas. In the event that the U.S. bases in Japan were attacked, we have the right to defend our own territory.

Q. Under the new treaty, will there not be an obligatory increase in troop strength?

A. No, but troop strength may very well increase as Japan's power rises.

Q. Japan permits the use of bases in order to preserve peace in the Far East, but will this not embroil us in far eastern conflicts in which our security is not at stake? Is it not conceivable that the United States will use her bases here as staging areas for military activities elsewhere?

A. No. According to the new prior consultation system, Japan has a veto over the use of facilities not directly relevant to Japan's security.

Q. Now that a thaw in East-West relations is developing, why does the government insist on such precipitate haste in establishing a military alliance with one side?

A. The easing of tensions is welcome but it has not brought any substantive change in, for example, the reduction of arms. In the meantime, Japan must provide for her security—and not by means of an outmoded treaty which puts her in an inferior position.

As the hearings continued throughout the month of April and into May, the Socialist strategy became clear: since they could not muster a majority to defeat ratification on the floor of the Diet, they would bottle up the measure in committee and prevent it from coming to a vote. But if the Socialists were determined to block ratification, the Kishi government (although not all Liberal-Democrats) was equally resolved to obtain Diet approval.

At this juncture there occurred one of those accidents of history the influence of which extends far beyond the immediate event.

On May 6 an American U-2 reconnaisance plane was shot down over the Soviet Union just as the final preparations were being made for the Big Four summit conference, scheduled to begin in Paris May 17. It quickly became apparent that this violation of Soviet air sovereignty had eliminated any possibility of fruitful discussions in Paris leading to a possible détente between East and West.

The Soviet government announced that any base from which U-2s operated was fair game for retaliation—and Japan among other nations had such airfields. When the Socialists asked if such bases would not draw Soviet attacks, the government replied that the U-2s based in Japan were collecting only meteorological data. This reply was not reassuring, and the contemplated visit of President Eisenhower took on an unpleasant tinge. Originally, he was to have come as a peacemaker following the summit meeting between East and West; now that the U-2 affair had exploded that possibility, the President, who insisted that the visit be carried out as planned, seemed to be going merely as a kind of military inspector-general of forward bases. And Japanese opinion was especially sensitive to the Socialist claim that the Americans were at bottom more interested in military bases than in Japanese security, which was an incidental by-product of the need to maintain a warlike and aggressive posture in East Asia to contain Communist China.

When the date of Eisenhower's scheduled visit, June 19, was announced, the question of timing became critical. Prime Minister Kishi desired treaty ratification (as a souvenir gift for the President, it was widely believed), but the treaty was still bottled up in committee and the 150-day term of the Diet was coming to its scheduled end on May 26. If the treaty was to be ratified, it was essential that the lower house act by May 20 and that the session be extended. The reason lay in constitutional provision and practice. Under Article 61 of the Constitution, a treaty concluded by the Cabinet automatically becomes effective 30 days after approval by the lower house—with the count of days being maintained only while the Diet is in session.[10] Hence, if there were to

---

[10] Article 60 provides for the resolution of deadlocks between the two houses on budget bills. If the House of Councilors fails to take action on a budget approved by the Representatives within 30 days, "the period of

be an effective treaty by June 19, the House of Representatives would have to ratify it by May 20 at the latest and the Diet session would have to be extended until at least June 19.

The Liberal-Democratic Party therefore on May 19 requested the Speaker of the House of Representatives and the President of the House of Councilors to institute proceedings to extend the Diet for an additional 50 days in accordance with the Diet Law that requires that extensions of sessions be determined by concurrent resolution of both houses. It was in the lower house that trouble developed when the Speaker in consultation with the Steering Committee called for a plenary session. Attempting to delay the proceedings, the Socialists resorted to the tactic of packing the corridor in front of the Speaker's office so that he could not emerge to call the session to order in the chamber of the House.

In the Special Committee on the Security Treaty, meanwhile, the Liberal-Democratic members had announced their intention of terminating further questioning, but as nightfall approached the discussions were still continuing with no end in sight; the committee thereupon went into recess. Late that evening, when the 10-minute warning bell rang, summoning the members of the lower house into plenary session, the Special Committee reconvened, and amidst great confusion and haste, terminated further debate, approved the treaty without hearing a formal report on the proceedings, and reported the measure out with a recommendation for Diet action.

Precipitate action was the result. When the main bell rang at 10:35 P.M., the Liberal-Democrats filed into the House Chamber. The Socialists, however, adopted the frequently used tactic of the boycott to register disapproval. In fact, they blocked the corridor leading to the Chamber. Trapped in his office, the Speaker sought to clear the hallway by appealing over the loudspeaker system. When this failed to bring the desired result, he reluctantly called in the police to remove the sit-ins. At 11:49 P.M. the Speaker, accompanied by parliamentary guards, finally reached the rostrum and in short order called the Representatives into session. The

---

recess excluded," the bill automatically becomes law. Article 61 stipulates that the same provision applies also to the conclusion of treaties.

assembled conservative party stalwarts, who of course constituted a majority, immediately approved the 50-day extension. It was then announced that the House would adjourn and then almost immediately reconvene at 12:05 A.M. to consider the Special Committee's recommendation on treaty ratification. The House was in turmoil as it reconvened, once again with only the Liberal-Democrats in attendance. No time was wasted in adopting the Special Committee recommendation. The treaty was approved, and the house was adjourned 13 minutes after it had reconvened.

The enraged Socialists charged that the decision to extend the Diet, taken only by Liberal-Democrat members, was improper, conveniently overlooking the fact that their behavior in attempting to physically block the plenary session itself was highly irregular. They declared that they would not approve the treaty and called for an immediate dissolution of the lower house, and in this action they were supported by the Democratic Socialists. The conservatives, in response, issued a statement declaring that the decisions of the Special Committee and the House were fully legal, as indeed they had been since there was no question about a lack of a quorum (one-third of the total membership).

The Kishi administration had undoubtedly acted within the law, but the immediate and massive outcry from the public suggests that the government had badly gauged the popular temper. The month of political turmoil that followed the May 19–20 disorders is a further indication of the unpopularity of the Kishi administration's actions. In the greatest mass movement in Japanese history, the people took to the streets in demonstrations and strikes, calling for the resignation of Kishi, dissolution of the House of Representatives, and rejection of the treaty. In an extraordinary party convention, the Socialists on June 6 decided to resign en masse from the House of Representatives and force the Kishi government out of office, but they did not go through with their plans when public disapproval of such action became apparent.

In view of the continuing disorders, the wisest course might have been to call off the Eisenhower visit, but the United States persisted. When James Hagerty, the President's press secretary, arrived at Tokyo International Airport on June 10 to prepare for the state visit, he was greeted by a howling mob of students and had to be rescued by helicopter. On the evening of June 15, student demonstrators tried to invade the House of Representatives, and in the ensuing melee they were ejected by the police and finally dispersed by tear gas. In this disturbance, a Tokyo University coed was trampled to death, and several hundred casualties were suffered by both students and police. On the following day, the Cabinet met and finally decided to withdraw its invitation to Eisenhower. Interpellated the next day in the Diet, Kishi declared that the rioting was directed by international Communism and that the government could not be brought down by mass demonstrations and acts of violence—an assertion that events were shortly to disprove.

The treaty had been sent to the House of Councilors where it had been studied by a Special Committee whose meetings were boycotted by the Socialists. The committee had reached no conclusion, and the decision of the lower house therefore automatically went into effect at midnight on June 18 in an atmosphere of extreme tension as 300,000 demonstrators, still protesting the ratification, surrounded the Diet compound. The exchange of ratifications following U.S. Senate approval on the 23rd completed the process.

Faced with continued opposition from without and from dissidents within his own party, who found in Kishi's mishandling of the treaty in the Diet a convenient excuse to attack him and bolster their own positions, the Prime Minister called his Cabinet into emergency session and announced his intention to resign. Immediately the party mechanism sprang into action and within a month, as the turmoil in the streets subsided, a new leader of the conservatives was selected and installed as Prime Minister. Kishi's "victory" in securing ratification had been a costly one personally, though not to his party, and he has been in political eclipse to this day.

The events just outlined suggest some of the characteristics of the Japanese legislative process. For example, a certain arrogance on the part of the government in its relations with the Diet is still discernible, a legacy from the Prussian-inspired administration of the past. Moreover, the usual mode of operation of the Diet in its inquiries of government measures is the formal interpellation. Furthermore, a favorite tactic of the Socialists, a more or less permanent minority party, is the boycott, here seen in exaggerated form. And finally, it may be noted that the Japanese have their own notion of how majority rule should operate.

One of the most difficult of all legislative problems is how to compromise differences between majority and minority parties. Above and beyond regular parliamentary procedures, there are certain tacit conventions that govern both sides, among them the idea that the majority will take into consideration the wishes of the minority since, theoretically, there is no bar to majority tyranny—a charge repeatedly flung at the Liberal-Democrats. It is likewise assumed that the minority will not filibuster or boy-cott sessions to the point of paralyzing the parliamentary process. In Japan, the notion that minority interests must be respected is singularly emphasized by the fact that the idea of majority rule as such was unknown in the traditional mode of decision-making, the usual process involving discussion, compromise without loss of face, and gradual arrival at a consensus agreeable, at least on the surface, to all parties.

The popular outcry against government tactics indicates that the traditional emphasis on consensus still has high appeal, even among the reformist groups, ironically enough.

Politically, neither party gained, and many people condemned both the ins and the outs impartially: public opinion polls showed large-scale rejection of unilateral voting by the government party, the sit-in tactics of the Socialists, and street demonstrations as modes of political action.[11] While the overall damage to the cause of parliamentary government was fairly severe, in the end the people accepted the decision of the majority party, the mob in the streets did not produce a revolutionary movement seeking to overturn the Constitution, and in the general elections held in the fall of the year the conservatives under Prime Minister

[11] Japan, Naikaku Sori Daijin Kambo, Kohoshitsu [Prime Minister's Office, Secretariat, Public Relations Office], *Zenkoku Seron Chosa no Genkyo* [Report on National Public Opinion Surveys], April, 1960–March, 1961, pp. 159–161.

Ikeda were returned to office with a comfortable majority in the Diet—a popular decision which the opposition accepted calmly enough even if with anguished frustration.

Principal Statutes Enacted by the 34th Diet

The struggle over ratification of the security pact so dominated the 34th Diet that it was later to be referred to as the Security Treaty Diet. Nonetheless, the Diet members also addressed themselves to other measures. The final count showed 207 legislative bills [12] introduced, 140 passed (including 5 holdover bills from the preceding session), 12 treaties considered, and 9 approved, and a total of 11,702 petitions received, of which the Representatives acted on 1203. The House of Representatives established four special committees (including the Security Treaty Committee) and the Councilors created one.

In addition to five budget bills and the ratification of the security pact, the Diet considered and enacted into law a number of measures which reflected conditions requiring national attention in 1960. The substance of some of the more significant measures and how they were enacted into law may be briefly summarized as follows:

LOCAL AUTONOMY MINISTRY LAW

In view of past criticism that local government was being neglected in part because of the subdepartmental status of the Local Autonomy Agency, the Cabinet proposed a revision of the agency law to elevate it to ministry status. When considered by the House of Representatives Cabinet Committee it met opposition from the Socialists, who regarded it as part of a government design toward greater centralization and a stronger bureaucracy. Nevertheless it was favorably reported out, passed by the House, approved by the Councilors, and enacted into law.

[12] Of these, 155 were Cabinet bills, 48 were Representatives' bills, and 4 were Councilors' bills.

REVISION OF THE HIGHWAY TRAFFIC CONTROL LAW

The existing law, providing for uniform traffic regulations throughout the country, dated back to 1947 and had been amended piecemeal over the succeeding years. By 1960 it was completely inadequate due to the steep rise in road traffic as car ownership increased and urban congestion worsened. The revised bill, which had popular and bipartisan support, was sent to the Local Government Committee of the House of Councilors where it was considered jointly with the Transportation Committee. Approved by the Councilors with minor modifications, it was then turned over to the House of Representatives where the Local Government and Transportation Committees considered it jointly and passed it without change.

EMERGENCY LAW TO PROMOTE MEDIUM AND SMALL ENTERPRISES

Japan is characterized as having a dual economy, typified on the one hand by giant enterprises utilizing the latest techniques in modern, highly efficient industrial plants, and on the other hand, by medium and small-scale businesses (often subcontractors for the bigger firms) which are undercapitalized, lacking in modern facilities, and relatively low in productivity. Since the government was gradually liberalizing the economy by removing barriers to freer trade, it became apparent that the rate of bankruptcy would rise among small firms as foreign goods entered the domestic market. In order to increase productivity, the government proposed a measure which would begin by classifying smaller business firms by type (e.g., textiles, opticals, sundry goods), and then provide for each type of industry specific methods for the rationalization of management and facilities and the regularization of competition. A Small Business Promotion Council would be established in the Ministry of International Trade and Industry to aid in the marketing of products. The government bill was first entrusted to the Commerce and Industry Committee of the House of Representatives where it was accepted as introduced and then moved to the House of Councilors where it was also approved without change.

REVISION OF EMERGENCY MEASURES LAW TO RATIONALIZE THE COAL INDUSTRY

The original law had been enacted to rationalize and stabilize the coal industry and make coal competitive with other energy sources, especially heavy fuel oil. Since a further drop in coal prices was forecast, the administration proposed that the pace of modernization efforts be stepped up. For this purpose, it suggested interest-free loans. It also proposed that inefficient producers be bought out and that such mines be retired. The proposed revision was submitted to the Commerce and Industry Committee of the lower house where it met the opposition of Socialist members, whose primary support comes from organized labor, including miners who would be adversely affected by the closing of mines and the introduction of coal-digging machinery. Despite the opposition, the bill was passed by both houses as introduced.

INSTITUTE OF ASIAN ECONOMIC STUDIES LAW

This institute had been established in 1958 as a private research foundation to study and promote economic cooperation and trade with the countries of Asia, Japan's "natural" geographic trading partners. To these ends it had conducted basic and statistical research with especial attention to developing areas, initially in South and Southeast Asia and subsequently in Africa and Latin America. Such research is essential to Japan's economic diplomacy, and the purpose of the law was to provide more generous funding by changing the status of the institute to a semigovernmental body financed by both government and private sources. The measure was approved unanimously by both houses.

MEDICAL FACILITIES BANK LAW

The government operates a number of financial organizations to supply equipment and long-term credit funds to specified businesses, e.g., the Small Business Finance Corporation set up in 1953. In view of the need for a special bank to advance loans for the establishment and improvement of private hospital and clinic facilities, the administration proposed the establishment of a Medical Facilities Bank to provide credit for the medical profession. Studied by the Social and Labor Committees of both houses, the bill readily gained approval and was enacted as submitted.

EMERGENCY FORESTATION AND WATER CONSERVATION LAW

This law arose out of the twin needs to provide relief through a 10-year program for the reconstruction of typhoon- and flood-damaged irrigation and water-storage facilities and to assure increasing water resources for an expanding industrial society. The law provided, therefore, for flood relief and water resources planning at both the local and national levels. The proposal was considered in joint committees (Construction-Agriculture and Forestry) in both houses and passed without alteration.

The legislative proposals briefly reviewed here are indicative of some of the concerns of the national government and also suggest the way in which the state responds in meeting the demands of a changing society. In the international sphere, a fundamental alteration of Japan's status required a change in her security status, and the formalization of her new role necessarily involved the legislative branch of the government. At the administrative level, the increasing centralization of government functions brought about a conversion of the Local Autonomy Agency to ministry status. Emerging needs and social changes led to water conservation and new traffic control measures. Above all, as stressed earlier, the government worked actively and positively through a continuing series of legislative enactments to transform or influence the economy of Japan, so that her industries would be able to compete effectively with the most efficient foreign producers in the markets of the world.

CHAPTER SEVEN

Party Politics

THE POVERTY of our conceptual vocabulary when dealing with political phenomena [1] is nowhere more evident than in a discussion of parties. Thus the word "party" is used to refer to the monolithic Soviet Communist Party as well as to either of the amorphous groups that coalesce periodically in the United States at election time under the Democratic and Republican labels. How then can the Japanese political interest groups which do not appear to fit either of the above two generalized types be described? To begin, groups which, in the fall of 1964, were represented in the National Diet were as follows: [2]

House of Representatives		House of Councilors	
Liberal-Democratic Party	289	Liberal-Democratic Party	146
Japan Socialist Party	144	Japan Socialist Party	66
Democratic Socialist Party	23	Democratic Socialist Party	10
Japan Communist Party	4	Japan Communist Party	3
		Clean Government Party	
		(Komeito)	15
		Green Breeze Society	
		(Ryokufukai)	4
		Second Chamber Club	
		(Dainiin Kurabu)	3

[1] For a general discussion on this question, see J. H. Kautsky, "The Western World and the Non-Western World," *American Behavioral Scientist*, April, 1964, pp. 25–29.

[2] As of September, 1964; unaffiliated members and unfilled seats excluded.

The two major parties, the Liberal-Democrats and the Japan Socialists, represent the conservative and reformist [3] mainstreams.[4] None of the minority groupings can be regarded as a serious contender for political power.

Perhaps the foregoing configuration of power in the Diet, which has held steady for most of the postwar period, is best described as a "one-and-one-half party system" characterized by a dominant party that monopolizes power and alone knows how to govern while opposed by a permanent minority group that at times seems "positively afraid of power." [5] (In this connection, it may be pointed out that the Socialists have not organized a shadow cabinet ready to take over the reins of government should the conservatives falter and lose their mandate from the people.) If a political party is defined as an organization committed to the attainment of supreme state power, the Liberal-Democratic Party in reality is not a single organization but a coalition of little conservative parties each of which feels certain that it will in the end gain hegemony over its rivals. It has been in the intraparty factional struggles, not in the formal election battles waged between the parties, that the real contests for power have in fact taken place. Factionalism, then, is one of the fundamental and enduring characteristics of Japanese political parties of all colorations; this topic will be discussed further later in this Chapter.

Another characteristic of Japanese parties is that they are shallowly rooted both in historical development and in organizational terms. The present organizations and their prewar predecessors, which trace their ancestry back only to the last quarter of the nineteenth century, began as national parties; only in recent years have they developed any extensive local bases. They have been organized from the top down, with power situated in large measure in party headquarters in Tokyo, and there are many election districts with inadequate local organizations, especially among the reformist parties. In Great Britain, in contrast, parties origi-

[3] The Japan Socialist, Democratic Socialist, and Communist Parties are referred to collectively in Japan as "renovationist" or "reformist" parties (*kakushinto*).

[4] See Table 3, "Postwar Evolution of Political Parties."

[5] Scalapino and Masumi, *Parties and Politics in Contemporary Japan*, p. 53.

nated at the local level and only later organized national unions, and to this day the local Conservative Party organizations preserve a great deal of autonomy in such matters as selection of candidates.

Japanese political parties have permanent headquarters and staffs; even the factions have independent offices. They are not the hastily organized, loose confederations of local entities that American parties tend to be. They are, moreover, characterized by fairly rigid discipline; voting in the Diet, for example, is normally along straight party lines. There are of course differences between the government and reformist parties in terms of organization, financing, and mode of operation.

Party Trends

The conservatives have dominated the postwar political scene and there seems little likelihood that their control of the government will be seriously challenged in the absence of an economic catastrophe brought on by maladministration or by a worldwide depression. As Japan gains in international power and influence, however, continued Liberal-Democratic rule will face the added risk of committing major diplomatic blunders that adversely affect Japan's security and her economic well-being.

The conservative advantage has been gradually reduced during the period 1952–1963 from a three-to-one edge to a two-to-one margin in both popular votes and number of lower house seats.[6] At each general election, while the size of the electorate has increased, the number of conservative voters has remained at about the 23 million range, while the opposition share of the electorate has doubled from 7.5 million in 1952 to 15 million in 1963. It was on the basis of this long-term trend that the Socialists were confidently predicting in the late 1950s that they would be able to command a majority in the lower house by the late 1960s, but the split of the Socialists in 1960 and the apparent slowing of the leftward drift among the electorate since that time have virtually ended any possibility of a Socialist administration in the

[6] See Table 4: Postwar Trends in General Elections.

TABLE 3. Postwar Evolution of Political Parties

	22nd General Election, 4-10-46	23rd General Election, 4-25-47	24th General Election, 1-25-49	25th General Election, 10-1-52	26th General Election, 4-19-53	27th General Election, 2-27-55	28th General Election, 5-22-58	29th General Election, 11-20-60	30th General Election, 11-21-63
CONSERVATIVE PARTIES:									
	Japan Liberal Party	Japan Liberal Party	Democratic-Liberal Party	Liberal Party	Liberal Party (Yoshida and Hatoyama factions)	Liberal Party	Liberal-Democratic Party	Liberal-Democratic Party	Liberal-Democratic Party
	Japan Progressive Party	Democratic Party	Democratic Party	Progressive Party	Progressive Party	Japan Democratic Party			
REFORMIST PARTIES:									
	Japan Socialist Party	Japan Socialist Party	Japan Socialist Party	Japan Socialist Party (Left and	Japan Socialist Party (Left and	Japan Socialist Party (Left and	Japan Socialist Party	Japan Socialist Party	Japan Socialist Party

Stage 1	Stage 2	Stage 3	Stage 4	Stage 5	Stage 6	Stage 7	Stage 8
Japan Cooperative Party	National Cooperative Party	National Cooperative Party					
		Right factions)	Right factions)	Right factions)		Democratic Socialist Party	Democratic Socialist Party
Japan Communist Party	Japan Communist Party	Japan Communist Party	Japan Communist Party	Japan Communist Party	Japan Communist Party	Japan Communist Party	Japan Communist Party
	Labor-Farmer Party	Labor-Farmer Party	Labor-Farmer Party	Labor-Farmer Party			
	New Farmers Party						
	Social Reform Party	⎤ Cooperative Party ⎦					

Adapted from *Senkyo Nenkan*, 1958–1959, and *Asahi Nenkan*, 1964.

near future. The combined percentage of votes obtained by Japan Socialist and Democratic Socialist candidates rose from 36.33 percent in 1960 to 36.40 percent in 1963, a negligible gain. Since the 1960 security treaty disturbances, the government party has emphasized a policy of conciliation and harmony, and inasmuch as the economy has continued to expand, bringing unprecedented prosperity to the people, the opposition has found it difficult to find an issue to exploit in order to increase its following.

Most disheartening of all to the opposition, the percentage of younger voters supporting the Socialists has progressively dwindled. Public opinion polls taken in 1956 and 1958 showed that the Socialists commanded the loyalty of 41.5–44 percent of the voters in the 20–35 year age bracket while the conservatives were able to count on only 33–35 percent of the same group.[7] By 1963, while the conservative share had remained stable, Socialist support had dwindled to about 30 percent of this vital young group.[8] A local Tokyo survey conducted by the Socialists themselves in late 1964 showed that the decline of support among the youngest voters had not been halted.[9]

The other minority parties—even the rapidly growing Clean Government Party, which represents the political arm of the militant Buddhist sect known as the Soka Gakkai—appear to have little future as bona fide contestants for control of the government.

Basic Party Orientations

Political platforms are notoriously untrustworthy guides to a party's basic outlook and policies, and yet the election enunciations of Japan's parties are instructive in showing the wide gap that separates the conservatives and reformist groups. The tendency for policy statements to degenerate into mere slogans is

[7] Fujiwara Hirotatsu, *Kokkai Giin Senkyo Yoran* [National Diet Elections], Kobundo, 1959, pp. 387–388.

[8] Calculated from figures in Tokei Suri Kenkyujo [Institute of Statistical Mathematics], *Kokuminsei no Kenkyu, Dai 3-Ji Chosa, 1963 Chosa* [Study of Japanese National Character, Third Survey of 1963], 1963, p. 77.

[9] *Japan Times Weekly*, Dec. 19, 1964, p. 4.

TABLE 4. Postwar Trends in General Elections and Party Affiliations of Representatives

Date of Election	Size of Electorate (in millions)	Votes by Party (in millions)				Diet Members by Party				Voting Percentage
		L-DP	JSP	DSP	JCP	L-DP	JSP	DSP	JCP	
1947	40.9	16.1	7.2		1.0	281	143		4	68%
1949	42.1	19.2	4.1		3.0	347	48		35	74
1952	46.8	23.4	7.5		.9	325	111		–	76
1953	47.0	22.7	9.2		.7	310	138		1	74
1955	49.2	23.4	10.8		.7	297	156		2	75
1958	52.0	23.0	13.1		1.0	287	166		1	77
1960	54.3	22.7 (57.56%)	10.9 (27.56%)	3.5 (8.77%)	1.2	296	145	17	3	74
1963	58.3	22.4 (54.67%)	11.9 (29.03%)	3.0 (7.37%)	1.6	283	144	23	5	71

NOTES: 1. L-DP, Liberal-Democratic Party. Figures for the period 1947-1955 reflect combined total of all conservative parties.
JSP, Japan Socialist Party, split 1952-1955 into left and right wings.
DSP, Democratic Socialist Party, split from JSP in 1960.
JCP, Japan Communist Party.
Miscellaneous groups excluded.
2. Voting percentage indicates percent of eligible electors voting.

SOURCES: *Asahi Nenkan*, 1964, p. 229; *Kokumin Seiji Nenkan*, 1964, pp. 687-689.

apparent everywhere, and the farther from political power, the shriller the sloganeering tends to become. The campaign platforms prepared by the Liberal-Democratic (L-DP), Japan Socialist (JSP), Democratic Socialist (DSP), and Japan Communist (JCP) Parties for the 1963 general election may be summarized, stripped of excessive verbiage, as follows: [10]

Basic Policy

L-DP.   Work for establishment of parliamentary government, for progress with proper respect for tradition and human rights, for a conciliatory spirit in Diet operation, and for a revision of the Diet Law to eliminate violence in legislative chambers.

JSP.   Work to change the existing politico-economic alliance which serves monopoly capitalism to a system based on the people, to elevate the position of the Diet, and to elect true representatives of the people through clean elections.

DSP.   Bury capitalism and weaken conservative political power by a rational development of welfare state policies; destroy the bogus opposition between L-DP and JSP forces and thus correct defects in Diet operations.

JCP.   Oppose revival of militarism and imperialism by the reactionary government party which, in subservience to U.S. wishes, promotes nuclear arms; abrogate the United States-Japan Security Treaty; and establish a coalition government with opponents of the security treaty.

Constitutional Revision

L-DP.   Revise the occupation-sponsored Constitution without reviving imperial sovereignty or rearming.

JSP.   Oppose revision aimed at rearmament, restriction of human rights, and debilitation of democratic government.

DSP.   Oppose revision altogether, both the L-DP's piecemeal attack and the JSP's strategem of supporting the Constitution until it gains political power, when it hopes to revise the Constitution.

JCP.   Oppose revision and develop further the pacifistic and democratic features of the Constitution; oppose proposed legislation curbing violence in the Diet as a hidden attack on constitutional guarantees.

[10] Adapted from *Asahi Nenkan* [Asahi Yearbook], 1964, p. 235.

Foreign Policy and Defense

L-DP. Increase defensive power so that it is commensurate with national power; strengthen mutual security ties with the United States; recognize right of U.S. nuclear submarines to enter Japanese ports.

JSP. Change the one-sided relationship with the United States, cancel the security treaty, and establish an independent neutralist diplomacy. Oppose nuclear rearmament; work for Sino-Japanese and Japan-Soviet peace treaties.

DSP. Oppose the L-DP's subservience to the United States and the JSP's pro-Communist, anti-American line and establish an independent foreign policy rooted in the popular will; provide minimum defense consonant with constitutional provisions, and gradually annul the security treaty; oppose entry of U.S. nuclear subs into Japanese ports.

JCP. Conduct an independent, peaceful, neutralist diplomacy; reject entry of nuclear subs and arms; oppose talks with Korea and isolation of China.

Economic Policy

L-DP. Double the national income; achieve full employment, price stability, balance of payments, and economic growth with stability; modernize medium and small enterprises and raise agricultural productivity.

JSP. Oppose income-doubling plan which leads to price rises, social unrest, and widening of qualitative gap between developed and underdeveloped sectors of the economy; reverse policies based on big business and work for a rationalized, socialized economy.

DSP. Modernize medium and small enterprises and agriculture and nationalize large enterprises; eliminate the concentration of capital in large enterprises and modernize the capital-flow system; prohibit usurious loans.

JCP. Oppose control of the Japanese economy by American monopoly capitalism and economic policies subservient to the United States; expand trade with socialist countries; develop democratic cooperatives among farmers.

Education

L-DP. Improve moral and ethical training; promote scientific and technical training; expand college education.

JSP.   Stop the drift to a reactionary takeover of education; provide compulsory free education through high school; protect academic freedom.

DSP.   Oppose the conservative attempt to create workers loyal to capitalism; provide compulsory high school education; and eliminate entrance examination problems.

JCP.   Oppose indoctrination to support revival of militarism and oppose state control of textbooks; provide compulsory free education; restore democratic election of education board members.

Public Order, Labor

L-DP. Strengthen police power; eradicate political violence; improve the social environment.

JSP.   Eliminate central (national) control of the police; control right-wing terrorists; enact basic employment law to increase employment.

DSP.   Reject individual and group political violence; democratize the police; extend minimum wage system; and systematize social security benefits.

JCP.   Oppose extension of police power and spying against labor unions and democratic organizations; disband right-wing terrorist organizations; shorten work week; and raise wages across the board.

National Livelihood

L-DP. Stabilize consumer prices; mass-produce houses; reduce taxes.

JSP.   Cut monopoly prices; regulate public utility rates and land speculation; cut income taxes; and rescind special tax provisions for big business.

DSP.   Cut monopoly prices of big business; regulate rise in public utility rates; reduce mass taxes.

JCP.   Oppose inflationary policies of U.S. and Japanese monopolies, high prices, and heavy taxes.

The basic business (free enterprise) and pro-American orientation of the Liberal-Democratic Party is obvious from these policy statements. Equally apparent is the fundamental commitment of the reformist parties to socialist solutions for economic and social problems and to neutralist or Communist-bloc sympathies in foreign affairs.

Party Organization

The bylaws and regulations of both of the major parties [11] provide for the recruitment and registration of dues-paying members. In 1964, the membership of the Liberal-Democratic Party was approximately 1.7 million, making it by far the largest political group in the nation. Its nearest competitor was the Japanese Communist Party with about 100,000 members, followed by the Japan Socialist Party with about 54,000. Bringing up the rear were the Democratic Socialists with 30,000.[12]

LIBERAL-DEMOCRATIC PARTY

The control exercised by the Liberal-Democratic Party headquarters over local associations is substantially less than that wielded by the Tokyo headquarters of the reformist parties. Annual party congresses, attended by Diet members and two delegates from each prefectural party association, meet to determine basic principles and policies and, every second year, to elect the party president and vice president.

Control of the party mechanism lies not in these deliberative bodies but in a council consisting of the President, the Vice-President, the Secretary-General, the Chairman of the Executive Board, and the Chairman of the Policy Board. At a slightly lower level are the chairmen of the National Organization Committee, the Diet Policy Committee, and the Party Discipline Committee. The highest decision-making body is the Executive Board, the 30 members of which are selected by Dietmen and by the Prime Minister. The House of Representatives elects 15 of its members, the House of Councilors, 7, while the Prime Minister appoints 8, the latter bearing the sobriquet "imperial appointees" (*chokusen*

[11] A convenient source for the bylaws is *Kokkai Nenkan* [National Diet Yearbook], 1962, pp. 48–57 for the L-DP and pp. 229–233 for the JSP.

[12] *Asahi Nenkan*, 1965, pp. 257–261.

TABLE 5. Liberal-Democratic Party Organization (1961)

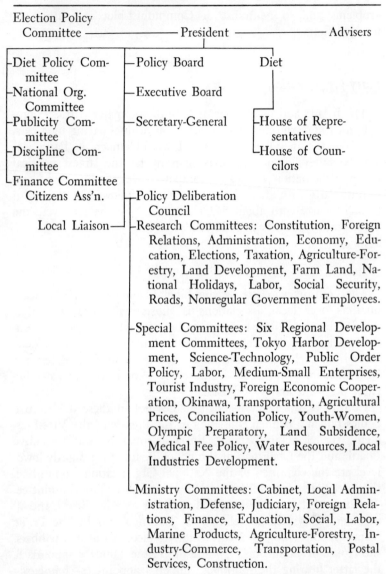

Election Policy
   Committee —————————— President —————————— Advisers

├Diet Policy Com-   ├Policy Board   Diet
│ mittee
├National Org.   ├Executive Board
│ Committee
├Publicity Com-   ├Secretary-General ├House of Repre-
│ mittee   sentatives
├Discipline Com-   └House of Coun-
│ mittee   cilors
└Finance Committee
    Citizens Ass'n.   ├Policy Deliberation
                     Council
    Local Liaison—├Research Committees: Constitution, Foreign
                      Relations, Administration, Economy, Edu-
                      cation, Elections, Taxation, Agriculture-For-
                      estry, Land Development, Farm Land, Na-
                      tional Holidays, Labor, Social Security,
                      Roads, Nonregular Government Employees.

                  ├Special Committees: Six Regional Develop-
                      ment Committees, Tokyo Harbor Develop-
                      ment, Science-Technology, Public Order
                      Policy, Labor, Medium-Small Enterprises,
                      Tourist Industry, Foreign Economic Cooper-
                      ation, Okinawa, Transportation, Agricultural
                      Prices, Conciliation Policy, Youth-Women,
                      Olympic Preparatory, Land Subsidence,
                      Medical Fee Policy, Water Resources, Local
                      Industries Development.

                  └Ministry Committees: Cabinet, Local Admin-
                      istration, Defense, Judiciary, Foreign Rela-
                      tions, Finance, Education, Social, Labor,
                      Marine Products, Agriculture-Forestry, In-
                      dustry-Commerce, Transportation, Postal
                      Services, Construction.

SOURCE: Togawa Isamu, *Seiji Shikin* [Political Funds], Uchida Rokakuho, 1961, Appendix.

somu), after the system of imperial appointees to the upper house under the old Constitution. What this system of selection means is that the Prime Minister's faction begins with 8 certain seats on the Executive Board and requires only 8 more for an absolute majority.

The Policy Deliberation Council (25 members) of the Policy Board studies the administrative aspects of policy decision and legislation. The Council tends to be dominated by men with bureaucratic backgrounds and by members of factions opposed to the party's mainstream. The 15 functional committees of the Policy Board, set up in parallel with the major government ministries, also tend to become the preserves of former bureaucrats with specialized knowledge. All Diet members of the conservative party are required to be members of one of these committees. There is a tendency for the Executive Board and Policy Board positions to be filled by party hacks since the more important posts—ministry heads and Diet committee chairmanships—go to top leaders of the party.[13]

SOCIALIST PARTY

The relationship between Tokyo headquarters and local associations of the Japan Socialist Party is based, according to party bylaws, on the principle of "democratic centralism." The highest organ of the party is, theoretically, the annual congress composed of headquarters officers and delegates from local associations. The congress elects the three principal officers, the Chairman of the Central Executive Committee, the Secretary-General, and the Chairman of the Control Committee.

The Central Executive Committee is the party's administrative organ and includes some 14 functional bureaus for general affairs, organization, publications, small business, etc. The Control Committee is the watchdog of the party, investigating infractions of party regulations and disciplining recalcitrant members when necessary.

[13] *Asahi Nenkan*, 1965, p. 54.

TABLE 6. Socialist Party Organization (1964)

```
                    National Congress
                            |
                    Central Committee ┐ Control Committee
                            |          ├ Audits
                    Central Executive  └ Advisers
                        Committee
                        (Chairman)
                    (Secretary-General)
                            |
  ┌─────────────────────────┘
 ┌Bureaus
 │    General Affairs (Policy)
 │    Organization
 │    International
 │    Publications
 │    Publicity
 │    Labor
 │    Farmers-Fishermen
 │    Medium-Small Enterprises
 │    Local Government
 │    Youth
 │    Women
 │    Citizen Activities
 │    Diet Business
 │       Planning Office
 │
 └Committees
      Election Policy
      Finance
      Policy Deliberation
      Diet Policy
         Diet Members Conference
         House of Representatives Members Conference
         House of Councilors Members Conference
```

SOURCE: Togawa, *Seiji Shikin; Kokumin Seiji Nenkan*, [Citizens' Political Yearbook], 1964, p. 794.

Party Finances

Japan's parties raise and spend enormous sums of money for a variety of purposes. As in Great Britain, the parties maintain permanent headquarters [14] and administrative and research staffs, and the expenses are high. They also issue a variety of publications (some of which are profitable sources of income) and convene periodic congresses to adopt basic policies and elect officers. The party presidency is the critical post especially for the majority party, since it is the president who is automatically designated Prime Minister. The biennial congresses which elect the party leader for the regular two-year term have become notorious for the free spending of money to buy delegate votes as the factions vie with each other in the contest to gain the Premiership, and it often seems to observers that the overweening ambition of the factional leaders is matched only by the infinite cupidity of the delegates. Money in quantity is also needed for elections, and Japanese politicians no less than their American brethren have shown astonishing virtuosity in circumventing the legal barriers to the raising and spending of funds.

Party finances are ostensibly regulated by two statutes, the Political Funds Law of 1948 and the Public Offices Election Law of 1950. Each in essence seeks to ensure fair and clean elections, the first by requiring the public reporting of political funds and their expenditure, and the second by spelling out rules for the election of all public officials, national and local. Each has signally failed to curb the corrupting influence of the excessive outlay of money in both intraparty and interparty politics.

The Political Funds Law requires the registration of all political organizations and the semiannual publication by local Election Management Commissions or by the Autonomy Ministry of all donations and expenditures. Fines and imprisonment are provided for violations. No limit is set on political contributions, but they must be reported.

[14] In 1964, the Socialists completed a new headquarters building in central Tokyo at a cost of $1.4 million.

The Public Offices Election Law regulates in detail unknown to American statutes all phases of the electioneering process from prenomination activities to certification of successful candidates. Included also are stipulations for the formal accounting, reporting, and publication of campaign fund expenditures. Of special significance is the formula that sets a ceiling on the amount that a candidate may legally spend on any one election. The formula, in its latest revision of 1961, is meant to ensure that inordinate sums are not spent, but unfortunately it has not noticeably curbed overspending. For lower house elections, the maximum is calculated as follows:

$$\frac{\text{No. of registered voters in election district}}{\text{No. of seats in election district}} \times ¥10.5 + ¥1,200,000$$

For the November, 1963, general election, this formula yielded a national average of about ¥2.54 million (about $7000) per candidate in legally allowable expenses,[15] ranging from a high of ¥4.14 million[16] in the Hyogo First District (includes the city of Kobe) with 740,123 qualified voters and 3 Representatives, to a low of ¥2.02 million in the Hyogo First District, which has only 226,789 registered voters and 3 Representatives.

Because of flagrant violations of the legal ceiling, and because of the need for more realistic limits on spending, the formula has been revised upward from time to time during the past decade. Even so, the actual amounts expended are generally assumed to be substantially above the lawful limit, and in some cases they are rumored to be as high as ¥20 million (about $55,000). In both the 1952 and 1960 general elections, a popular and cynical view was that ¥20 million would ensure victory while ¥10 million would only lead to defeat.[17]

[15] Japan, Jichisho, Senkyokyoku [Autonomy Ministry, Election Bureau], *Sosenkyo no Tebiki* [General Election Handbook], Teikoku Chiho Gyosei Gakkai, 1963, p. 167.

[16] Japan, Jichisho, Senkyokoku, *Shugiin Giin Sosenkyo . . . Kekka Shirabe* [House of Representatives General Election . . . Results], 1963, pp. 25, 46. A simple calculation reveals that the high should be in the neighborhood of ¥3.79 million while the low should be about ¥1.9 million. The apparent error in the official figures is unexplained.

[17] See Chitoshi Yanaga, *Japanese People and Politics*, p. 292; and Togawa Isamu, *Seiji Shikin* [Political Funds], Uchida Rokakuho, 1961, p. 36.

Virtually all candidates report expenditures substantially lower than the limit in case later checks should reveal additions that must be made to the amount initially reported. In the 1960 general election, for example, when the legal ceiling in the Tokyo Third District was ¥1.35 million, the conservative candidate reported an expenditure of ¥637,788, his Socialist opponent reported ¥925,423, and it was assumed that the actual spending came to many times these amounts.[18] One writer has estimated that a minimum of ¥5 million is required to conduct a modern campaign, while those with means spend from ¥10 to ¥20 million.[19]

The election law calls for fines and imprisonment for infractions of the allowable expenditures provision, but few if any violators are prosecuted for the same reason that the Corrupt Practices and Hatch Acts in the United States have been ineffective in limiting campaign spending: in neither country are there adequate provisions for enforcement. In Japan, the Election Law does not provide for the investigation and prosecution of violators, nor has the Autonomy Ministry been given the staff needed to conduct inquiries. Instead, the police and women's and youth groups which are organized to spot voting irregularities tend to concentrate on the more visible forms of corruption such as outright vote buying—the largest category of election violations. In the 1963 general election, not a single instance of spending above the legal ceiling was reported.

How Parties Raise Money

Financial statements submitted by the political parties to the Autonomy Ministry for 1963 show that the income for the Liberal-Democratic Party that year was ¥4.09 billion (about $1.1 million), ¥2.5 billion for the Communist Party, ¥331 million for the Japan Socialists, and ¥138 million for the Democratic Socialists.[20] These totals represent only the visible part of the ice-

[18] Towaga, *Seiji Shikin, op. cit.*
[19] *Ibid.*, p. 47.
[20] *Japan Times Weekly*, Dec. 19, 1964, p. 4.

berg, since they do not include additional billions of yen contributed separately to factions and local party organizations.

How are these astronomical sums raised? The Liberal-Democrats, as the recognized party of big business, naturally turn to the world of finance and industry. The Japan Socialists and the Democratic Socialists, on the other hand, find their chief support in their own membership and in the giant labor confederations with which they are politically allied. The Communist Party relies on individual membership dues and, it is widely assumed, donations from foreign Communist parties including that of China.[21]

Parties have both internal and external sources of revenue. A basic and steady source of income for the government and opposition parties alike is party and legislative research dues extracted from Diet members by party business offices. In the case of the conservatives, these dues which in 1961 were assessed at the rate of ¥30,000 per month (deducted from a base monthly salary of ¥150,000) amounted to ¥10.3 million, a sum which constituted about 20 percent of monthly party expenditures of ¥50 million. The deficit was made up by receipts from external sources, that is, donations from business enterprises.

In contrast, the Socialist Party derived 57 percent of its total income in 1961 from membership and research dues. An additional 25 percent came from the sale of party literature (periodicals and pamphlets); Diet members are required to sell from five to ten subscriptions for periodicals. The remainder came from labor and business donations, in particular from the political action committees of labor unions established for the sole purpose of raising funds for the party.[22]

The superior efficiency of the Liberal-Democrats reveals itself especially in fund-raising activities which, for the party itself, are controlled by the important Finance Committee. In a speech addressed to a citizen's group in 1963,[23] Secretary-General Maeo Shigesaburo admitted frankly that the party leadership had decided in 1961 to seek a broader base of support in order to correct

21 *Ibid.*
22 Data on dues from Togawa, *Seiji Shikin*, pp. 82, 133.
23 The address is reported in *Kokumin Seiji Nenkan*, 1964, pp. 825–826.

the poor image of the conservatives as a captive of big business. To this end, the party had organized a separate foundation called the Citizens Association (*Kokumin Kyokai*) the main function of which was the open channeling of funds to the Liberal-Democratic Party.

The Citizens Association was in fact an attempt to correct a series of shortcomings in the financing of party activities. The periodic scandals arising out of the flow of political funds to the conservatives had indeed created an image of venality; the constant dunning for donations by the various elements in the conservative alliance had also led to a revolt on the part of the donors themselves. Moreover, one of the desired objectives in the overall planning for party modernization was the elimination of factions, and this could not be done as long as the factions continued to seek and obtain financial support independently of the party.

The problem is a long-standing one. A predecessor of the Association was the Economy Reconstruction Conference (*Keizai Saiken Kondankai*) organized in January, 1955, at the behest of such financial leaders as the heads of the Federation of Economic Organizations and the Chamber of Commerce, who were seeking ways to systematize their giving through a central pool that would collect and disburse funds to the two conservative parties then in existence. The announced objective was the giving of "political funds without corruption," i.e., in an above board manner with no strings attached. Voluntary contributions were to be solicited from business firms; all funds were to be passed on to the parties without the donors' names attached. Initially, the amount raised by the Conference was somewhat less than the total contributions that had been raised separately, and by mid-1960 it had collected some ¥2.5 billion and disbursed practically all of it to the conservatives, with smaller amounts being given to the Socialist Party.[24]

Despite the success of the Conference, opposition developed on at least two counts: first, that it was too narrowly based, seeking contributions primarily from business organizations; and second, that the various conservative factions had continued to seek sup-

[24] Togawa, *Seiji Shikin, op. cit.,* pp. 175–176.

port from firms already committed to pooled giving. The problem is regrettably only too familiar for organizations as disparate as the conservative party of Japan and united fund drives in American communities. The sums collected, though massive, are not enough to go around, and the units of the larger organization are convinced that they can raise more money through their own efforts.

Following the November, 1960, general election in which Prime Minister Ikeda consolidated his hold on the party, the liberal-minded Keizai Doyukai (Japan Committee for Economic Development) issued a report recommending that both the conservative and reformist parties take steps to rationalize party finances, beginning with the establishment of party finance committees to unify receipts of political funds. It also suggested that the Conference, originally created as an ad hoc body, was undesirable for the healthy development of parliamentary government and that it should be disbanded. These recommendations were carried out in March, 1961.

The Liberal-Democratic Party's Finance Committee initially was to have five members, as does its counterpart in the British Conservative Party, but at the insistence of Prime Minister Ikeda, who wanted as large a base as possible, a 42-member committee was set up with Ikeda as chairman. Subcommittees responsible for a specific industry—steel, coal, electric power, etc.—were formed, with all of the important factions proportionately represented.

The next step was the organization of the Citizens Association in July, 1961, established with the objective of converting the Liberal-Democratic Party to a "true citizens' party" engaged in "collecting clean funds for clean government" so that the "voice of the people would be directly reflected in government"—according to its own promotional literature. Individual membership fees started at ¥100 per month and rose to ¥10,000, while corporate membership dues were set at ¥1000 to ¥100,000 per month.[25] Unlike its predecessor, the Citizens Association of course does not contribute to opposition parties.

According to a 1963 report by the Autonomy Ministry, the

[25] *Ibid.*, pp. 179–183.

Citizens Association received the bulk of its income from membership dues supplied by 30,000 individuals and 3000 corporations. A lesser but still substantial sum comes in the form of lump sum donations given largely by trade associations (e.g., ¥8 million from the Japan Textile Association) and business firms (e.g., ¥2 million from the Japan Cold Storage Company). Meanwhile, the conservative party itself listed the Citizens Association as its chief source of income (some 42 percent). Other top contributors to the party were the Chiyoda Association, the National Confectionary Industry Association, Yawata Iron and Steel Corporation, Kyushu Electric Power, Sambo Development Corporation, and the Paper and Pulp Association.[26]

That the Citizens Association has not been an unqualified success despite the large sums it has raised is evident from continued efforts by the party to eliminate causes of donor dissatisfaction. There is still grumbling that the conservatives have merely added another money-seeking organization to all the others, and that appeals still press in from the various factions and from the Finance Committee itself under which the Citizens Association nominally operates.

The principal thrust of reform forces in the party is toward dissolving the factions, which are regarded by the public as the source of corruption and by the institutional donors as unnecessary duplication. One result was the recommendation in late 1963 by the chairman of the Policy Committee, Miki Takeo, that such long-standing fund-raising organizations as the Shuzankai of the Sato faction and the Kochikai of the Ikeda faction be abolished. Miki also suggested that all fund-raising be centered strictly in the party, with the annual amount given by any one individual or corporation being restricted to ¥300,000. The recommendation on abolition of factional support was followed, but early in 1964 a new cluster of "clubs" and "societies" had sprung up, and the impression remained that the old factions had merely reclothed themselves in new names.

The Socialist Party reported receipts of approximately ¥97.8 million for the first half of 1963—less than the ¥108.6 million

[26] A detailed breakdown is given in *Kokumin Seiji Nenkan*, 1964, pp. 713–716, 834.

reported by one of the factions, Sato's Shuzankai, of the conservative party.[27] The party's primary external source of support
is labor, especially the General Council of Japan Labor Unions
(known by its Japanese acronym, *Sohyo*) and the Council's Political Action Committee, which contributes separately. Substantial sums are also received from business sources, but usually as
fractions of similiar donations to the Liberal-Democratic Party,
as shown in the following table adapted from an Autonomy Ministry survey:

Selected Contributors to the Liberal-Democratic
and Socialist Parties, 1963.

Firm	L-DP	JSP
Yawata Iron and Steel	¥10 million	¥2 million
Japan Sugar Industry Council	6	1
Tokyo Gas	3	1
Nippon Steel Tube	2.78	1
Matsushita Electric	.6	.15
Fukuoka Bank	7	3
Asahi Glass	3.5	3
Bridgestone Tire	5	0
Idemitsu Kosan (Oil)	3	0

SOURCE: *Kokumin Seiji Nenkan,* 1964, pp. 716, 718.

The Democratic Socialists reported the lowest income of ¥27.4
million. Their main support came from the middle-of-the-road
Japan Federation of Labor (Sodomei)[28] and the All-Japan Sea-
men's Union. A handful of business backers, led by Ueda Mining Company, also contributed, although none of the major
industrial supporters of the Socialists and Liberal-Democrats felt
it necessary to give to this small minority party. The Communist
Party, though numerically the smallest party in the Diet with
only seven members—four in the lower and three in the upper
house—was nevertheless the most affluent after the conservatives
insofar as reported revenue was concerned. It reported an in-

[27] See Table 7: Income of Principal Political Parties.
[28] Reorganized as *Domei* in 1964. See Chapter Nine for further discussion.

come in 1963 in excess of ¥744 million, all from individual donors.[29] The Clean Government Party is supported almost completely by the Soka Gakkai, a Buddhist organization of recent origin.

The Yawata Steel Case

The present system of fund-raising, which works to the benefit of the conservatives, has been challenged by a case still pending in the courts. In 1961, a shareholder in the Yawata Iron and Steel Company brought suit against two of the firm's directors on the novel ground that the ¥3.5 million donation to the Liberal-Democratic Party during 1960 contravened the Commercial Code as well as the company's articles of incorporation and was therefore illegal. The main argument was that the law prohibits activities beyond the scope of a corporation's normal and legitimate activities—in this case, the manufacture and sale of iron and steel products. The Tokyo District Court in 1963 decided in favor of the plaintiff, rejecting the defense argument that political donations were sanctified by custom and that they were in the nature of socially obligatory contributions to philanthropic and educational causes. Both conservative and reformist parties attacked the ruling as being inconsistent with social reality as recognized elsewhere in the law, e.g., in the Political Funds Regulation Law.

The reason for the across-the-board condemnation of the court ruling is not hard to find since all parties, both of the right and the left (except for the Communists) are dependent for financial support on big business, and without such backing their very existence would be endangered. The Finance Committee chairman of the Socialist Party admitted as much when the ruling was first announced, while a Democratic Socialist spokesman dismissed it as "just one opinion from judicial circles."[30]

Most seriously affected among the conservatives are the factional leaders who are almost completely dependent on business

[29] *Kokumin Seiji Nenkan*, 1964, pp. 718–719.
[30] *Japan Times*, Apr. 6, 1963, p. 1.

TABLE 7. Income of Principal Political Parties
and Organizations (1960–1963)

Organization	Jan.-June 1963	1962	1961	1960
CONSERVATIVES				
Lib.-Dem. Party HQ	¥1293 m. (4090)*	¥2418 m.	¥738 m.	¥1890 m.
Citizens' Association	540	940	119	—
Sato Faction	109	531	200	329
Kono Faction	66	403	114	132
Ikeda Faction	34	308	92	396
Fujiyama Faction	38	118	73	56
Ono Faction	23	184	42	—
Miki Faction	20 Jan.–June	71		
Kishi Faction (Shin'yukai)	7	61	58	66
Kishi Faction (Tokakai)	(Dissolved in late 1962)	Jan.–June 46	98	214
Ishii Faction	3	140	55	—
House of Councilors Doshikai	4	45	Unkn.	10
REFORMISTS				
Japan Communist Party HQ	317 (744)*	731	379	208
Socialist Party HQ	98 (331)*	267	104	219
Japan Dem. Educ. Pol. League	71	92	17	33
Japan Nat. Railway Union Pol. League	16	30	28	32
Dem.-Soc. Party HQ	27 (139)*	139	42	186

Adapted from Autonomy Ministry survey, as given in *Asahi Nenkan*, 1964, p. 244.
*Jan.-Dec., 1963, totals as reported in *Japan Times Weekly*, International ed., Dec. 19, 1964, p. 4.

PARTY POLITICS   147

friends to supply their money needs, and whose influence waxes
and wanes according to their ability to gain regular and sizeable
funds. While newspaper opinion supported the court decision
as a healthy corrective to corrupting influences, others remained
skeptical and indicated that the ruling would merely increase the
flow of illegal funds, thus corrupting the parties to an even
greater extent.[31]

The case is still under appeal to the Supreme Court. Meanwhile, the Cabinet Bureau of Legislation has issued a statement
declaring that in its opinion contributions are "necessary and
inevitable expenses . . . to smooth business activities,"[32] and
firms have continued unabashedly to donate to both government
and opposition parties alike. For the 1963 general election, for
example, the Federation of Economic Organizations set as its
goal the collection of ¥1 billion from its member trade associations to be delivered to the Citizens Association.[33] Among the
Federation officials who determined the new goal (¥100 million
more than the amount solicited for the previous campaign), was
vice-president Ojima Arakazu, better known in his capacity as
Chairman of the Board of the Yawata Iron and Steel Company,
one of the defendants in the 1961 court action.

Factionalism in Japanese Politics

According to the Japanese political scientist Maruyama Masao,
power elites in Japan were traditionally characterized by extreme
factionalism, with the groups engaging in endless disputes and
schisms resulting essentially from differences in personal ties and
loyalties of the boss-follower (oyabun-kobun) type.[34] The boss-

[31] Ibid., Apr. 8, 1963, p. 1.
[32] Ibid., Apr. 10, 1963, p. 2.
[33] Ibid., Oct. 25, 1963, p. 1.
[34] As cited in I. I. Morris, Nationalism and the Right Wing in Japan,
Oxford University Press, 1960, p. xxii. See also R. A. Scalapino and J.
Masumi, Parties and Politics in Contemporary Japan, University of California Press, 1962, pp. 18–20. For an analysis of the oyabun-kobun relationship
in connection with industrial workers, see J. W. Bennett and I. Ishino, Paternalism in the Japanese Economy; Anthropological Studies of Oyabun-Kobun
Patterns, University of Minneapolis Press, 1963.

follower group (in Japanese, *ha* or faction), which constitutes a legacy from Japan's feudal past, is the primary unit in National Diet politics. The factional leader must have political experience and skills of a high order. He has normally been returned repeatedly by his constituency to his seat in the Diet and has served as a cabinet minister, and because he has the right connections, he has access to both funds and positions with which to reward his followers. In return, the followers are expected to show unswerving loyalty to their leader whose ultimate goal is the Premiership itself, with cabinet and high party posts going to his faithful followers.

The traditional boss-follower pattern of social behavior has been strongly reinforced by certain aspects of the postwar election system. Miki Takeo, L-DP Secretary-General and a leader in the party modernization movement, headed an Organization Study Committee which issued a report in 1963 calling for a number of reforms to rid the party of factionalism. As a practical politician's analysis of the causes of faction, the Miki report is worth noting. The causes given were: appointment policy, method of raising funds, the manner in which the party president is elected, and the electoral system for Diet members.[35]

The appointment of ministers of state and of high party officials and the selection of approved L-DP candidates are made so that a factional balance will be attained, and this policy leads to further continuation of factions. The Miki report recommended a new policy of selecting the "right men for the right post" without regard to faction through the establishment of a personnel bureau in party headquarters. The designation of approved candidates would be the work of a permanent business office to be set up under the Election Policy Committee.

With respect to fund-raising, the report recommended the centralizing of these activities in the party to eliminate the financial base of factionalism. Individual politicians would no longer need to depend on affluent patrons but would rather look to the party for needed support. Turning to the existing method of electing the party president at biennial congresses marked by the excessive spending of money to buy the needed votes, the committee called

[35] The report is condensed in *Kokumin Seiji Nenkan* [Citizens' Political Yearbook], 1964, pp. 827–828.

for maintaining the principle of the open election of the president but restricting the number of candidates through the creation of a screening mechanism and the lengthening of the term of office to three years to cut down the frequency of voting. (Neither recommendation has been accepted.) Finally, factionalism is strengthened by the existing multimember election district system which pits members of the same party against each other on the same ballot.

The causes of faction, then, are many, and none of the political parties has undertaken serious steps to eliminate them. At the beginning of 1965, the factional line-ups of the 289 Liberal-Democrats in the House of Representatives stood as follows: Ikeda, 48; Kono, 47; Sato, 45; Miki, 37; Funada, 29; Kishi-Fukuda, 21; Fujiyama, 20; Kawashima, 18; Ishii, 14; and Independent, 10. The 145 L-DP members of the House of Councilors were grouped under the following eight factions: Sato, 50; Funada, 11; Ikeda, 11; Ishii, 18; Miki, 12; Kono, 20; Fujiyama, 12; and Independent, 11.[36]

Conservative factions are classified by a number of systems—for example, "ins" vs. "outs,"[37] or as "main stream" vs. "anti-mainstream." But this is not very useful since the opportunistic factions do not appear to combine in any meaningful fashion. Another analysis divides the factions into the "bureaucrats' factions" and the "pure politicians' factions" represented by the group of the former government official Sato Eisaku on the one hand, and the faction of the long-time Dietman Miki Takeo on the other.[38] The bureaucratic factions, which have dominated the government to date, do not necessarily combine against the politicians, and vice versa. However, the day of bureaucratic dominance may soon be over: already six of the nine L-DP factions may be described as being led by "pure politicians." If there has been any pattern at all, it may be found in the frequent alignment of the Ikeda-Sato-Kishi bureaucratic group against the Kono-Miki-Ishii alliance of "politicians."

[36] *Mainichi Daily News,* Monthly International Edition, Jan. 1, 1965, p. 1.

[37] See for example H. Ikeda, "Ins and outs of Japan's Factions," *Japan Times Weekly,* Dec. 5, 1964, p. 4.

[38] H. H. Baerwald, "Japan: the Politics of Transition," *Asian Survey,* Jan. 1965, pp. 33–42.

The Japan Socialist Party is torn by factional disputes even more than the conservatives, but the causes appear to be somewhat different. Socialist differences between the two broad groups —the left-wing mainstream and the right-wing antimainstream— are said to be based primarily on ideology. The Socialists include broadly ranging reformist groups from the conservative former Social Democrats to the old Marxist Farmer-Labor Party. In such circumstances, it is only natural that cliques arise out of ideological differences. Socialist factions thus have the general reputation of being "policy cliques" as against the "personality cliques" of the conservatives,[39] but this of course is not the whole story, and one cannot dismiss the factors which contribute to faction among the conservatives.

The Socialist Party mainstream was for many years a right-wing alliance of the factions of party chairman Kawakami Jotaro,[40] Secretary-General Narita Tomomi, the liberal-minded Wada Hiroo, and Eda Saburo, who was Secretary-General in 1960 when the party adopted the so-called "structural reform" policy aimed at the gradual rather than the revolutionary recasting of the nation's political and economic structure along Marxist lines. This alliance was challenged by adherents of Suzuki Kozo, and when he was elected chairman in 1965 his leftist coalition became the new party mainstream.

The Electoral Process

Constitutional and legal provisions as well as political considerations govern the timing of general elections for the House of Representatives. Elections are required once every four years—the constitutionally determined term of the lower house—but the full term is normally cut short by a dissolution of the house [41] and the calling of a general election. No Diet in the postwar period has lasted its full constitutional life; the 18-year period 1946–1963 has seen nine general elections.

[39] Kona Takao, *Seikai no Uchimaku* [Inside Politics], Toyo Seiji Keizai Kenkyujo, 1963, p. 94.
[40] Kawakami died in 1965 a few months after stepping down as chairman.
[41] See Chapter Three for detailed discussion.

When the House of Representatives is dissolved, the government must call a general election within 40 days. The actual date of the election must be announced at least 25 days in advance and candidates must register their candidacies with the local Election Management Commission 15 days before the polling takes place. Electioneering is supposedly restricted to the period between registration and the eve of the election, but this limitation is generally disregarded because of the difficulty of determining where normal political fence-mending activities end and campaigning commences, often well in advance of the official notification of dissolution. For example, Japan's 30th general election—in a series beginning in 1890—was called for November 21, 1963, after the government dissolved the House of Representatives on October 23. All 467 seats were at stake, and since it had been common knowledge since the spring of the year that the Ikeda administration was planning to go to the electorate in the late fall, informal electioneering was well under way several months before election day.

Members of the House of Councilors are elected for a term of six years, and since the upper house is not dissolved, the Councilors serve the full term. Half of the members are elected every three years.

The Constitution stipulates that local officials be directly elected, and the Election Law provides specially for the simultaneous election of prefectural governors, mayors of cities and towns, village heads, and members of city, town, and village assemblies. The normal term of office is four years, and biennial elections are held in April to elect approximately half of all locally elected officials and assemblymen. In the local elections of April, 1963, some 47,495 officials were sent to office by voters throughout Japan.[42]

Candidates for Election

The number of candidates running for office in general elections has steadily decreased during the postwar period, falling

[42] *Japan Report*, Mar. 15, 1963, p. 3.

from a high of 1590 contestants for the 466 House of Representatives seats open in 1947 to a low of 917 candidates for the 467 available seats in 1963. This averages out to less than 2 candidates per seat, but there is a tendency for the urban constituencies to offer an excessive number of candidates while the rural election districts run fewer aspirants for office. The most extreme cases were the 7 Tokyo districts which put up 119 candidates for 27 seats whereas the rural Toyama Second District ran only 4 nominees for the 3 contested seats.[43]

Ideally, each political party should enter a candidate for each seat, but this has not been the case in any recent election. The selection of candidates is determined by central party officials (on the basis of local recommendations, to be sure) and is not determined by local conventions or primaries. For the 1963 general election, the local chapters of the Liberal-Democratic Party suggested over 400 names to Tokyo headquarters, and the party's Election Policy Committee (with Prime Minister Ikeda as chairman) narrowed this down to a group of 359 official candidates. The breakdown by party was as follows:[44]

	L-DP	JSP	DSP	JCP	Minor	Unaffil-iated	Total
Candidates	359	198	59	118	64	119	917
	(39%)	(22%)	(6%)	(13%)	(7%)	(13%)	
Elected	283	144	23	5	—	12	467

The legal requirements for candidacy are minimal, the Election Law merely requiring citizenship and a minimum age of 25 (30 or more for the House of Councilors and for prefectural governorships). As in Great Britain, there is no residence requirement, so that theoretically the best-qualified statesmen that the nation can offer will run for office regardless of their place of residence,[45] but there is a tendency for local men to stand in their home constituencies, except perhaps in the great urban districts of Tokyo-Yokohama and Kyoto-Osaka where nationally known figures may be imported by the parties. Certain classes of public

[43] *Asahi Nenkan*, 1964, p. 231.
[44] *Kokumin Seiji Nenkan*, 1964, pp. 688–689.
[45] Local Assemblymen are required to be electors in their own districts, and hence must satisfy the three-month residence requirement.

officials—civil servants and judges, for example—are banned from seeking elective office unless they first resign, and no individual may simultaneously be a member of both houses of the Diet. Candidates must file for election with local Election Management Commissions and accompany their applications with deposits ranging in amount from ¥200,000 ($555) for Councilors standing for election from national constituencies to ¥10,000 ($28) for city assemblymen. The deposit fee, originally borrowed from English practice in 1925, is designed to discourage frivolous candidacies, and it is forfeited if the office seeker fails to poll a certain percentage of the votes.[46] It is criticized by some as a stratagem of the monied parties to restrict the activities of the less affluent parties.[47]

Election Districts

For lower house elections, the 46 prefectures of Japan are divided into 118 election districts on the basis of population—the lightly settled prefectures like Saga and Kochi comprising a single constituency and the more populous prefectures like Tokyo having as many as seven. Each district sends from three to five representatives to the Diet, with the exception of the special Amami district in southern Japan, which is allotted a single seat—the number again being determined by the population of the district. Unlike the single-member constituencies of Great Britain and the United States in which the winner takes all usually by a majority, the Japanese multimember single-vote constituency results in three to five winners, each with a minority of the total votes cast.

The multimember district tends to exacerbate intraparty factional rivalry for the simple reason that the candidate's most formidable rivals quite often are members of his own party

[46] In elections for the House of Representatives, the candidate must poll

$$\frac{1}{5} \times \frac{\text{Valid Votes Cast}}{\text{Number of Seats in District}} \text{ or forfeit his deposit.}$$

[47] See for example Soma Masao, *Nihon no Senkyo Seiji* [Japan's Election Politics], Aoki Shoten, 1963, p. 25.

and not of the opposition.[48] Consider as an extreme case the sad fate of Representative Ozawa Taro, Liberal-Democratic incumbent who in 1963 faced the formidable task of running not only against his Socialist opponents but against two of the best-known politicians in the country, former Prime Minister Kishi Nobusuke and future Prime Minister Sato Eisaku.[49] Seven candidates contested the 5 seats alloted to the First District of Yamaguchi Prefecture: 3 Liberal-Democrats, 2 Socialists, a Democratic Socialist, and a Communist. Altogether the conservatives polled 188,583 votes which, if distributed evenly among the 3, would have ensured re-election for all. But Sato gained 94,785 votes, Kishi 49,877, and Ozawa only 43,841. Sato's great pulling power reduced Ozawa's total, with the result that his Socialist and Democratic Socialist opponents with 50,000–66,000 votes took the other 3 seats.

Since the absolute number of conservative voters has remained at about 23 million for the past decade and a half, each candidate must fight for his fair share of the conservative vote, and naturally this is more easily done at the expense of his colleagues than of his opponents in the opposition parties. While Ozawa could hardly attack his distinguished fellow party members, quite often the conservative candidates run against each other with more vigor than they do against the Socialists. Moreover, they seek support (i.e., election funds) from allies in other electoral districts. The leader of such an alliance is the factional head, whose principal aim is to gain enough adherents of his own or through a coalition with other party leaders to obtain the party presidency itself.

The multimember district thus contributes to the extreme factionalism that marks Japanese politics, but an even graver drawback is the tendency for the system to exaggerate a failing not

[48] The voter can of course cast only one ballot, and he must therefore select only one of many candidates from the same party.

[49] Sato and Kishi are full blood brothers, the first brothers to become Prime Ministers in Japan's history. Sato was born a Kishi but adopted his wife's family name in accordance with customary procedure when the family of the wife lacks a male heir. Actually, the "original" family name, at least as far back as the generation of the father of the two, was "Sato," since Kishi père was originally born a Sato and was "adopted" by his wife's family which lacked a male heir.

unknown in the United States, viz., inequality of representation between urban and rural constituencies caused by uncorrected apportionment. The current allocation of seats (generally 3-5 per district) was made in 1950 on the basis of the 1946 population figures, and although the Election Law calls for reapportionment every 5 years, nothing has been done to correct the extreme imbalances that have developed in the past 15 years. The 1946 census was abnormally weighted in favor of the countryside to begin with because of the forced evacuation of the major cities during the war, and in the 2 decades since, Japan has become rapidly urbanized as agricultural workers have streamed into the urban industrial centers. The net effect is that the cities are underrepresented in comparison to the villages. The Hyogo First District (includes city of Kobe) with 740,123 qualified voters in 1963, for example, was alloted 3 representatives. Seven candidates stood for election, and the top 3 received upwards of 78,000–100,000 votes, while 2 who received 46,000–51,000 votes were defeated. On the other hand, the 3 seats in the rural Hyogo Fifth District with 226,789 registered voters were contested by 6 candidates. The top winner received 48,462 votes, while the other 2 winners polled 40,000–46,000 votes—less than those who had been defeated in the First District of the same prefecture.[50] Actually the national swing was even greater; in the Tokyo Fifth District, 80,000 votes were not sufficient to win, while in the rural Ishikawa Second District 34,874 elected a Diet member.[51] In other words, the spread is from a low of one representative per 128,000 people in the Hyogo Fifth to a high of one per 390,000 in the Tokyo Second.[52]

The correction of these gross inequities in representation, the necessity for which is recognized by all, has inevitably bogged down in partisan politics. When Prime Minister Hatoyama attempted in 1956 to introduce a bill providing for single-member constituencies, the newly drawn election districts were heatedly criticized as favoring the conservatives, and the plan, attacked as a "Hatomander," was discarded. Basic reform is still in the

[50] Figures as given in *Asahi Nenkan*, 1964, p. 288.
[51] *Ibid.*, p. 282.
[52] Soma, *Nihon no Senkyo Seiji* [Japan's Election Politics], *op. cit.*, p. 70.

future although redistricting has long been studied by a government Commission on the Election System, one of the latest proposals being to increase the number of lower house seats by 20 to 486 and thus remove some of the objections to reapportionment.

The basis for representation in the House of Councilors is quite different, 100 of the 250 members being elected from the nation at large and the remainder being allocated to the 46 prefectures roughly according to population—but with a minimum of 2 to each prefecture and a high of 8 (in Tokyo and Hokkaido). It was hoped that the Councilors from the national constituency would be nationally known scholars and statesmen, who would act as a stabilizing influence on the supposedly more volatile members of the lower house and other Councilors from the regular districts. But the upper house has not attracted an unusual quota of distinguished scholars; it rather tends to draw those who have money enough to run as national delegates at large or those who belong to small fringe groups that concentrate their votes on their candidates. Thus, 2 of the 3 Communist Party members of the House of Councilors are elected from the national constituency, as are 11 of the 15 Clean Election Party members.

The Voting Public

Since the first election for the House of Representatives in 1890, the franchise has been gradually broadened with the result that today virtually all adults are registered and eligible to vote. In 1950, out of a total population of 93.3 million, some 56.1 million were of legal voting age (20 years or over), and of this number, some 54.3 million (97 percent) were eligible to vote.[53] Under the original Election Law of 1889, the franchise was limited to male subjects of the Emperor 25 years of age or more, who had established legal residence in a constituency for at least one year and who had paid a direct national (property) tax of ¥15 or

[53] See *Asahi Nenkan*, 1963, p. 250, and *Kokumin Seiji Nenkan*, 1964, p. 687.

more per year. These qualifications limited the franchise to a mere 450,000 individuals—or 1.5 percent of a total population of about 30 million. Over the years, under pressure of public opinion, the property tax qualification was progressively lowered and was finally eliminated altogether in 1925 when the Election Law was revised to bring universal male suffrage to Japan. The percentage of voters jumped in the subsequent election to approximately 20 percent of the total population and remained more or less at this level until the end of World War II. The occupation-instituted revision of the Election Law dropped the voting age to 20 and opened the vote to women on a basis of complete equality, with the result that now about 57 percent of the total population are eligible to vote.

QUALIFICATIONS

Under the current Public Offices Election Law of 1950, which governs both national and local elections, voter qualifications are kept to an irreducible minimum. Basically, the law regards as eligible all Japanese citizens who have attained the age of 20 and who have established residence in a particular city, town, or village for a period of three months. Excluded are those legally judged incompetent, prisoners serving sentences, and convicted violators of the Election Law. There are no poll taxes, literacy tests, or any other device to restrict the franchise; in the 1963 general election, some 212,039 illiterates were aided in casting their ballots.[54]

REGISTRATION

Not only are restrictions against voting kept to a minimum, but the government also takes positive steps to register voters. Primary responsibility for registering, in fact, rests not with the individual but with the Election Management Commission of each city, town, and village, which is required by law to prepare each year a basic list of electors. This work commences in Sep-

[54] Japan, Jichisho, Senkyokyoku, *Shugiin Giin Sosenkyo . . . Kekka Shirabe* [Results of House of Representatives General Election], 1963, p. 83.

tember and the initial list is completed in October. During most of November the election lists are displayed for public inspection and for the correction of omissions and errors. The basic list becomes final on December 20 and is valid until it is superseded one year later.

Voting, therefore, tends to be regarded more as duty than a right, and this fact is especially noticeable in the rural areas where the traditional values are still firmly entrenched and the voting percentages are significantly higher than in the more liberal urban constituencies.

Voting Behavior

The American voter has been intensively studied for over three decades and a variety of conclusions has been reached concerning the factors which influence his voting behavior. Thus, it may be said that party loyalty tends to be passed on from father to son; that voter participation in presidential elections ranges from 50 to 60 percent of those over 21; and that men, whites, Catholics, and urban dwellers generally vote more frequently than women, Negroes, Protestants, and inhabitants of rural constituencies. Also, middle-aged citizens, college graduates, and professional men and business managers have better voting records than the young, grade school graduates, and unskilled workers with low incomes.[55]

In Japan, where the two major parties assumed their current form only a decade ago—although both of course trace their ancestries back through prewar parties to turn-of-the-century organizations—it is still too early to say that party loyalty is "inherited." Indeed, whether there is any kind of patterned transfer of allegiance from generation to generation remains to be studied in the Japanese case. Insofar as overall voter participation is concerned, the figure is significantly higher in Japan than in the United States, with about 75 percent of all eligible voters casting their ballots in general elections (for the House of Representatives, and hence for the Premiership), although the percentage has been

[55] See for example V. O. Key, *Politics, Parties and Pressure Groups*, 3rd ed., Crowell, 1952, pp. 565–588.

slipping toward the 70 percent mark in recent years. Racial and religious considerations are generally irrelevent in the case of Japanese elections, and the rate of voting among males is only slightly higher than among women.[56] In all other demographic aspects but one, Japanese and American voting behavior exhibit similar tendencies. As in the United States, the older, wealthier voters with high status incomes and jobs vote at a higher rate than the younger, poorer, and low-income citizens.[57] The exception, and it is a vital one with far-reaching consequences, is in the urban-rural variable. In Japan, the rural constituencies regularly turn out about four-fifths of all eligible voters while in the urban districts of such great metropolitan centers as Tokyo and Kyoto, only two-thirds of the registered voters cast ballots. Professors Kyogoku and Ike, who have studied this phenomenon in detail, attribute the disparity in voting habits to more efficient mobilization of the electorate in rural areas rather than to greater political consciousness.[58] It is, of course, the solid rural vote that has been the mainstay of the conservative Liberal-Democratic Party throughout the postwar period.

PARTY PREFERENCE

As shown in Table 8, according to a national opinion survey of 1963, twice as many people preferred the Liberal-Democratic Party as preferred the Socialist (43 percent *vs.* 22 percent), while 22 percent professed to no party allegiance. In actual elections over the past 10 years, the conservatives have garnered about 55 to 58 percent of the votes as against 26 to 30 percent for the Socialists.[59] The size and composition of those who profess no party affiliation are remarkably similar to the so-called "independent" vote in the United States. In both countries, the per-

[56] In 1963, 72 percent of eligible male voters as against 70 percent of women exercised their right to vote. *Asahi Nenkan*, 1964, p. 228.

[57] Tokei Suri Kenkyujo, *Nihonjin no Kokuminsei*, Shiseido, 1961, p. 317.

[58] J. Kyogoku and N. Ike, *Urban–Rural Differences in Voting Behavior in Postwar Japan*, Tokyo, 1959. Reprinted as Stanford University Political Science Series, no. 66. See also Fujiwara Hirotatsu, *Kokkai Giin Senkyo Yoran*, p. 317.

[59] *Kokumin Seiji Nenkan*, 1964, p. 688.

TABLE 8. Demographic Analysis of Electorate: Party Preference

	Liberal-Democrat	Socialist	No Party
National average	43%	22%	22%
Sex			
Male	47	22	19
Female	40	21	25
Age			
20–24	27	32	29
25–29	38	30	21
30–39	39	25	24
40–49	48	20	19
50–59	52	16	24
60–	53	8	21
Education			
Elementary	42	14	25
Middle school	44	23	21
High school	43	25	23
College	42	26	20
Occupation			
Professional	33	37	21
Managerial	42	13	35
White collar, big business	34	32	23
White collar, small–medium business	42	30	20
Family enterprise	48	17	26
Small business owner	62	10	19
Agricultural-fishery	59	12	16
Blue collar, big business	19	51	15
Blue collar, small–medium business	30	26	30
Day labor	35	28	17
Unemployed	40	20	26
Voting rate			
Always vote	47	24	16

Table 8 (*Continued*)

	Liberal-Demo-crat	Socialist	No Party
As often as possible	41	20	29
Don't vote	27	15	40
Population classification			
6 largest cities	41	23	25
200,000–	37	27	21
100,000–200,000	46	15	31
50,000–100,000	36	22	25
To 50,000	45	18	25
Towns-villages	47	22	17

Adapted from national random sample survey made by Institute of Statistical Mathematics, Tokyo. See Tokei Suri Kenkyujo, *Kokuminsei no Kenkyu Dai 3-ji Chosa* 1963 *Chosa* [Japanese National Character; Third Survey of 1963], p. 77. "Don't knows" and minor party supporters (13 percent) excluded.

centage hovers at about 20, and the "independents" are found in all classes and occupational strata, constituting about one-third of the managerial group (the highest) and about one-sixth of the agricultural class (the lowest).

Degree of education appears to have little effect on party preference. It is true that elementary school graduates—who in 1963 constituted 21 percent of the sample—support the Socialists the least, but the effect of schooling as a factor in preference may be expected to decrease. The percentage of those with minimum education has been steadily dropping, and according to figures released by the Ministry of Education in 1964, more than 99 percent of all Japanese children undergo 9 years of education (elementary and middle school), approximately 71 percent go on to high school, and about 16 percent then continue on to college.[60]

As expected, the conservatives find their most stable support among the agricultural masses—farmers and fishermen, who comprise 16 percent of the electorate, the largest single bloc of voters. They are also supported by a high percentage of small business entrepreneurs (11 percent of the sample), by the numerically small managerial class (2 percent), and by substantial

[60] *Japan Times Weekly*, Nov. 21, 1964, p. 5.

numbers of white collar workers (9 percent). The Socialists, on the other hand, find their main support in organized labor (blue collar workers), comprising 15 percent of the sample, especially in large-scale enterprises (7 percent). Significantly, labor in the smaller business firms (8 percent) vote conservatively as frequently as they do Socialist. Professional people (the "intelligentsia") also support the Socialists.

AGE DIFFERENTIALS

The conservative appeal, which rises with age, is stronger than the Socialist appeal among all age groups except the lowest (20–24), in which the Socialists outdraw the Liberal-Democrats 32 to 27 percent. This is small consolation to the Socialists, however, since in the decade 1950–1960 their appeal to voters in the 20–35 age brackets had been consistently higher than the conservatives'. As was indicated earlier, it would appear that the Socialist claim to youth is on the wane; according to fragmentary surveys made in late 1964, the Socialists are losing their attractiveness even to the youngest segment of voters.

PERSONALITY vs. PRINCIPLE

Japanese voters are often criticized as lacking in political maturity and voting more often for personalities than principles. How accurate is this view of the electorate?

In a nationwide survey conducted prior to the 1958 general elections, voters were asked to indicate the considerations which determined their selection of particular candidates. Multiple choices were permitted, and not surprisingly most of the respondents indicated party (40.3 percent) and personality (53.1 percent) as the governing considerations.[61] If we assume that devotion to party may be equated with commitment to principle (let us say to a conservative vs. a reformist principle), it is fairly clear that personality considerations do indeed overshadow principle. In a

[61] Japan, Naikaku Sori Daijin Kambo [Prime Ministers Office, Secretariat], *Zenkoku Seron Chosa Kikan no Genkyo* [Reports of National Public Opinion Survey Organizations], 1958, p. 106.

1962 survey, when asked to indicate whether the party or the man was decisive in the selection of candidates, some 38 percent of the respondents said party and 34 percent said the man, while 17 percent stated that no such simple formula was applicable and 11 percent were uncertain.[62] There is thus no easy answer, but perhaps the criticism as put is overly simplistic to begin with. The formation of basic attitudes, of which voting is merely one manifestation, still remains a matter of conjecture; additional research is required before the basic determinants in the decision process are clarified.

[62] Japan, Naikaku Sori Daijin Kambo, *Zenkoku Seron Chosa no Genkyo* [National Public Opinion Survey Reports], 1961–1962, p. 94.

CHAPTER EIGHT

Political Economy

Economic Interest Groups and Politics

A UNIVERSAL PHENOMENON of the technological society in twentieth-century western democracy is the existence of a variety of groups seeking to influence the government to their private advantage. These pressure groups are normally united on the basis of common economic or other interests. Although they profoundly affect the governmental process, they have apparently not yet reached a stage at which the societies in which they operate have found it necessary to systematize controls over their activities either by legislative or constitutional means. The largely theoretical advocacy of functional representation may be regarded as one aspect of this problem.

The term *pressure group* to denote such organizations is not strictly applicable to the Japanese species of trade and professional associations, although it may be appropriate for labor unions. In the United States, such groups are normally regarded as external to the government; with their national headquarters in Washington, D.C., they exert pressure from the outside especially on the legislative branch of government. The lobbying activities of, for example, the National Association of Manufacturers, the American Medical Association, and the AFL-CIO readily come to mind. In Japan, though in formal terms the interest groups also exist outside the constitutional government, the relationship between the two is much closer than in the United States. The government and the trade associations in particular constitute, in a sense, mutual interest groups, with the point of contact lying primarily in the executive bureaucracy rather than in the legislature. The labor unions with their close ties with the opposition parties are by and large excluded. In fact, because of the dominance of the government in the postwar period by the conservatives, and because of the very close—one might even go so far as to say symbiotic—relationship between government and industry, it may be concluded that the interest groups constitute an organic part of the governing mechanism, with the political parties serving as middlemen. The term *political economy*, out of fashion for over half a century but regaining popularity to describe the government of today's post-Keynesian societies, is particularly appropriate in the case of Japan to indicate the intermeshing of political and economic forces.

A number of factors are responsible for the close interplay between industry and government, with businessmen acquiescing to controls and interference while, at the same time, influencing national policy to an extent perhaps unknown in the freer economy of the United States. The remarkable homogeneity of Japan's industrial and governmental leadership has already been mentioned in Chapter Four. The Japanese historical experience in modernization has also left its imprint. Japanese capitalism in large measure was government-initiated and supported, especially in its beginning stages when it was faced with the superior competition from European nations. In the 1870s, the government, alarmed at the flood of foreign textiles,[1] founded model factories and extended extensive credit for rapid mechanization of cottage industries. Protective policies for all the major industries—shipbuilding, iron, steel, etc.—saw these "enterprises" through their infancy and beyond. Here nationalism rather than the profit motive appeared to fuel early industrialization, and patriotic enterprising and imported technology have characterized Japanese industry to this day.[2]

---

[1] Ironically, the same problem has now appeared on the horizon as textiles from Hong Kong and Southeast Asia based on "cheap" labor threaten to undersell native products in Japan.

[2] In fiscal 1963, Japan imported $146 million worth of foreign industrial techniques and exported only $6.5 million of its own technology. This kind of induction of industrial knowledge has been increasing in recent years, and the trend seems destined to continue. See *Japan Economic Journal*, Dec. 8, 1964, p. 3.

With the beginning of the great worldwide depression in 1929, government intervention increased as steps were taken to enforce rationalization of industries and reduction of unnecessary competition. As Japan embarked on her continental adventures with the invasion of Manchuria in 1931 and of China in 1937, government controls became even more severe with the passage of the Essential Industries Regulation Act of 1931 and the National Mobilization Act of 1938.

The quick pace of Japan's industrialization in the nine decades between Perry and Pearl Harbor was thus largely due to government leadership and support. Yet this same historical development, which has had many gratifying results in economic growth, has also led according to some critics to a stultification of competition among Japanese entrepreneurs and an undue reliance by management on governmental instruction and largesse.[3] The truth of the matter is that the Japanese businessman will probably never reach the levels of open competitiveness ascribed to his American counterpart; he will undoubtedly remain dependent on the government.

There are at least three ways in which the interest groups intermesh with the government machinery. The close tie between the Liberal-Democratic Party and the world of business and finance has already been discussed, as well as the relationship between the reformist parties and labor. Trade associations interact with the government in two additional ways: by supplying members to the numerous advisory commissions and committees which are set up to study administrative and legislative policy and by directly advising the government on economic policy.

Advisory Commissions

Advisory commissions are organized by the government and often conduct studies over extended periods and with heavy investments in personnel. For example, the government set up in 1961 the Commission on the Industrial Structure (*Sangyo Kozo*

[3] M. Sekiguchi, "The Backgrounds of Business Creed in Japan," *Keio Business Review*, 1963, pp. 94–124.

Chosakai) to advise the Ministry of International Trade and Industry (MITI) on basic industrial policy with special reference to
the ideal structure to be created as Japanese industry shifted
toward a freer and more "open" economy in the 1960s. Some 331
scholars, experts and representatives of industry, finance, and government were mobilized, and their investigations were backed by
a staff of 500 and the personnel of MITI.[4] Two years later, the
Commission, which was headed by Ojima Arakazu,[5] issued recommendations calling for a market structure built generally on the
price mechanism and operating under free competition. Characteristically, it added several vital reservations, including partial price
controls and measures to prevent excessive competition.

The activities of other advisory commissions appear regularly in
the press, more often than not reporting that a commission-gov-
ernment recommendation curbing competition has been accepted
by a particular group of firms or that a commission finding has
been adopted as government policy. Late in 1964, for example,
Japanese oil refiners, controlled by MITI under the Petroleum
Industry Law, accepted a Petroleum Industry Commission recommendation restricting the expansion plans of the refiners.[6] A few
weeks later, the Power Resources Development Adjustment Council, which is headed by Prime Minister Sato himself and which of
course includes industry representatives, decided to restrict the
import of oil-burning thermal generators in order to protect Japanese electrical machinery firms.[7]

Business Interest Groups

There are four national associations of employers that work
to influence government economic policy. They are Keidanren
(Keizai Dantai Rengokai, or the Japan Federation of Economic
Organizations), Nikkeiren (Nihon Keieisha Dantai Remmei, or

[4] I. Hoshii, "Reshaping Japan's Industrial Structure," *Orient/West*,
March-April, 1964, pp. 84–89.

[5] Ojima is Chairman of the Board of Yawata Iron and Steel Co. and
vice-president of Keidanren, discussed below in this chapter.

[6] *Japan Economic Journal*, Nov. 10, 1964, p. 8.

[7] *Ibid.*, Dec. 1, 1964, p. 20.

Japan Federation of Employers' Associations), Nissho (Nihon Shoko Kaigisho, or Japan Chamber of Commerce and Industry), and Keizai Doyukai (Japan Committee for Economic Development). Affiliated with one or more of these national federations are numerous specialized bodies, such as the Iron and Steel Association, the Coal Association, and the Shipbuilders' Council.

KEIDANREN (JAPAN FEDERATION OF ECONOMIC ORGANIZATIONS)

This is a national federation of leading industrial, commercial, financial, and trade associations as well as some 750 individual enterprises. According to its own literature, Keidanren "serves as an organization through which business circles in Japan can express their views to the public and to the government. . . . The Federation secures from business and industry leaders their mature views on domestic as well as international problems and submits these to the government to be reflected in its policies."[8]

The Federation is thus quite frank in its self-assessment as an influencer of government policy. Because its members represent Japan's industries, and because its officers and standing committee chairmen are themselves leading businessmen and industrialists, it is able to present to the government unified and coherent programs that reflect the needs of the business community. It goes without saying that such proposals receive a sympathetic hearing.

Keidanren operates through 30 standing committees representing the various interests of its membership: foreign trade, economic cooperation, taxation, finance, banking, steel, and mining. It is through these functional committees (and special committees established to study urgent problems as they arise) that specific industry needs are called to the attention of the government. Committee relationships with government agencies are especially close, and on occasion such high-ranking officials as administrative vice-ministers and bureau chiefs are invited to attend committee meetings.

Committee ties extend also to their functional counterparts not only in the Diet but also in the Liberal-Democratic and Socialist

8 *Keidanren Review*, no. 1 (1964), Introduction.

Parties. One illustration is Keidanren's Finance Committee, which is in contact with the Finance Committees of both houses, the Finance Ministry, and the Finance Subcommittees of the Policy Committees of both parties. There is an additional layer of contact: the individual trade associations are paired with the various bureaus and agencies of the government. Thus, the Iron and Steel Association maintains close liaison with the Iron and Steel Section, Bureau of Heavy Industries, MITI; the Shipowners Association with the Shipping Bureau of the Ministry of Transportation; and the All-Japan Federation of Banking Associations with the Bureau of Banks, Finance Ministry.[9]

Keidanren influence extends to the very top level of government. During the early stages in the drafting of the fiscal 1965 budget, for example, Keidanren, together with the other three economic organizations, decided to ask the government to streamline its economic programs. They thus arranged for policy consultations with the Finance and MITI ministers to exchange views on fiscal, tax, and trade policies, as well as for a final series of talks with the Prime Minister himself.[10]

NIKKEIREN (JAPAN FEDERATION OF EMPLOYERS' ASSOCIATIONS)

Originally formed in 1948 to counter the increasing power of labor unions stimulated by the occupation, Nikkeiren (with a membership of about 500 organizations) in recent years has concentrated more on developing rational labor policies and promoting cooperation between labor and management. It operates through 15 specialized committees in the formulation of recommendations to be made to government agencies and the Diet. These committees include Unemployment Policy, Business Rationalization, Social Security, Labor Legislation, and Medium and Small Enterprises. Their points of access are the Labor and Welfare Ministries, the Labor and Social Welfare Committees in both houses of the Diet, and the Labor Subcommittee of the Policy Committee of the Liberal-Democratic Party.

[9] Shinobu Seizaburo, *Nihon Seiji Tokuhon* [Japanese Government Reader], Toyo Keizai Shimpo Sha, 1960, pp. 117–118.

[10] *Japan Economic Journal*, Aug. 25, 1964, p. 2.

NISSHO (JAPAN CHAMBER OF COMMERCE AND INDUSTRY)

The chief concerns of Nissho, representing 445 chambers in various cities throughout the nation, are the promotion of foreign trade, the strengthening of small and medium scale enterprises and the development of local and regional industries. Its contacts are therefore with the Foreign, International Trade and Industry, and Transportation Ministries, as well as with the Small and Medium Business Bureau of MITI.

KEIZAI DOYUKAI (JAPAN COMMITTEE FOR ECONOMIC DEVELOPMENT)

The Keizai Doyukai was organized in 1946 by a group of young, progressive businessmen then in the middle ranks of management, many of whom have now reached board chairmanship and company presidency ranks. It differs from the other business organizations in being an association of individual members, now numbering some 1000 executives in managerial positions. Its influence is more diffuse and of a more general nature than the other three, and in keeping with its espousal of forward-looking programs, it was one of the prime movers in Japan's recent adoption of trade liberalization policies. The Keizai Doyukai was behind the establishment of the Japan Productivity Center, the objective of which is to increase the efficiency of industrial operations by studying the most up-to-date techniques and processes. It has worked to cement relationships with like-minded groups in foreign countries (for example, with the U.S. Committee for Economic Development)[11] and to promote the modernization of management and the training of the next generation of business leaders; it is a vociferous advocate of management's responsibility to society.

Labor Interest Groups

If the conservatives are allied with business, the reformist parties find common cause with labor. Indeed, among the leftist

[11] See the joint publication issued by the United States and Japan Committees for Economic Development, *Japan in the Free World Economy*, 1963.

unions, there is an interlocking directorate of union and party officials, particularly at the local level.[12] The schismatic tendencies and developments of the Socialists are reflected in turn by the factionalization of the labor movement, and the combinations, recombinations, and name changes occur with bewildering rapidity. In late 1964, there were two major confederations: Sohyo, allied with the Japan Socialist Party, and Domei, allied with the Democratic Socialist Party.

Japan labor unions tend to be small (average membership: 187), more than 80 percent being "enterprise" unions—autonomous union shops enrolling all of the workers of a single plant or enterprise rather than all of labor in a particular craft or industry. The majority of these local unions and their federations are affiliated with one of four national loosely knit confederations: Sohyo (Nihon Rodo Kumiai Sohyo Gikai, or General Council of Trade Unions of Japan); Domei (Zen Nihon Rodo Sodomei, or Japanese General Federation of Labor); Shin Sanbetsu (Zenkoku Sangyo-betsu Rodo Kumiai Rengo, or National Federation of Industrial Labor Unions); and Churitsu Roren (Churitsu Rodo Kumiai Renraku Kaigi, or Federation of Independent Labor Unions).

SOHYO

The oldest (founded 1950) and largest of the national organizations with a membership at the end of 1964 of 4.2 million,[13] Sohyo's principal adherents include such giants as the 590,000-member Japan Teachers' Union and the 760-000-member National Local Government Workers' Union, as well as such smaller groups as the 2000-member Ministry of Finance Workers Union. About 75 percent of its members are government or public workers. Its chairman is Ota Kaoru of the Japanese Federation of Synthetic Chemistry Workers Union. Sohyo was originally founded as an anti-Communist federation and its mainstream faction continues the tradition against the opposition of the Communist-leaning antimainstream faction. In 1964 the mainstreamers under Ota successfully engaged in a power struggle

[12] C. H. Uyehara, "The Social Democratic Movement," *Annals of the American Academy of Political and Social Science*, Nov. 1956, p. 59.
[13] *Asahi Nenkan*, 1965, p. 437.

with the internal opposition over a half-day general strike of communications workers called by the chairman. The strike, which had been called for April 17, was suddenly denounced as meaningless by the Communist Party and its supporters in the anti-mainstream faction of Sohyo. The issue was actually settled without a strike as the result of a summit conference between Ota and Prime Minister Ikeda, but the angered mainstream faction succeeded later in expelling the dissident unions and consolidating its hold on the federation.

Sohyo in its federation convention of 1961 decided to place emphasis on "economic tactics" (as against political or class warfare), but it remains the main financial and ideological support of the Japan Socialist Party through which it seeks to attain its political goals. Where regular parliamentary procedures appear to have little prospect of success, it does not hesitate to resort to strikes and mass demonstrations: it was one of the prime movers behind the anti-security treaty disorders of 1960.

DOMEI

The newest of the confederations, with a membership of 1.47 million, Domei was formed in November, 1964, as the successor to a series of conservative federations. Among its constituent bodies is Zenkanko (a generic designation for four government workers' unions). It is committed to "democratic trade unionism" and supports the Democratic Socialist Party.

SHIN SANBETSU AND CHURITSU ROREN

Shin Sanbetsu, with a 1964 membership of only 58,000 members, is the smallest of the national federations. Its chief aim now is the creation of a united front of all labor unions. Together with Churitsu Roren, which has 936,000 members, it often supports Sohyo on political and economic issues.

Labor and the socialist parties are mutually supportive. The fact that labor unions constitute the chief source of campaign funds for the Socialists has already been mentioned. Labor also frequently nominates its members as candidates for the Diet subject to approval by the parties. On the other hand, Socialist Diet members are frequently sent by the party to mediate labor union disputes, and Joint Diet Tactics Committees are set up to coordinate party-labor activities when the legislature is in session.[14] Compared to the influence that businessmen can bring to bear on government, the voice of labor is weak indeed, and this is of course due to its identification with the permanent out party. Among the Socialists themselves, there is an awareness that their close association with labor may in the end turn them into a class party, reduce their appeal to all groups in society, and perpetuate their minority status. Still, the majority opinion appears to be that the Socialist tie with labor, which goes back to the turn of the century when the first labor unions were organized, is not strong enough. Since the 1960 security treaty disturbances in which Sohyo played a major role, the Socialist Party has attempted to increase its control over the labor movement. It has organized Party Members' Associations within the major unions with the ultimate objective of gaining the decisive voice in the direction of the labor movement.[15] The strategy appears to be to utilize the labor organizations in strikes, street demonstrations, and other mass actions—the Socialists have long been identified with the ban-the-bomb movement—as an extraparliamentary force in the political struggle with the conservatives.

[14] C. H. Uyehara, *op. cit*.
[15] Kokumin Seiji Nenkan, 1964, pp. 785–790.

CHAPTER NINE

Constitutional Revision

THE QUESTION of constitutional revision has inevitably become politicized over such issues as the position of the Emperor in the Japanese scheme of government, rearmament, and the preservation of individual rights. Ironically, it has been the conservatives who have pushed for revision over the opposition of the reformist Socialists and Communists, who have become the staunchest supporters of the MacArthur Constitution. To date, the government party has not yet seriously attempted to force a vote since it has never been able to muster the necessary two-thirds majority of the full membership of the Diet.[1] One consequence is that the amending process itself has become a constitutional issue, and there are today advocates of a reversion to the previous system under which amendments could be effected by a two-thirds majority of a quorum, which consists of two-thirds of the two houses.

The Commission on the Constitution

Japanese opinion toward the Constitution has been ambivalent from the time it was adopted by the Imperial Diet in 1946, one side of the Japanese character rejecting it as an instrument imposed by the Supreme Commander for the Allied Powers,[2] the other side embracing it fervently as a fundamental charter pro-

[1] Amendments passed by the Diet are subsequently referred to the people in a referendum or special election; ratification is effective if the amendment is approved by a simple majority of all votes cast. Constitution, Article 96.

[2] See Chapter Two.

tecting the human rights of the people. The movement to revise the Constitution to accord with political reality became especially acute after Japan regained her independence in 1952. It was at this time that the San Francisco Treaty of Peace went into effect, and Japan came face to face with the problem of providing for her security without a constitutionally valid means of defense. The hostile world Japan re-entered that year as a newly sovereign nation had not been envisaged in 1946 when hope for the United Nations as an instrument of international peace and security loomed large in the thinking of both Japanese and American officials alike. It had seemed then under the first flush of idealism that Japan could safely "forever renounce war as a sovereign right" and proclaim that "land, sea, and air forces, as well as other war potential, will never be maintained" (Article 9 of the Constitution).

It was the need to root out the discrepancy between the constitutional provisions denying armed forces and the creation of a defense establishment in the early 1950s that led to a re-examination of the Constitution, although earlier, the voice of the right had been heard demanding a reappraisal of the symbolic position of the Emperor and his elevation to a more realistic status as head of state. In 1954, therefore, the conservative Liberal and Progressive Parties issued a statement calling for overall revision of the Constitution and the establishment of a commission to study the question. They were immediately opposed by the reformist parties which demanded cessation of the modest rearmament then under way, the dissolution of the security forces, and the preservation of the "peace Constitution" without change. Their position, spelled out in party platforms of 1954, has not altered substantially to this day.

The conservatives' attempt to introduce a bill for the establishment of a Commission on the Constitution was initially unsuccessful, but in 1956 the newly formed Liberal-Democratic Party pushed through a bill creating the Commission under the aegis of the Cabinet. The law provided for a membership of some 50 persons, 30 selected from the Diet and 20 from among "persons of learning and experience." A secretariat and specialist advisers were also added to aid in the investigation. The government party, wishing to establish a nonpartisan body, requested cooperation from the Socialists and suggested that the membership from the Diet be allocated roughly in proportion to party strength, with 20 seats going to the conservatives and 10 to the Socialists. But the Socialists had been opposed to revision from the very outset and therefore boycotted the Commission, refraining to the end from participating directly in the hearings and studies of the Commission. They based their decision on the technical ground that the setting up of the Commission in the executive branch was unconstitutional in view of the fact that Article 96 of the Constitution specifies that amendments are to be initiated by the Diet. When the Commission findings were published in 1964, the report[3] was automatically attacked as a partisan document.

Beginning in 1957, the Commission held a series of public hearings at both the national and local levels. The opinion of foreign constitutional lawyers was also solicited. The objective of the Commission—"to deliberate on the Constitution"—was so broad that almost any aspect of the modern Japanese state could have been investigated. Actually, the Commission narrowed its interests to the following points: the circumstances surrounding the drafting of the Constitution in 1945–1946 by SCAP and by the government, the position of the Emperor, the renunciation of war, the rights and duties of the citizen, the Diet, the Cabinet, the administration of justice, national finances, local government, and the Constitution as the supreme law of the land. The remainder of this chapter will be devoted to a discussion of two of these points: the renunciation of war and the position of the Emperor.

Renunciation of War

Nothing better illustrates the haste in which the Constitution was drafted—haste which left little time for a realistic appraisal of the facts of international life—than the famous Article 9 renouncing war.

[3] Okurasho Insatsukyoku [Ministry of Finance Printing Bureau], *Kempo Chosakai Hokukusho*, 1964.

Aspiring sincerely to an international peace based on justice and order, the Japanese people forever renounce war as a sovereign right of the nation and the threat or use of force as a means of settling international disputes.

In order to accomplish the aim of the preceding paragraph, land, sea, and air forces, as well as other war potential, will never be maintained. The right of belligerency of the state will not be recognized.

The high idealism of a nation basing its security on the pacifistic intentions of a world weary with war is even clearer in the Preamble to the Constitution:

We, the Japanese people, desire peace for all time and are deeply conscious of the high ideals controlling human relationships, and we have determined to preserve our security and existence, trusting in the justice and faith of the peace-loving peoples of the world.

But within four years China had succumbed to Communist armies and a year later Korea was in flames. Korea was the touchstone; for Japan, during her long colonization of that unhappy land, had justified her seizure of her closest continental neighbor by insisting that the peninsula, in unfriendly hands (for example, Russian), constituted a dagger pointed at the heart of Japan. By 1951, General MacArthur, in a New Year's message to the Japanese people, was enunciating a rationale for rearmament which its advocates have used ever since: the inherent right of self-defense. The Supreme Commander put it in these terms:

If . . . international lawlessness continues to threaten the peace . . . it is inherent that this ideal [renunciation of war] must give way to the overweening law of self-preservation, and it will become your duty [as Japanese] . . . to mount force to repel force.[4]

---

[4] Quoted in M. Royama, "Problems in Self-Defense," *Annals of the American Academy of Political and Social Science*, Nov., 1956, p. 167. Actually, in his New Year's message of 1950 (the Communists had seized effective control of the China mainland a few months earlier), MacArthur had followed the same reasoning in arguing that Article 9 could not be interpreted as a "negation of the right of self-defense against unprovoked attack." Quoted in D. H. Mendel, *Japanese People and Foreign Policy*, University of California Press, 1961, p. 64. For a discussion of the Japanese Supreme Court ruling on Article 9, see Chapter XI.

The self-defense principle was recognized in the United States-Japan Security Treaty signed in 1951, which stipulated that Japan as a sovereign nation possessed the "inherent right of individual or collective self-defense referred to in Article 51 of the Charter of the United Nations." Japan has ever since accepted the responsibility of providing for, and indeed increasing, her defensive capability. The National Police Reserve of 75,000 men created shortly after the outbreak of the Korean War in 1950 was changed in late 1952 to a National Safety Force, and its strength was stepped up to 110,000 men. Its basic mission remained that of a police force, that is, the maintenance of internal peace and order and the protection of life and property. The land force was supplemented by a modest coast guard of 7590 men and some 18 patrol frigates and 50 landing support craft leased from the U.S. Navy.

In June, 1954, the police forces were militarized with the establishment of the Defense Agency as an external organ of the Prime Minister's Office, superseding the National Defense Board. One reason the Agency was not set up as an independent ministry was the fear that such a bold move would make it highly visible as a de facto war ministry, and hence make it vulnerable to attack as being clearly unconstitutional. Under the Defense Agency, headed by a civilian director-general, were created Land, Sea, and Air Self-Defense Forces (that is, an army, navy, and air force). Their mission, as spelled out in the Self-Defense Forces Law, clearly indicates their new status: they are charged with guarding "the nation's peace and independence" and defending "the nation against both direct and indirect invasion in order to preserve the safety of the nation."[5]

This transformation was brought about primarily on the prompting of the United States, which had begun a year earlier a program of Mutual Security Assistance to Japan. Because Japanese leaders doubted that the nation was strong enough economically to bear the heavy burden of rearmament, they had used the convenient excuse of the constitutional ban on rearmament to explain Japan's slowness in setting up a defense establishment. In March, 1954, however, after months of negotiations, the Diet

[5] Self-Defense Forces Law of 1954, Article 3, Sect. 1.

finally approved the Mutual Defense Assistance Agreement with the United States under which Japan agreed to prepare to defend herself against direct external aggression. Two months later the police forces were converted to full-fledged military forces. Today, as the result of a gradual buildup over the years, Japan has a substantial defense establishment of close to 246,000 men armed with modern weapons, tanks, jet fighters, and warships.[6]

PUBLIC OPINION AND REARMAMENT

Popular opinion has been running against any constitutional amendment which would, in effect, legitimize Japan's de facto rearmament. During the period 1952–1957, sentiment favoring revision of Article 9 remained fairly constant at around 30 percent of those polled, while the number of those opposed to revision climbed from 32 percent to 52 percent.[7] The high rate of opposition continued into the 1960s, but support for revision declined to 20 percent.[8] These percentages were obtained in reply to questions which, with slight variations, were put in the following terms: "In your opinion, should the constitutional provision denying Japan the right to have armed forces be revised?" In a nationwide survey conducted in 1962, however, a substantial change in wording produced quite different results. The respondents were asked to agree or disagree with the following statement: "One hears the view expressed that Japan's right to defend herself should be clarified by amending the Constitution, and that in order to provide for defense, the right to possess arms should be recognized." Some 29 percent agreed, 26 percent disagreed, 22 percent replied that they could not fully agree or

[6] *Asahi Nenkan*, 1965, pp. 308–309. Reserves and civilian employees are excluded from the count. Japan's rate of investment in defense continues to be the lowest among major nations of the world. In 1963, for example, it stood at 1.38 percent of the national income as against 11.3 percent in the United States and 7.5 percent (in 1962) in Great Britain. See Zaisei Chosakai [Public Finance Study Association], *Kuni no Yosan* [The National Budget of Japan], Doyu Shobo, 1964, p. 221.

[7] D. H. Mendel, *Japanese People and Foreign Policy*, p. 74.

[8] Japan, Naikaku Sori Daijin Kambo [Prime Minister's Office, Secretariat], *Kempo ni Kansuru Seron Chosa Sogo Hokoku* [General Report on Public Opinion Surveys Relating to the Constitution], 1961, p. 33.

disagree, and 23 percent indicated they had no opinion.[9] Regardless of how the question is phrased,[10] popular support for revision of Article 9 remains at a low level, and opinion is not likely to change on the question for some time.

Members of the Commission on the Constitution, on the other hand, favored revision of the Constitution by an overwhelming margin, especially with respect to Article 9. Although they were fully agreed on the need to uphold the idealism of the peace provisions, they nevertheless felt that it was unrealistic under existing international conditions to deny Japan the right to maintain arms for defense, and that regardless of the constitutionality of existing forces, it was necessary to amend Article 9 to harmonize constitutional theory with practice.[11] That the Commission reached these conclusions should not be surprising in view of the fact that it was dominated by the conservatives.

Majority opinion in the Commission on related issues followed the same general line. Thus, it was felt that Japan as an independent nation possesses the right to self-defense even though "war as a sovereign right" was "forever" renounced. Moreover, since the maintenance of defensive strength was permissible, it therefore followed that the Self-Defense Forces were perfectly legal. Cooperation with the United Nations and participation in collective security arrangements involving military forces under whatever name were unconstitutional.[12]

Despite the strong majority recommendations, the government has not yet taken any steps toward amendment except to commit the Commission report to the Cabinet Bureau of Legislation for study. Soon after he took office in the late fall of 1964, Prime Minister Sato declared in reply to an interpellation in the Diet that he planned no changes in the Constitution, stating merely

[9] Japan, Naikaku Sori Daijin Kambo, *Kempo ni Kansuru Seron Chosa* [Public Opinion Surveys Relating to the Constitution], no. 8 (1963), pp. 27, 31.

[10] Drastic changes in the percentage of those favoring or opposing constitutional revision can of course be caused by altering the wording or even manner of posing questions. See Hayashi Chikio, "Kaiken Rongi to Seron Chosa" [The Dispute on Constitutional Revision and Public Opinion Surveys], *Chuo Koron*, Sept. 1964, pp. 102–111.

[11] *Kempo Chosakai Hokokusho*, pp. 526–528.

[12] *Ibid.* On the question of constitutionality of the Self-Defense Forces and the Security Treaty as tested in the courts, see Chapter Ten.

that he hoped all the people would take an interest in the matter.[13] Today, Article 9 has become the symbol of the deep Japanese commitment to peaceful means of resolving international disputes, and it will require political astuteness and resolve of the highest order if amendment is to be effected in the near future. Reformist threats to plunge the nation into a political crisis to defend the Constitution have undoubtedly influenced the government to adopt a cautious policy, but even more important is the continued unpopularity of amendment and rearmament.

Position of the Emperor

The Emperor is today a powerless symbol of the state who derives his status from the sovereign people. The conservatives have long agitated for revision of the Constitution to restore some measure of the power the Emperor previously enjoyed. Opinion in the Commission on the Constitution was split, with the advocates of reform pushing for a change in status from symbol to "head of state" together with an alteration of functions to correspond to that status. They were opposed by upholders of the status quo who saw no need to change either his status or his functions.[14]

The amount of public support for change has steadily lessened in the past 15 years while the opponents of amending the Constitution to restore some of the prewar glory and power to the throne have remained steadily strong. In polls conducted by the Prime Minister's Office during the period 1958–1962, support for revision dropped from 33 to 19 percent of national samples, while opposition increased from 50 to 54 percent.[15]

This issue, which was very much alive in the early 1950s and which actually provided the initial impetus to the movement to revise the Constitution, may now be regarded as dead. Neither the logic of parliamentary government nor political pressure from the grass roots require that the government do anything about increasing the powers of the Emperor.

[13] *New York Times*, Nov. 27, 1964, p. 15.
[14] *Kempo Chosakai Hokokusho*, pp. 489–492.
[15] Naikaku Sori Daijin Kambo, *op. cit.*, p. 17.

CHAPTER TEN

Recent Trends in Law
and Local Government

Development of Japanese Law

JAPANESE LAW today represents an amalgamation of the civil and common law traditions, and this, one authority suggests, is largely fortuitous. Thus, in her drive to modernize in the final quarter of the nineteenth century, Japan adopted the civil law under French and German influence primarily because the common law was not codified. The foundation was thus laid over a native tradition having Chinese origins; later, defeat in World War II and occupation by U.S. forces introduced, again by historical accident, a massive overlay of rules and principles of common law derivation.[1]

The Japanese code makers of the Meiji period initially relied on French models, but within a short period of time German influence was predominant. Thus the revised Penal Code of 1907, the Code of Criminal Procedure of 1922, the Civil Code of 1898, and the Code of Civil Procedure of 1890 were patterned on German counterparts. The Commercial Code of 1893 was eclectic. It has been noted elsewhere that the Meiji Constitution of 1899 was itself Prussian in orientation.

The Constitution and these five codes—together referred to as the "Six Codes"—represent a systematized series of laws which

---

[1] K. Takayanagi, "The Development of Japanese Law, 1868–1961," in A. T. Von Mehren (ed.), *Law in Japan*, Harvard University Press, 1963, p. 37. Dr. Takayanagi, professor of law emeritus of Tokyo University, served as chairman of the Commission on the Constitution.

had in essence been stabilized by the turn of the century. The elimination of the authoritarian aspects of the codes and the introduction of various principles from the common law tradition have produced remarkable changes, some of which have already been discussed in Chapter Two.

Two major revisions of the Penal Code are the elimination of crimes against the imperial household (including the crime of lese majesty) and the deletion of adultery as a crime. Both of these revisions are in support of the constitutional guarantees of equality under the law regardless of sex, social status, or family origin (Article 14). Previously, crimes against members of the imperial family were bracketed with high treason and carried special punishments. Obviously, discrimination based on social status or family origin was unconstitutional; the offending chapter of the Criminal Code was therefore stricken from the books. Under the old statute, a wife and her paramour caught in an adulterous act were punishable, but a wife had no legal recourse against a philandering husband surprised in similar circumstances. Since discrimination against women was constitutionally banned, and since it would have proved politically and socially unwise to extend the law to cover errant husbands, a compromise solution was adopted: the adultery provision was dropped altogether.

The common law influence is most evident in provisions of the Constitution and in the revised Code of Criminal Procedure protecting the rights of accused individuals from the time of arrest to judgment. These include the right of habeas corpus, the right to a speedy trial before an impartial tribunal, the right to counsel, and guarantees against double jeopardy and self-incrimination. The inquisitorial powers of presiding judges have been greatly modified, and the right to cross-examine witnesses has been newly introduced.

The Judicial System

The prewar centralized judicial system has been continued (there are no independent local or police courts) with major modifications to ensure the autonomy of the judicial branch invested by the Constitution with the "whole judicial power" (Article 76). Under the old Constitution, the judiciary was decidedly subordinate to the executive branch. The administration of the courts was a responsibility of the Ministry of Justice which, through its procurators (prosecutors), was also charged with the investigation and prosecution of criminal activities. In effect the executive branch was policeman, prosecutor, and judge.[2] Today, the functions are split, with judges and procurators no longer employees of the same ministry. Investigative functions are in the hands of the police under the jurisdiction of the National Public Safety Commission. Procurators remain in the Ministry of Justice, while the courts function theoretically as a completely independent branch of the government, though honoring the constitutional principle of legislative supremacy. One curious attempt to assert the principle of popular sovereignty lies in the constitutional provision for review of judicial appointments in general elections (Article 79), but to date no justices appointed by the Cabinet[3] have been denied popular approval.

The prewar courts had limited power of judicial review. They were permitted to determine the constitutionality of a law only with respect to form and not substance: that is, they were bound to accept as constitutional any measure passed by the Diet, sanctioned by the Emperor, and promulgated with due formality. It was up to the legislature to determine whether the substance of any particular law agreed with constitutional stipulations, and the courts could not impeach their interpretations.[4] Actually, it was the practice of the government to submit any bills affecting the Constitution to the Privy Council, the watchdog of the Constitution, for prior approval.

Today the constitutionality of all laws, ordinances, administrative regulations, and official acts of the government is subject

[2] The jury system, used from 1928 until it was suspended during World War II, has not been revived.

[3] The Cabinet appoints all justices except the Chief Justice (Article 79) who is appointed by the Emperor "as designated by the Cabinet" (Article 6). Since the Emperor has no discretionary power in the matter, in effect, the Cabinet appoints all judges.

[4] T. Takeuchi, *War and Diplomacy in the Japanese Empire*, Doubleday, 1935, p. 63.

to review by the courts, responsibility for final arbitration in matters of interpretation lying with the Supreme Court. This is not to say that the doctrine of judicial review as it is known and practiced in the United States is fully accepted in Japan. The Supreme Court has not been a forceful and positive advocate of its own power, and the future of judicial review is still uncertain.[5]

The present court system comprises a Supreme Court in Tokyo with 15 justices; 8 high courts in Tokyo, Osaka, Nagoya, Hiroshima, Fukuoka, Sendai, Sapporo, and Takamatsu functioning as appellate courts; a District Court in each of the 46 prefectures with four in Hokkaido; 49 Family Courts adjudicating domestic and juvenile disputes; and some 570 Summary Courts in the principal cities, towns, and villages functioning as the initial trial courts of the nation.

Constitutional Interpretation: Some Landmark Cases

The postwar Constitution is based on three principles, all of which were either nonexistent or imperfectly realized in the Meiji Charter: popular sovereignty (from which flow the secondary principles of legislative supremacy and local autonomy, both of which theoretically make the people and not the central government the supreme political power), renunciation of war, and guarantees of fundamental human rights. The principle of popular sovereignty does not lend itself readily to constitutional interpretation, although it is the premise on which many of the Supreme Court's decisions are based in controversial questions involving, for instance, the basic freedoms and legislative supremacy. The section renouncing war has produced only two Supreme Court cases (see below). According to Professor John Maki, the bulk of the Court's decisions relating to constitutional interpretation concern the people's rights and freedoms.[6]

[5] The Court to date has declared only two laws unconstitutional, and in both cases the laws at the time of decision were no longer in full legal force. M. Ito, "The Rule of Law: Constitutional Development," in Von Mehren (ed.), *Law in Japan*, p. 238.

[6] John Maki, *Court and Constitution in Japan, Selected Supreme Court Decisions, 1948–60*, University of Washington Press, 1964, p. xxxvii.

The reason is not hard to find: the concept of fundamental individual rights was, like the railroad and the steamship, imported from the West and is therefore fairly new to Japanese political philosophy. It was a foreign transplant first weakly nurtured by the political parties, then suppressed especially under the military rule of the 1930s, and finally revived by occupation forces convinced that Japanese democracy could not flourish without a written guarantee in the organic law of the land. The civil rights movement in presurrender Japan was not marked by intense political controversy or extended litigation seeking to define the nature and scope of basic rights. The natural outcome in recent years, therefore, has been a spate of suits seeking concrete definitions and interpretations of the abstract principles enunciated in the Constitution.

The Meiji Constitution included a catalogue of rights enjoyed by "subjects" of the Emperor. Article 29, for instance, specified that "Japanese subjects shall, within the limits of law, enjoy the liberty of speech, writing, publication, public meetings, and associations." But the "limits of law" were made narrow indeed, and the result was that these basic liberties were virtually strangled.

In contrast, Article 21 of the new Constitution flatly states: "Freedom of assembly and association as well as speech, press, and all other forms of expression are guaranteed." The comprehensive catalogue of rights in Articles 10–30 casts the widest possible net and includes many principles alien to Japanese experience. Thus the fundamental human rights are regarded as "eternal and inviolate." Individualism, equality under law without regard to social status or sex, universal adult suffrage, the right of peaceful petition for redress of wrongs, freedom of thought and conscience, and academic freedom all are guaranteed, as are the right to minimum standards of "wholesome and cultured living," the right to equal education, and the right to work and bargain collectively. Articles 31–40 specify individual rights and duties before the law, and include habeas corpus, guarantees against illegal seizures, searches, and torture, the right to a speedy trial, and freedom from self-incrimination.

These rights of the individual are not, however, absolute, for they are restricted by the higher demands of the common good. According to Articles 12 and 13 of the Constitution:

The freedoms and rights guaranteed to the people by this Constitution shall be maintained by the constant endeavor of the people, who shall refrain from any abuse of these freedoms and rights and shall always be responsible for utilizing them *for the public welfare*.

All of the people shall be respected as individuals. Their right to life, liberty, and the pursuit of happiness shall, *to the extent that it does not interfere with the public welfare*, be the supreme consideration in legislation and in other governmental affairs. [Italics added.]

Insofar as restricting the basic freedoms through constitutional interpretation is concerned, these "public welfare" clauses may be regarded as the counterparts of the "within the limits of law" reservation of the Meiji Constitution. The Supreme Court has consistently interpreted the "public welfare" clauses to justify the constitutionality of any statute limiting freedom of expression, and accordingly has been attacked for abridging the absolute rights guaranteed by the Constitution.[7] But Professor Maki points out that there has been no practical restriction or erosion of freedoms under the Court's interpretations and denies that the Supreme Court has betrayed its role as guardian of the Constitution.[8]

Another criticism of the Supreme Court is that it has been passive in its relations with the executive and legislative branches. In essence, the charge is that the Court, while jealously guarding its right to the "whole judicial power," denies that it has the right to check the executive and legislative branches which are, in the final analysis, accountable only to the sovereign people. It can be cogently argued that the principle of responsibility to the people is closer to the democratic ideal of responsible government than any system relying on an excessive commitment to judicial supremacy.[9] Still, it would appear that in balance the Court has a fairly limited vision of its overall power and of its function of constitutional interpretation. Especially in its role as

[7] See, for example, the criticism by M. Ito, professor of law at Tokyo University, in his article, "The Rule of Law: Constitutional Development," in Von Mehren (ed.), *Law in Japan, op. cit.*, pp. 205–238.

[8] Maki (ed.), *op. cit.*, p. xliii.

[9] *Ibid.*, p. xliv.

interpreter, it has tended to narrow rather than broaden the scope of individual rights.

THE TOKYO ORDINANCE CASE: THE PUBLIC WELFARE TEST

This case illustrates the manner in which the Supreme Court has given precedence to the public welfare test ahead of, according to some of its critics, the guarantees of basic rights. At issue was the validity of a Tokyo Ordinance regulating parades and demonstrations and banning them if advance permission (through application to the local police station) had not been obtained. Such a prohibition would appear to limit the freedom of expression guaranteed by the Constitution by requiring prior approval. Article 21 grants freedom of assembly and expression and forbids censorship; prior approval and restraint may be regarded as the classic restriction of free expression through censorship. Hence, under a liberal interpretation of the Constitution, any prior restraint would appear to be unconstitutional. In the Niigata Ordinance Case of 1954, the doctrine of prior restraint had been admitted and the Court had suggested a definite standard for determining the constitutionality of laws abridging the basic freedoms.[10] That is, a general prior restraint would be held unconstitutional, but a restraint with specific limitations would not necessarily be held invalid.[11] In this earlier case, the Court had dismissed the appeal of the defendants, stating that the ordinance was constitutional because it did not attempt to restrict demonstrations by a general system of licensing.

On the basis of this test, the Tokyo District Court in 1959 declared invalid a Tokyo ordinance requiring licenses for "assemblies, processions, and demonstrations" since it imposed a general prior restraint on freedom of expression. It therefore refused to authorize the detention of students demonstrating without license against the then pending revision of the United States-Japan Security Treaty. When the case was appealed to the Supreme Court by the Tokyo district procurator, the Court re-

10 The Niigata and Tokyo Ordinance cases are translated in full in Maki, *op. cit.*, pp. 70–116.
11 *Ibid.*, p. 75.

versed the decision of the lower court and supported the validity of the Tokyo Ordinance on the grounds of the public welfare test. "To decide whether it conforms with the Constitution," the Court declared in its formal judgment, "is to decide whether it improperly restricts the freedom of expression guaranteed by the Constitution by exceeding the requirements set forth in the Constitution that prohibit the abuse of freedom and enjoin the maintenance of the public welfare." [12] Although the Court therefore admitted that the crux of the problem was the proper balance between freedom of expression and the public welfare, it concluded that even though the Constitution prohibits censorship or prior restraint, local authorities still had to adopt minimum measures necessary to maintain law and order in advance of any public event.

This ruling has been attacked on the grounds that the Court in its reasoning indulged in a kind of "word magic" and that it maintained that the traditional right of the state to maintain peace and order is superior to the more recently established right of freedom of expression.[13] Insofar as the power of judicial review is concerned, it would appear that the Court limits its area of competence and tends to shy away from a finding of unconstitutionality on the implicit assumption that any legislative act is in itself constitutional if the overall effect is reasonable.

THE POPORO CASE: ACADEMIC FREEDOM DEFINED

Article 23 of the Constitution states merely that "academic freedom is guaranteed." In the first test of the scope of academic freedom, the Court in 1963 again adopted a narrow rather than broad interpretation. The case involved a performance staged by students of the Poporo Theatrical Group of Tokyo University in conjunction with an "anticolonialism struggle day" for which donations were solicited and received. During the performance, an undercover policeman had been discovered and subjected to a kangaroo court by students who objected to what they regarded as an unwarranted invasion of the university campus by the

[12] *Ibid.*, p. 88.
[13] Ito, "The Rule of Law," pp. 236–238.

authorities. Subsequently, one of the students was arrested for attacking the officer. The Tokyo District Court acquitted the student on the grounds that the entry of the police officer into the Tokyo University campus was in violation of the guarantee of academic freedom, and therefore jeopardized academic freedom and university autonomy.

The Supreme Court, in overturning the ruling of the Tokyo District Court which had been upheld by the Tokyo High Court, declared that two conditions must be met before the rights of academic freedom and university autonomy could be extended to student activities: such events must come within the scope of academic activities, and they must be attended only by students of the university concerned. Since neither of these conditions had been met, the performance did not come under the guarantee of academic freedom, and accordingly the presence of the police officer was not in violation of the Constitution. It concluded that the privileges and immunities of academic freedom extended only to purely academic activities and the publication of the results of such undertakings.[14]

THE SUNAKAWA CASE: INTERPRETATION OF ARTICLE NINE

Over the years, the continued U.S. military presence in Japan now nearing the end of its second decade has generated considerable popular opposition which, from time to time, has flared into rioting and violence.[15] The Sunakawa Incident of 1957 was one such case. When Japanese government surveyors attempted to conduct preliminary studies preparatory to the elongation of runways at Tachikawa Airfield (a U.S. Air Force base) near the village of Sunakawa, they met the resistance of land-hungry "farmers" who had the area under cultivation. Rioting developed, and some of the "farmers" trespassed on the airfield, and were promptly arrested for illegal entry onto an American base. It quickly became apparent that the farmers were led by a small

---

[14] *Japan Report*, May 31, 1963, pp. 5–6.

[15] For a brief survey of popular attitudes toward U.S. bases, see D. H. Mendel, *The Japanese People and Foreign Policy*, University of California Press, 1961, Chapter Four.

group in the vanguard of a movement to expel American forces altogether from Japan; the case became a constitutional issue when the Tokyo District Court held that the law under which the trespassers were arrested was unconstitutional. The law was invalid, the court held, because it had been enacted to support the United States-Japan Security Treaty of 1951, in itself unconstitutional because it contravened Article 9, which forbids the maintenance of war potential. The defendants were not guilty, according to the court's judgment, because they had been charged under an illegal enactment, and criminal penalties cannot be imposed under Article 31 of the Constitution "except according to procedure established by law."

The Supreme Court quashed the original finding and returned the case to the Tokyo District Court. In its judgment, it confined itself strictly to the narrow issue of the constitutionality of U.S. forces in Japan and avoided the broader, and vastly more vital issue of the legality of Japan's own military forces. Earlier, in 1950, Suzuki Mosaburo, Secretary-General of the Socialist Party, brought suit to have the National Police Reserve declared unconstitutional inasmuch as the newly formed force constituted "war potential" in contravention of Article 9. The Court did not decide the issue, and it dismissed the case on the ground that while it has the final say on constitutional interpretation it does not have the right to determine in the abstract the constitutionality of a law in the absence of a specific concrete case.[16] To date, therefore, the Supreme Court has yet to rule on the constitutionality of this cornerstone of Japan's "peace constitution."

Nevertheless the Court clearly adumbrated the rationale for any future interpretation of various stipulations of Article 9 which, if taken at face value, would appear to prohibit the maintenance of armed forces of any kind. How else can the flat assertion that "land, sea, and air forces, as well as other war potential, will never be maintained" be interpreted? The Supreme Court on this occasion showed how, and in doing so followed the reasoning first used in 1950 to justify the creation of the paramilitary National Police Reserve: that the Constitution

---

[16] For a translation of the Court's decision, see Maki (ed.), *op. cit.*, pp. 362–365.

"naturally . . . in no way denies the inherent right of self-defense." [17]

The Court also reasoned that in order to compensate for an inadequate defensive capacity arising out of constitutional restrictions on rearmament, Japan as a sovereign nation has the right to seek to base her security on the peace-loving peoples of the world through the instrumentality of the United Nations. But if the Security Council of the United Nations is unable to provide for her security, then Japan has the further right to seek other guarantees. Article 9, according to the Court, does not forbid requests to a second country to maintain national security; nor does the introduction of war potential by a second country constitute Japanese "war potential" forbidden by the Constitution. It went on to declare that the intent of the provision renouncing war forever was to ban "aggressive war." [18]

As to the constitutionality of the Security Treaty itself, the Court denied that it had jurisdiction, stating that the treaty was of a "highly political nature" the ultimate judgment of which must be left to "the political review of the sovereign people." [19] Once again the Court had chosen to regard as nonjudicable a partisan question, and even its critics were inclined to agree that such highly controversial questions must be left to political settlement.[20]

The cases selected for discussion here tend to emphasize the passivity of the Supreme Court in its relations with the executive and legislative branches, and its timidity in extending basic rights. On the other hand, the Court has jealously guarded its independence from Cabinet and Diet encroachment on what it regards as its sole preserve, the judicial power. Moreover, its interpretations of the Constitution have not been so unreasonable as to erode away in any substantial way the basic guarantees of freedom. The Court's decisions also have given concrete meaning

---

[17] Formal judgment of the Supreme Court as cited in *ibid.*, p. 303. The formal judgment is translated in pp. 302–361.

[18] *Ibid.*, p. 304.

[19] *Ibid.*, pp. 305–306.

[20] Ito, "The Rule of Law," p. 238.

to the abstract principles enshrined in the text of the Constitution, and it has consistently worked to establish the rule *of* law [21] as enacted by the people through their representatives in a nation where the traditional mode was rather rule *by* law from above.

Trends in Local Government

Prior to the institution of postwar reforms designed to promote grass-roots democracy, Japanese local government was marked by a high degree of centralization with government authority flowing from the ministries in Tokyo through appointed prefectural governors to the cities, towns, and villages. In this respect the system reflected the pattern of European continental local government after which it had been designed. There was little or no tradition of home rule, and one consequence was that until very recent times there was little politicization of government at the local level, and experience in urban or prefectural politics was not regarded as being particularly beneficial in gaining national eminence.

Local government in postwar Japan has been characterized by two contrary developments: an initial attempt to create a viable system of autonomous government followed by a "reverse course" trend toward recentralization which is now gathering swift momentum.

LOCAL AUTONOMY REFORMS

In an attempt to democratize the authoritarian system then in force, the occupation-instituted reforms aimed at promoting local autonomy; in this objective they were only partially successful. The principle of local autonomy was enshrined in the Constitution; thereafter, any law enacted by the National Diet relating to the organization and operation of "local public entities" (prefectures, cities, towns, and villages) had to be in accordance with

---

[21] Maki (ed.), *op. cit.*, p. xlv.

the principle. Chief executives and legislative assemblymen were made elective and localities were granted the right to self-administration, enactment of their own regulations and ordinances, and management of their property. Thus the principles of home rule in the British-American tradition were adopted and legislation was enacted creating the necessary mechanisms and safeguards. By the end of 1964, some 45 statutes were in existence, and these may be subsumed under one of the following categories: those relating to (1) the basic Local Autonomy Law of 1947 regulating organization and operations; (2) the local civil services; (3) local finance and taxation; (4) local elections; and (5) police, firemen, and education.[22]

Control over the primary functions of local government—education, preservation of law and order, and public works—is assigned to the localities by the Local Autonomy Law of 1947 (since frequently amended). Occupation reformers were especially interested in reducing the power of the central government in education and in peace preservation. It had been through Education Ministry controls over teachers, curricula, and textbooks that generations of school children had been indoctrinated in the ethics of an Emperor-centered state. And it was through control of the national police system that the Home Ministry exercised stringent controls over subversive and unpatriotic activities. A system of locally elected school boards having jurisdiction over education was instituted, and the Home Ministry was abolished and police functions transferred to local constabularies and national rural police.

The basic reforms in the election of public officials and the decentralization of education and police have worked to create a substantial measure of popular control over local affairs—the primary objective of the reformers. For a number of reasons, however, the ideal of complete local independence from central control has not been realized, and if recent trends continue it is likely that the powers of local public entities will be further reduced in the not too distant future.

[22] Suzuki Shun'ichi, *Shin Chiho Jichi Seido*, Zentei Shimpan [The New Local Government System, rev. new ed.], Gakuyo Shobo, 1964, pp. 19–23.

THE DRIVE TO RECENTRALIZATION

Local public entities in Japan serve both as autonomous bodies serving local needs and as administrative subunits of the national government. Professor Kurt Steiner has pointed out that the legal distinction between the two tends to break down in practice, and that in some cases mayors and village heads spend up to 80 percent of their time on functions assigned to them by Tokyo.[23] In spite of their nominal independence, the localities receive general guidance from the central authorities in the form of model laws, notifications, and warnings transmitted through prefectural offices. There is therefore the tendency to slip back into the traditional pattern of relationships, and this has proved to be a strong predisposition in the recentralization now taking place.

There are other reasons, not the least of which is the inadequacy of the financial base for local operations. It was indeed the inability of the villages and smaller towns to afford their own police that led in 1954 to the partial recentralization of the police system. The existing system of local urban police and national police in rural areas was supplanted in that year by the creation of 46 prefectural police forces, each operating under the existing prefectural public safety commission composed of private citizens. These commissions are under the jurisdiction of the National Public Safety Commission—an external agency of the Prime Minister's Office. Operational standards for the prefectural police are determined by the Police Agency which operates under the National Public Safety Commission. The police therefore have been partially recentralized, but the localities retain a measure of control through membership of their citizens on the prefectural commissions.

In the field of education, the system of locally elected boards of education and local control of school finances which had been in effect in the prefectures and the five major cities of Japan since

[23] "Japanese Village Government," *Far Eastern Quarterly*, Feb. 1956, p. 195.

1948 (in other cities and towns since 1952) was revised in 1956. Board of Education members are now appointed by prefectural governors and mayors with the consent of local legislatures.

Fiscal independence, moreover, has been severely compromised by the direct and indirect controls exercised by the central government through specialized grants and subsidies and local allocation (equalization) grants. A major share of local expenditures now comes from the national treasury; in recent years it has been rising steadily and in 1961 reached 43 percent of total expenditures (as contrasted to 12 percent in 1935).[24] Also, because localities were encountering fiscal difficulties, the national government in 1955 enacted a Local Finance Rehabilitation Law which provides for the reconstruction of local finances through government-approved loans and procedures. This involves the submission of local budgets to the Autonomy Ministry and therefore leads to indirect controls over fiscal policy.

The announced objectives of the Autonomy Ministry in recent years, moreover, indicate that there will be a further tightening of controls. This appears to be primarily due to natural developments that have been taking place in the past decade and a half as the Japanese economy has registered a spectacular growth, and the country has rapidly been urbanized. The old political boundaries no longer appear as natural or rational units in the new economy, and the latest bywords are regional economic development and regional political federation. The Autonomy Ministry in this situation is interested in developing coordinated area attacks on problems that are no longer strictly local or even regional in character. It is interested also in raising the standard of administration at the local level, and above all it seeks to create a healthy fiscal base of operations.[25]

The evolution of regionalism under the sponsorship of national agencies, which will probably further diminish the powers and functions of the municipalities, appears to be more or less inevitable given Japan's geographic foundations. The present bounda-

[24] Japan, Jichisho [Autonomy Ministry], *Chiho Jichi Benran* [Local Government Handbook], 1964, pp. 38–39.

[25] Japan, Jichisho, *Chiho Zaisei Tokei Nempo* [Local Financial Statistics Annual], Chiho Zaimu Kyokai, 1964, p. 1.

ries for the 46 prefectures were set about 90 years ago when the nation was still primarily agricultural and the communications network was primitive. In today's industrialized society, in which motorized transportation and electronic communications have shrunk an already small island nation into even narrower confines, the 3405 cities, towns, and villages [26] and 46 prefectures seem to be too numerous for efficient regional and national growth. In this situation, the movement to reduce the number of primary local units continues, and at the same time, proposals have been put forth seeking to cut down the number of prefectures. In 1964, for example, the Autonomy Ministry drafted a plan to create regional prefectural federations which would have the right to issue ordinances and float bond issues. A secretariat consisting of prefectural governors in the federation would have the power to draft ordinances, manage finances, and engage in regional planning. Other proposals seek to amalgamate existing prefectures or to divide all of Japan into from seven to nine districts each with a centrally appointed chief executive.[27] Clearly all such plans envisage a further weakening of the principle of local autonomy.

POLITICIZATION OF LOCAL GOVERNMENT

One recent trend needs to be noticed here. Even as recently as 10 years ago, partisan politics had not penetrated to the local level, and especially in town and village elections, virtually all candidates ran as independents and shunned party labels.[28] Moreover, the number of National Diet members who gained experience in local politics before venturing onto the national scene was inordinately low. In the 1955 general election, for example, only 108 of 467 members of the lower house had had previous

[26] Down from a high of 15,861 municipalities in 1889 when the present system of cities, towns, and villages was adopted. The decrease in number has been brought about by a series of amalgamation promotion laws. The targets for the latest such law, enacted in 1953, were generally fulfilled by 1964, and in 1964 the Autonomy Ministry began studying revision of the law to promote further amalgamations. See *Chiho Jichi Benran*, pp. 18–19.

[27] *Asahi Nenkan*, 1965, p. 524.

[28] Steiner, "Japanese Village Government," p. 195.

experience at the local level: 28 as municipal councilmen, 57 as prefectural assemblymen, 19 as mayors, and 4 as governors.[29]

Following the formation of the two major parties in 1955, however, elections at all levels have become increasingly politicized. In village assemblies the number of "independents" remains high, but even here party labels are more and more frequently encountered. The preponderent majority of prefectural assemblymen are now party affiliated, whereas the governors and mayors lag behind in proclaiming their associations. The party affiliations of local officials in 1964 were as follows: [30]

Office	L-DP	JSP	Independent
Governors	24	1	20 (21)
Mayors	77	20	459 (452)
Village Heads	113	15	2708 (2713)
Pref. Assemblymen	1739	527	166 (141)
City Councilmen	2940	1674	11,868 (11,875)
Village Assemblymen	1865	1068	54,887 (55,566)

These trends, if continued, would appear to indicate that groundwork is being laid for increasing political independence at the local level, but this will only be true if the parties themselves evolve a strong measure of independence from headquarters.

[29] Hoshino Mitsuo, *Nihon no Chiho Jichi* [Japan's Local Government], Toyo Keizai Shimpo Sha, 1960, p. 8.
[30] *Asahi Nenkan*, 1965, p. 523. Minor parties and factions not shown. Figures for 1963 in parentheses.

CHAPTER ELEVEN

Foreign Relations

FROM PREHISTORIC until relatively recent times, the outside world to the Japanese meant China. China was the source of all the great civilizing influences: Buddhism, naturalized in the "Central Kingdom" after its Indian beginnings; Confucianism, which molded the Japanese character; the Chinese styles of writing, art, and architecture; and law and the social and political institutions of the successive dynasties. This transcendent reliance on Chinese culture was modified somewhat when the vanguard of the expanding western powers—Portugal, Spain, and Holland—reached Far Eastern waters in the sixteenth century. But Japan soon adopted a policy of national seclusion, leaving the West only a peephole through the Dutch outpost on Deshima. Her contact with China remained uninterrupted, but her isolation from the western world was not broken until the arrival of Commodore Perry's four black steamships in Edo (Tokyo) Bay in July, 1853. Subsequently, Japan has been subjected to the tug of two forces, one pulling her toward the traditional fount of civilization across the China Sea, and the other drawing her toward Europe and America. These two influences have been paramount in the formation of modern Japanese foreign policy, and currently the western attraction has gained the upper hand.

In the first decades following the appearance of Perry's armed warships, which revealed the nation's weakness for all the world to see, the main thrust of Japanese diplomacy was directed toward preservation of independence. Western imperialism was at flood tide and appeared ready to engulf Japan; security was to be gained by strengthening the nation militarily and economically. The slogan of the day therefore became "Prosperity and Arms."

Japan soon assured her independence under American tutelage

in diplomatic affairs, and then she turned her attention toward gaining equality. By the end of the nineteenth century, she had eliminated unequal treaties, and she then began to direct her national energy toward gaining recognition as a world power. She showed her mettle by defeating the Chinese in the War of 1894–1895 and the Russians in the war of 1904–1905. The latter victory, together with the Anglo-Japanese Alliance of 1902, established Japan as a maritime power with ties to the most important naval power of the West. At the same time, she advanced onto the Asian continent by annexing Korea and carving out a sphere of influence in Manchuria.

Having sided with the Allies in World War I, Japan attended the Versailles Peace Conference as the first nonwestern nation in modern times to be regarded as a major power; but when she sought to have her newly-won status recognized by having the principle of racial equality written into the League of Nation's Covenant, she was rebuffed largely because of the opposition of British and Australian delegates. Japan turned her back on the western democracies within a decade and embarked on a policy of militarism and further continental expansion with the aim of creating a self-contained empire which she was finally to call the Greater East Asia Co-Prosperity Sphere. Her attempt to establish herself as a continental power ended in the disaster of Hiroshima.

Since the end of World War II, and especially since the recovery of independence in 1952, Japan's foreign policy has once again been based on alliance with a western power. To ensure her security, she has chosen to ally herself with the United States; to increase her economic strength, she relies on continued expansion of international trade. The American alliance and trade therefore constitute the two pillars of her foreign policy, but as her economic power has risen and she has regained stature in the international community, the idea of Japan as a third force has presented itself as an increasingly attractive alternative.

Alliance with the West

The formation of foreign policy is, in Japan, a function of partisan politics, for the fervent conservative commitment to the

West and the equally intense reformist sympathy for neutralism rule out any possibility of a unified policy. It cannot be assumed, however, that the individual parties themselves are united on foreign policy. The conservatives are split on the question of recognizing Peking as the legitimate government of China; the Socialist Party is for a program of positive neutralism and an opening to the left—that is, rapprochement with China and closer relations with the Soviet Union; and the Democratic Socialists espouse a strong autonomous policy free of excessive influence from both major power blocs of the world. Moreover, among Socialists there is substantial rank-and-file support for alignment with the United States, and among conservatives there is considerable neutralist sympathy.[1]

Public opinion surveys of the last 15 years have consistently shown strong support for the government's prowestern orientation as against Communist bloc or neutralist affiliations, and in addition the United States invariably comes out on top of various popularity polls as the "best liked" foreign country. The correlations between party strength, foreign policy, and national popularity are striking evidence of the influence of public opinion on the shaping of the overall orientation of foreign policy.[2]

The basic choice, as these polls reveal, is not between the West and the Communist bloc but rather between alliance with the West and a policy of neutralism. Indeed, this and the related question of pacificism have been the most divisive issues in postwar Japan, and it is only in recent years that the neutralist appeal seems to have lost some of its attraction. There is a strong emotional tinge to the neutralist appeal, and it seems likely to continue as a force in Japanese politics.

The Quest for Military and Economic Security

The ties that bind the United States and Japan in an alliance across the Pacific are both military and economic, and this fact is reflected in the Preamble to the Treaty of Mutual Cooperation and Security of 1960.

[1] See D. H. Mendel, *The Japanese People and Foreign Policy*, University of California Press, 1961, pp. 46–48.
[2] See Table 9: Party Preference and Foreign Policy.

TABLE 9.   Party Preference and Foreign Policy

	1964	1961
POLITICAL PARTY PREFERENCE		
Liberal-Democratic Party	39.3%	35.2%
Socialist Party	21.7	21.8
Democratic Socialist Party	2.2	3.6
Others, Don't Knows	36.8	39.4
INTERNATIONAL AFFILIATION		
Free World	42.9	38.7
Communist Bloc	1.1	1.0
Neutral	26.9	33.1
Don't Know	29.1	27.2
COUNTRIES LIKED BEST (NAME 3)		
United States	50.3	42.9
United Kingdom	32.1	34.4
Switzerland	30.1	31.5
France	26.1	27.9
West Germany	16.5	11.7
India	9.2	18.0
COUNTRIES DISLIKED MOST (NAME 3)		
Soviet Union		48.6
Red China		32.3
Korea		41.2
United States		8.0

SOURCES: Data for 1964 from Jiji Press survey of May, 1964 as given in *Japan Report*, June 30, 1964, pp. 7-8. Data for 1961 from Japan, Naikaku Sori Daijin Kambo [Prime Minister's Office, Secretariat], *Zenkoku Seron Chosa no Genkyo* [Report on National Public Opinion Surveys], 1961, pp. 94, 101-102.

"Japan and the United States of America,

Desiring to strengthen the bonds of peace and friendship traditionally existing between them . . .

Desiring further to encourage closer economic cooperation between them . . .

Considering that they have a common concern in the maintenance of international peace and security in the Far East,

Having resolved to conclude a treaty of mutual cooperation and security,

Therefore agree. . . ."

The two parties agreed to "seek to eliminate conflict in their international economic policies," to "encourage economic collaboration," and for each party to "act to meet the common danger" in the event of an armed attack. The use of land, sea, and air bases was granted to U.S. forces "for the purpose of contributing to the security of Japan." [3] The treaty therefore underscores the dual nature of the alliance in its military and economic aspects.

THE MILITARY ALLIANCE

When Japan renounced war as an instrument of national policy in her new Constitution, she thereby rendered herself defenseless and placed her trust in the peace-loving peoples of the world acting through the United Nations. According to Yoshida Shigeru, the conservative Prime Minister under whose guidance Japan eventually signed the peace treaty as well as the first United States-Japan Security Treaty in 1951, it was the Socialist government of Katayama Tetsu which first suggested to Washington that Japan enter into an alliance with the United States for the purpose of ensuring her security.[4] Even to the Socialists, it was apparent that Japan could not, in a world split into the Free World and Communist camps, maintain her independence by appeal solely to the United Nations.

Alliance with America for security has thus been one of the key principles of Japanese foreign policy and is enshrined in the Security Treaty of 1960. With her relatively small armed forces of less than a quarter of a million men, Japan is no match for either her traditional enemy in East Asia, Russia, or for Communist China, now in possession of nuclear weapons. Her air

[3] The text of the treaty may be found in *Contemporary Japan*, May, 1960, pp. 564–565.

[4] Yoshida Shigeru, *The Yoshida Memoirs*, Heinemann, 1961, p. 265. The memorandum to Washington was drafted by Foreign Minister Ashida Hitoshi and Chief Cabinet Secretary Nishio Suehiro. The latter is now chairman of the Democratic Socialist Party.

force of close to 40,000 men supplied with outmoded F-86 jet fighters and a smaller group of F-104J fighters is complemented by U.S. Air Force units based in Japan proper, with additional units operating from Okinawa. Similarly, her small navy of approximately 35,000 men operates a pocket navy with no ships larger than destroyers and is supplemented by the power of the U.S. Seventh Fleet. Her army of some 171,000 men, organized into 13 divisions, is regularly called out for such non-military duties as disaster relief.[5] While U.S. troop strength in Japan has steadily decreased since the signing of the peace treaty, there still remained at the end of 1964 about 40,000 men, mostly in the Air Force. They were supported by Army, Air Force, and Marine units amounting to 60,000–70,000 men stationed in Okinawa.[6]

Japan therefore relies heavily on the American military to ensure her security, and one of the causes of friction now developing between Tokyo and Washington is the slow pace of Japan's rearmament. Still, the benefits are not all one-sided. Aside from the military value of the air and naval bases for units operating far from North America, Japan also contributes to U.S. security simply by remaining in the western camp. Consider for a moment the American position in East Asia if Japan were to opt for neutralism or go over to the Communist side.

For one hundred years, the primary aim of American diplomacy in East Asia was to ensure the independence of China, and it was adherence to this principle that led the United States into World War II. Always implicit in the doctrine that the territorial integrity of China should be upheld was the assumption that China would be ruled by a government friendly to the United States. Since the Communist takeover of the mainland in 1949, however, Washington has been confronted by a hostile government in Peking that regards America as its chief enemy.

To preserve her right to her presence in the western Pacific—a

[5] Japan has resisted all pressures to dispatch troops overseas even for U.N. peace-keeping activities, arguing that to do so would be unconstitutional in view of the renunciation of force as a means of settling international disputes.

[6] Figures on Japanese and U.S. troop strength as given in *Asahi Nenkan*, 1965, pp. 309, 564.

right won through victory over Japan in World War II—the United States has sought through a policy of containment of Communist expansionism to stabilize an outer perimeter defense line extending from Alaska through the Japanese archipelago (and touching continental Asia in South Korea) southward through the mighty complex of airbases in Okinawa through the Nationalist Chinese-held island of Formosa and the friendly Republic of the Philippines to Vietnam and Thailand. The strategic key is Japan, with its modern industrial plants and highly trained and energetic people. Control of this industrial complex by the Communist powers could force the United States to retreat to the doubtful shelter of the Hawaiian Islands. Should Japan renounce her present prowestern stance and turn first to neutralism and then to alliance with the Communist camp the consequences for U.S. security would be incalculably grave; for Japan has the industrial and technological capacity, still largely unused, to produce not only nuclear weapons but also the ballistic missiles, aircraft carriers, airplanes, and submarines needed to deliver them.

THE ECONOMIC ALLIANCE

Ever since defeat in World War II shattered Japan's dreams of autarky and empire, her political leaders have necessarily placed their trust in the free movement of goods in international trade as the best means of assuring economic stability. The miracle that has in recent years transformed the economy has already been referred to in some detail in Chapter One. Let it suffice to re-emphasize here that Japan's prosperity is linked directly with an expanding world economy in which her share has increased steadily year by year; that the nation is heavily dependent on external sources for essential raw materials; and that without a vigorous and enlarging trade made possible by a stable international order, her economy would subside to politically unacceptable levels.

Japan's foreign trade is based essentially on the importation of raw materials and the exportation of processed goods. Raw cotton from the United States and wool from Australia are re-exported in the form of yarns, textiles, and clothing to American markets; iron ore from Malaysia and Goa and coking coal from American and mainland Chinese mines are converted to steel and steel products for export to western customers. Raw materials account for more than half of Japan's imports while finished and semifinished products amount to more than 90 percent of exports.

The necessity for trade accounts in large measure for her continued close association with the United States, Japan's top trading partner. In recent years, some 30 percent of Japan's total exports and imports have been with her best customer and supplier. On the other hand, Japan is, after Canada, the top buyer of American products—agricultural raw materials (cotton, soybeans), foods (wheat, corn), coal, timber, and machinery (office machines, aircraft). In return, Japan sends to the United States textiles and clothing, fish and marine products, steel plate and metal-working machines, and electronic and optical equipment. The total trade between the two nations, including capital transactions, amounted in 1963 to close to $6 billion;[7] the balance of trade in normal years is unfavorable to Japan.

As the economic relationship has deepened, friction has inevitably arisen as the products and services offered by the two have come more and more into open competition with each other on international markets. Japanese businessmen complain that their textile quotas for American buyers are overly restricted and threaten to abandon the "voluntary" quotas holding down shipments; and they argue that limitations on North Pacific fisheries should be liberalized, and that Japan Air Lines should be permitted to operate over North America. American businessmen, on the other hand, would like to see a further liberalization of controls on precisely those categories in which they are most competitive: heavy electrical machinery, electronic computers, and automobiles. It is apparent that the two countries are adopting harder lines on economic issues, while Japanese government spokesmen speak bravely about the necessity for adopting a spirit of "competitive cooperation" or "cooperative competition" as the guiding principle for the further development of economic co-

---

[7] *Japan Report*, Sept. 30, 1964, p. 5.

operation and development.[8] Annual cabinet–level talks by the joint United States-Japan Committee on Trade and Economic Affairs were initiated in 1961 in an atmosphere of relaxed friendliness, but by the time of the third meeting in January, 1964, distinct tensions had arisen over a variety of issues from capital transactions to trade with mainland China.[9]

As Japan assumes a stronger stance in international affairs commensurate with her growing economic strength, these relatively minor differences will likely become aggravated rather than lessened. Meanwhile, other issues of graver consequence threaten the alliance: differences over the control of the Ryukyus (Okinawa), over U.S. military actions in Vietnam, and over China policy. While the United States recognizes Japan's "residual sovereignty" over the Ryukyu Islands chain, populated by close to 800,000 people linguistically and culturally close to the Japanese, Washington is not yet ready to relinquish control over the strategically placed islands won by conquest and since converted into a gigantic air base. Under the terms of the 1960 security treaty, the effectiveness of U.S. bases in Japan proper is limited by the need to obtain prior Japanese approval before making major changes in troop or weapons deployment. This means that U.S. forces in Japan are not equipped with atomic weapons, that nuclear submarines can enter Japanese ports only at the risk of endangering relations between the two countries, and that the United States finds it impossible to utilize the bases as staging areas for troop movements in East Asia. American armed forces on Okinawa, however, are under no such inhibitions, and it is not likely that the United States will readily give up this formidable bastion of power in Pacific waters.

In the past, the Japanese have tended to emphasize the economic aspects of the alliance while Americans have tended to look upon their ties with Japan primarily in politico-military terms. Japanese leaders, especially among the ruling conservative party, have thought in terms of trade, discriminatory tariffs, "voluntary" restrictions on exports, and fishery rights; while American spokesmen have regarded Japan as an ally in the per-

[8] *Ibid.*
[9] *Ibid.*, Jan. 31, 1964, pp. 7–13.

imeter defense of the United States against Communist aggression and as a democratic model sponsored by America for the
uncommitted nations to emulate. There are indications that these
basic differences in outlook and approach are changing, as, on
the one hand, American interests increasingly come into open
competition with Japanese goods on the international market,
and, on the other hand, stepped up military activities by the
United States in Asia force the Japanese people and their leaders
to accept the consequences of their alliance with America.

Japan has passed from a one-sided dependence on the United
States to a new phase of independent participation in international society, but for the immediate future she will continue to
rely on the treaty with the United States to ensure her security.
However, treaty revision will be considered in 1970, and in
1965 the opposition Socialists were already making plans to termi-
nate Japan's obligations and direct her future toward neutralist
and pro-Communist lines.

Japan and China

"Japan," the Japanese ambassador reminded an American audience, "is first of all an Asian nation, and although we maintain
formal diplomatic relations with Nationalist China, it is impossible for us to cut ourselves off from all contact with mainland
China. We cannot erase, after all, our long historical involve-
ment with the Chinese, we cannot obliterate our geographic
proximity to the mainland, we cannot ignore our ancient and
deep cultural affinity with its peoples." [10]

It is not only geographic proximity and historical and cultural
ties that influence Japanese attitudes toward China; economic
and security considerations also affect the thinking of both
Japan's masses and leaders. Prime Minister Sato put it in these
terms:

We have developed cultural and economic relations [with China]
under the policy of separation of political and economic matters,

[10] Ambassador Takeuchi Ryuji in a speech to the Japan Society of Oregon,
March 12, 1965, as quoted in *Japan Report*, March 15, 1965, pp. 2–4.

and we shall continue to do so. While our trade with the mainland accounts for a mere 2 percent of our entire trade, it is our view that if improvements can be effected, through such contacts, in the welfare and livelihood of the Chinese on the mainland, as with the rest of Asia, this would lead the way in the long run to peace and stability in Asia.... While Japan does enjoy close and friendly ties with the United States, her nearest neighbors are the two most powerful Communist countries in the world, the Soviet Union and Communist China.[11]

Japan is officially committed to a policy of separating politics from economics, which means that she will continue to withhold recognition from the Peking regime [12] and oppose the latter's entry into the United Nations. At the same time, Japan encourages the development of business and cultural relationships at the private level; for while the mainland trade may be currently miniscule, in prewar days it amounted to almost 25 percent of foreign commerce [13] and the potential demand of 700 million customers appears unlimited. Moreover, China was the traditional supplier of certain basic industrial raw materials—iron ore, coking coal, salt, and soybeans—until the outbreak of the Korean War cut off the continental supply and Japan turned to the United States and other nations to supply these needs.[14]

Revival of trade with mainland China is, however, beset with a number of technical, economic, and political difficulties. The properties and quality of Chinese raw materials—generally cheaper than those available elsewhere—are not always suitable for Japanese industrial use. China requires in exchange industrial plant facilities, heavy machinery, rolling stock, and tons of chemical fertilizers, for which long-term credit must be extended. But capital-starved Japan, heavily dependent on American loans, is peculiarly vulnerable to U.S. pressure in this respect, and credit

[11] In an address to the National Press Club, Washington, D.C., January 12, 1965, as given in *Japan Report*, Jan. 20, 1965, pp. 3–6.

[12] Public opinion is mixed on the question of recognition. One poll taken in 1964 had 37.1 percent of the people favoring recognition of Peking, 10.5 percent opposed, and an usually high percentage of 52.5 percent "don't knows." *Japan Report*, June 30, 1964, p. 8.

[13] *Nippon: a Charted Survey of Japan*, 1964, p. 74.

[14] Takase Kiyoshi, *Nitchu Boeki* [Sino-Japanese Trade], Ashi Shobo, 1964, p. 197.

is not easily forthcoming. The anticipated sale of a complete vinylon plant collapsed in 1965 when the Japanese government refused to extend export credit to the Osaka manufacturer through the official Export-Import Bank. The Chinese, on their part, have also tended to use trade as a political weapon, as in 1958 when Peking broke off commercial relations because of the hostility of the conservative regime of Kishi Nobusuke, an outspoken critic of Communism. In this instance, the steel industry, which had concluded a five-year barter agreement to exchange finished steel products for coal and iron ore, found that its anticipated source of raw material, for which it had patiently negotiated over an extended period of time, had suddenly vanished for political reasons. Among planning-conscious businessmen, such an erratic source of supply cannot be relied upon, and this is another reason for the slow development of the trade. Nevertheless, since 1962 commerce between the two nations has picked up on the basis of a private five-year accord negotiated between Japanese business interests and Chinese government authorities,[15] and in 1964 Chinese-Japanese trade was expected to reach $300 million, a new high but still only one-tenth the value of the trade between Japan and the United States.[16] But after Sato Eisaku, Kishi's brother, assumed the Premiership in November, 1964, Peking's attitude hardened, and whether the upswing in the trade will continue remains to be seen.

Japan faces a dilemma in her China policy because of her desire to retain friendly relations not only with the United States but also with the Nationalist Chinese government now sequestered on Taiwan (Formosa). Japan recognizes the Nationalist regime of Generalissimo Chiang Kai-shek as the legitimate government of China and has concluded a treaty of peace with her. There is a sentimental feeling of gratitude toward Chiang for guaranteeing the safe return of Japanese troops from mainland China following the end of hostilities in 1945 and also for not

[15] This is the Liao-Takasaki Trade Agreement, signed by the late Takasaki Tatsunosuke, then chairman of the Japan-China Overall Trade Liaison Council and a pro-Peking stalwart of the Liberal-Democratic Party, and Liao Cheng-chi, president of the China-Japan Friendship Society of China.

[16] *Japan Economic Journal*, Aug. 11, 1964, p. 11.

insisting on reparations. Additionally, trade with Taiwan, at the $230 million level,[17] was surpassed by trade with mainland China only in 1964. But above all, Japan is restrained by the attitude of Washington, although in her approach to the China problem it is likely that she will increasingly take steps that will meet the disapproval of her American ally.

In addition to economic considerations, Japan must also take into account her military weakness vis-à-vis her two Communist neighbors from whose air and missile bases her densely populated cities lie within easy striking distance. War under such circumstances would be an invitation to *hara-kiri*. As the Japanese periodically and almost pridefully now remind the world, they are the only ones who have been atom-bombed, and they are acutely sensitive to any possibility of a recurrence of the experience. The explosion of a nuclear device by the Chinese Communists in 1964 followed by the escalation of the Vietnamese war (which, if generalized, could involve Japan) appeared to affect Japanese attitudes both toward America and China. The Japanese are not as ready as their American friends to denounce Chinese aggression and expansionism.[18]

The ruling Liberal-Democratic Party is not united on the question of Japan's China policy. While most party members readily agree with Prime Minister Sato that Japan as an Asian nation stands in a special relationship with China, there have long been pro- and anti-Peking groups in the conservative party. Those who call for closer relationships with China have formed a policy study group in the L-DP called the Asian-African Problems Association. Prominent in this association are such conservatives as Fujiyama Aiichiro, former financier, foreign minister, and head of one of the larger party factions (and as such contender for the prime ministry), and Dietman Utsunomiya Tokuma, a frequent visitor to Peking. They are opposed by another group

[17] Japan, Tsusho Sangyosho [Ministry of International Trade and Industry], *Tsusho Hakusho, Soron* [International Trade White Paper, General Report], 1964, pp. 264–267.

[18] For example, see the critical reception accorded W. W. Rostow, chairman of the State Department's Policy Planning Council, during his visit to Japan in late April, 1965, as reported in the *Japan Times Weekly*, May 8, 1965, p. 1.

called the Asian Problems Study Association, headed by the out-spoken anti-Communist Kaya Okinori, a former justice minister. Kaya, with Prime Minister Sato, advocates a cautious approach to the China problem.[19] In an attempt to heal the breach and harmonize policy on this critical issue, the party leadership in early 1965 invited representatives of the two associations to join the party's Foreign Affairs Committee which was specially en-larged to accomodate them. At the same time, Secretary-General Miki Takeo was singled out to serve as overall coordinator of China policy both for the party and for the Cabinet.

It appears unlikely that there will be a drastic change in Japan's China policy in the near future. Intraparty politics among con-servative factions would appear to rule out any such a possibility since the pro-Peking group is still a minority and in the periphery of party power. Japanese opinion, moreover, still supports a pro-American, anti-Communist orientation, and these basic attitudes do not appear headed for change despite the periodic noisy out-bursts of anti-Americanism by student activists and the reformist parties.

Japan's Search for a New Identity

Hiroshima not only shattered Japan's dreams of empire: it also destroyed the sense of mission that had fired her patriots in the grandiose plan to bring the four corners of the world under the realm of the divine Emperor. It was, according to the old ide-ology, the special destiny of the Japanese people to rule Asia, and when Hiroshima revealed the unreality of this dream, pride of race also crumbled. Twenty years later the Japanese people are still struggling to establish a new identity and to find a new sense of purpose. When a special advisory commission to the Ministry of Education issued an interim report on the "Image of the Ideal Japanese," it raised a furor since it contended that the emphasis on individual liberty, which has been at the center

[19] See D. C. Hellman, "Japan's Relations with Communist China," *Asian Survey*, Oct. 1964, pp. 1085–1092; and *Japan Times Weekly*, Feb. 20, 1965, p. 4.

of the struggle to create a new identity, had gone too far and that the old national virtues should be re-emphasized.[20]

The old ultranationalism has been so thoroughly discredited that it would appear impossible to revive, as the public opinion polls reveal on such issues as restoration of imperial rule and rearmament. Nonetheless, with economic recovery has come a return of pride in the fact of being Japanese. In the area of foreign relations, this is manifest in a growing independence in her relations especially with the United States. At the same time, she is moving more in the direction of establishing herself as a third force in international politics.[21] This movement to date has taken two forms: commitment to the United Nations and other international agencies, and service as an impartial mediator in East-West and North-South relations. The new image that Japan is attempting to project therefore contains elements of the highest idealism; but at bottom it is based on a coldly realistic appraisal of Japan's position in the world of today. Japan is too exposed, geographically, militarily, and economically, to be able to afford a bellicose posture in international politics. She must perforce rely on the maintenance of international order to protect her very existence.

In his 1965 policy speech to the Diet, Prime Minister Sato emphasized that it was a cardinal principle in Japan's foreign policy to make positive contributions to enhance the United Nations' prestige and functions.[22] This is merely a restatement of a conservative foreign policy principle enunciated when Japan gained admission to the United Nations in 1956. Even before that date she was an active participant in such bodies as the Food and Agriculture Organization; the United Nations Educational, Scientific, and Cultural Organization; the Economic Commission for Asia and the Far East; the World Health Organization; and the International Monetary Fund. As a member of the General Agreement on Tariffs and Trade, Japan works to promote

20 For a discussion of the report, see *Mainichi Daily News*, Monthly International Ed., Feb. 1, 1965, p. 6.

21 This is of course not a new idea since it has been current from the time Japan regained her independence and began the search for a new role in international relations.

22 Address given in *Japan Report*, Jan. 31, 1965, pp. 2–3.

the orderly development of international trade, and in 1964, she became the first nonwestern nation to become a member of the Organization for Economic Cooperation and Development, one of the major agencies devoted to economic cooperation in the Free World.

Japan's new sense of mission, furthermore, casts her in the role of an independent third force mediating differences between contending East-West forces and between North-South nations at disparate levels of development. In particular, she sees herself as occupying a unique position in Asia as a bridge between the United States and China over such conflicts as the war in Vietnam. She has sought also tentatively to act as an Asian leader by settling her differences with the Republic of Korea and by offering to mediate the confrontation among Indonesia, Malaysia, and the Philippines.

Another way in which Japan has shown her willingness to emerge from her isolation is in the area of economic and technical aid. Japan sees herself as the model for the newly developing nations of the South—in Asia, Africa, and Latin America—and as the transmitter of economic, political, and social ideas from the industrialized North. It is in the nonmilitary fields of economic, cultural, and technical exchange that Japan seeks to exert international influence.

There are many difficulties lying in the path of Japan's attempt to realize such ambitions, not the least of which are her own timidity in assuming a larger role and her unwillingness to rearm to a level consistent with her aspirations. The memory of Imperial Japan bent on conquest by brutal arms is still green in the minds of her neighbors in Asia, and this has dampened Japan's enthusiasm for leadership. Her suitability as an economic and political model for emerging nations is open to question, since her own development has been more or less unique, or, if any comparison can be made, closer to western than to Afro-Asian developmental patterns. But above all, there is an inherent contradiction between Japan's attempt to play a neutralist role and her continued alliance with the United States, the leader of one of the great power blocs.

It is the conservative party leadership that has advocated alliance with the West, and in this they have been opposed by the Socialists who opt for neutralism and pacificism as the only realistic role appropriate for Japan today. It would appear that the conservatives are slowly moving toward the Socialists' position on this issue but without the Marxist trappings and leftward bias of the latter.

To summarize, Japan seeks to create a new image for the nation first, as an impartial mediator between two hostile camps now being splintered by polycentric pressures as the individual nations assert their independence from central control, whether from Washington or Moscow, and second, as a model for the economic development of the emerging South while utilizing the democratic parliamentary institutions of a free society. Meanwhile, she continues her reliance on the American alliance to provide security. Japan's announced objectives are thus beset with contradictions, and she may yet be forced to choose between continued alliance with the West and a stronger commitment to neutralism.

But the significance of the Japanese political experience of the past century lies precisely in the fact that apparently contradictory eastern and western approaches to the fundamental problems of government have been harmonized with surprising success. In particular, Japan has been able to adapt western parliamentary democracy to an eastern mold, and she has thus provided a governing system capable of dealing successfully with the first problem of politics: the responsible use of power. It is a notable accomplishment and provides this object lesson: that western democracy need not be copied entire but may be successfully adapted without complete denaturation to accord with national conditions and needs. This elementary lesson may well be the most important contribution the Japanese people will be able to make in the world of politics.

SELECTED READINGS

GENERAL WORKS AND HISTORY

Beckmann, George M., *Modernization of China and Japan*, Harper & Row, 1962.

Japanese National Commission for UNESCO (comp.), *Japan: Its Land, People and Culture*, (rev. ed.) Printing Bureau, Ministry of Finance, 1964.

Kawai, Kazuo, *Japan's American Interlude*, University of Chicago Press, 1960.

Reischauer, Edwin O., *Japan, Past and Present*, (3rd ed., rev.) Knopf, 1964.

Sansom, George B., *A History of Japan*, Stanford University Press, 1958-1963, three vols. (Stanford Studies in the Civilizations of Eastern Asia.)

Sansom, George B., *Japan; a Short Cultural History*, (rev. ed.) Appleton-Century-Crofts, 1943.

Sansom, George B., *The Western World and Japan*, Knopf, 1950.

Yanaga, Chitoshi, *Japan Since Perry*, McGraw-Hill, 1949.

CULTURE AND NATIONAL CHARACTER

Beardsley, Richard K., John W. Hall, and Robert E. Ward, *Village Japan*, University of Chicago Press, 1959.

Benedict, Ruth, *The Chrysanthemum and the Sword; Patterns of Japanese Culture*, Houghton Mifflin, 1946.

Bennett, John W. and Iwao Ishino, *Paternalism in the Japanese Economy: Anthropological Studies of Oyabun-Kobun Patterns*, University of Minnesota Press, 1963.

Dore, R. P., *City Life in Japan: a Study of a Tokyo Ward*, University of California Press, 1958.

Matsumoto, Y. S., *Contemporary Japan: the Individual and the Group*, American Philosophical Society, 1960. (Transactions of the American Philosophical Society, n.s., vol. 50, part 1.)

Norbeck, Edward and George de Vos, "Japan," in F. K. L. Hsu (ed.), *Psychological Anthropology*, Dorsey Press, 1961, pp. 19–27.

Silberman, Bernard S. (ed.), *Japanese Character and Culture: a Book of Selected Readings*, University of Arizona Press, 1962.

Smith, Robert J. and Richard K. Beardsley, *Japanese Culture: its Development and Characteristics*, Aldine, 1962. (Viking Fund Publications in Anthropology, no. 34.)

ECONOMY, GEOGRAPHY, LABOR

Ackerman, Edward A., *Japan's Natural Resources and Their Relation to Japan's Economic Future*, University of Chicago Press, 1953.

Allen, G. C., *A Short Economic History of Modern Japan, 1867–1937, with a Supplementary Chapter on Economic Recovery and Expansion, 1945–1960*, Praeger, 1963.

Ashikaga, Tomomi, *Agriculture in Japan*, Japan FAO Association, 1963.

Ayusawa, Iwao, *Organized Labor in Japan*, Foreign Affairs Association of Japan, 1962.

Cohen, Jerome B., *Japan's Postwar Economy*, Indiana University Press, 1958.

Dore, R. P., *Land Reform in Japan*, Oxford University Press, 1959.

Hall, Robert B., *Japan: Industrial Power of Asia*, Van Nostrand, 1963.

Levine, Solomon B., *Industrial Relations in Postwar Japan*, University of Illinois Press, 1958.

Lockwood, William W., *The Economic Development of Japan: Growth and Structural Change, 1868–1938*, Princeton University Press, 1954.

Ogura, Takekazu (ed.), *Agricultural Development in Modern Japan*, Japan FAO Association, 1963.

Smith, Thomas C., *The Agrarian Origins of Modern Japan*, Stanford University Press, 1959. (Stanford Studies in the Civilizations of Eastern Asia.)

Trewartha, Glenn, *Japan, a Geography*, University of Wisconsin Press, 1965.

POLITICS, GOVERNMENT, LAW

Beckmann, George M., *The Making of the Meiji Constitution: the Oligarchs and the Constitutional Development of Japan, 1868–1891*, University of Kansas Press, 1957.

Burks, Ardath W., *The Government of Japan*, (2nd ed.) Crowell, 1964.

Cole, Allen B. and Naomichi Nakanishi, *Japanese Opinion Polls with Socio-Political Significance, 1947–1957*, Fletcher School of Law and Diplomacy, Tufts University, 1958, three vols.

Ike, Nobutaka, *The Beginnings of Political Democracy in Japan*, Johns Hopkins Press, 1950.

Ike, Nobutaka, *Japanese Politics: an Introductory Survey*, Knopf, 1957.

Japan, Commission on the Constitution, Secretariat, *Comments and Observations of Foreign Scholars on Problems Concerning the Constitution of Japan [of] 1946*, Tokyo, 1964.

"Japan Since Recovery of Independence," *Annals of the American Academy of Political Science*, vol. 308 (Nov., 1956), pp. 1–174.

Kyogoku, Junichi and Nobutaka Ike, *Urban-rural Differences in Voting Behavior in Postwar Japan*, Tokyo, 1959. (Proceedings of the Dept. of Social Sciences, College of General Education, University of Tokyo.) Reprinted as Stanford University Political Science Series, no. 66.

McNelly, Theodore, *Contemporary Government of Japan*, Houghton Mifflin, 1963.

Maki, John M. (ed.), *Court and Constitution in Japan: Selected Supreme Court Decisions, 1948–60*, University of Washington Press, 1964.

Maki, John M., *Government and Politics in Japan: the Road to Democracy*, Praeger, 1962.

Maruyama, Masao, *Thought and Behaviour in Modern Japanese Politics*, Ivan Morris (ed.), Oxford University Press, 1963.

Morris, I. I., *Nationalism and the Right Wing in Japan; a Study of Postwar Trends*, Oxford University Press, 1960.

Patrick, Hugh T., *Monetary Policy and Central Banking in Contemporary Japan*, University of Bombay, 1962. (University of Bombay Series in Monetary and International Economics, no. 5.)

Quigley, Harold S. and John E. Turner, *The New Japan: Government and Politics*, University of Minnesota Press, 1956.

Scalapino, Robert A., *Democracy and the Party Movement in Prewar Japan: the Failure of the First Attempt*, University of California Press, 1953.

Scalapino, Robert A., and Junnosuke Masumi, *Parties and Politics in Contemporary Japan*, University of California Press, 1962.

Smith, Thomas C., *Political Change and Industrial Development in Japan: Government Enterprises, 1868–1880*, Stanford University Press, 1955. (Stanford University Publications; University Series: History, Economics, and Political Science, no. 10.)

Steiner, Kurt, *Local Government in Japan*, Stanford University Press, 1965.

Supreme Commander for the Allied Powers, Government Section, *Political Reorientation of Japan, September 1945 to September 1948*, U.S. Government Printing Office, 1949, two vols.

Von Mehren, A. T. (ed.), *Law in Japan: the Legal Order in a Changing Society*, Harvard University Press, 1963.

Ward, Robert E. and Dankwart A. Rustow (eds.), *Political Modernization in Japan and Turkey*, Princeton University Press, 1964. (Studies in Political Development, no. 3.)

Yanaga, Chitoshi, *Japanese People and Politics*, John Wiley, 1956.

FOREIGN RELATIONS

Griswold, A. Whitney, *The Far Eastern Policy of the United States*, Harcourt, Brace & World, 1938.

Maki, John M. (ed.), *Conflict and Tension in the Far East: Key Documents, 1894–1960*, University of Washington Press, 1961.

Mendel, Douglas H., *The Japanese People and Foreign Policy: a Study of Public Opinion in Post-Treaty Japan*, University of California, 1961.

Reischauer, Edwin O., *The United States and Japan*, (3rd ed.) Harvard University Press, 1965.

Scalapino, Robert A., "The Foreign Policy of Modern Japan," in Roy C.

Macridis (ed.), *Foreign Policy in World Politics*, (2nd ed.) Prentice-Hall, 1962.

Schwantes, Robert S., *Japanese and Americans; a Century of Cultural Relations*, Harper & Row, 1955.

Takeuchi, Tatsuji, *War and Diplomacy in the Japanese Empire*, Doubleday, 1935.

Ward, Robert E., *The Position of Japan in the Far East and in International Politics, 1965–1970*, Technical Military Planning Operation, General Electric Co., 1958. (TEMPO Report RM 58TMP–41.)

PERIODICALS AND YEARBOOKS

Asian Survey, Berkeley, Institute of International Studies, University of California, monthly.

Contemporary Japan, Tokyo, Foreign Affairs Association of Japan, irregular.

Economic Survey of Japan, Tokyo, Economic Planning Agency, Japanese Government, annual.

Japan Annual of International Affairs, Tokyo, Japan Institute of International Affairs.

Japan Economic Journal (Nihon Keizai Shimbun), International Weekly Edition, Tokyo, Nihon Keizai Shimbun Sha.

Japan Quarterly, Tokyo, Asahi Shimbun-Sha.

Japan Report, New York, Consul-General of Japan, biweekly.

Japan Times Weekly, International Edition, Tokyo.

Journal of Social and Political Ideas in Japan, Tokyo, Center for Japanese Social and Political Studies, triannual.

Nippon: a Charted Survey of Japan, Tokyo, Tsuneta Yano Memorial Society, annual.

Statistical Yearbook of Japan (Nihon Tokei Nenkan), Tokyo, Prime Minister's Office, Bureau of Statistics.

INDEX